D0890076

Major Cities of the Biblical World

MAJOR CITIES
OF THE
BIBLICAL WORLD

Edited by *R. K. Harrison*

Thomas Nelson Publishers
Nashville • Camden • New York

Published in Nashville, Tennessee by Thomas Nelson Publishers, Inc., and distributed in
Canada by Lawson Falle, Ltd., Cambridge, Ontario.

Printed in the United States of America.

Scripture quotations noted RSV and NIV are from the Revised Standard Version of the
Bible copyrighted 1946, 1952, © 1971, 1973; and from The Holy Bible: New International Version. Copyright © 1978 by the New York International Bible Society. Used by
permission of Zondervan Bible Publishers.

Library of Congress Cataloging in Publication Data
Main entry under title:

Major cities of the biblical world.

  Bibliography:
    1. Near East—History—To 622. 2. Cities and towns—
Near East—History. 3. Bible—History of contemporary
events, etc. I. Harrison, R. K. (Roland Kenneth)
DS62.2.M26   1985   939'.4   85-10508
ISBN 0-8407-7520-2

CONTENTS

13 January 1981

71954

LIST OF ILLUSTRATIONS

INTRODUCTION

One has only to glance briefly at such material as the historical writings of the Old Testament and the Book of Acts in the New Testament to become aware of the bustling, turbulent life of the Near East in the biblical period. People migrated from place to place, cultures that have become known to us for their magnificence rose and fell, and individuals of great renown left their imprint on history.

This book attempts to capture something of the vitality and achievements of the ancient Near Eastern peoples by focusing upon specific cities rather than individuals or empires for that purpose. The cities selected were all important in various ways during the biblical period, and the findings of archaeology have been enlisted in order to illustrate more clearly the roles that these centers of culture played in scriptural narratives.

Some sites, such as Jericho and Jerusalem, have a lengthy history of human occupation, while others, such as Alexandria, are of more recent origin. A few cities such as Ebla, Mari, and Nuzi, will be new to many readers because they are not mentioned in the Bible. They are included, however, because the kind of culture which they represent has an important bearing upon the Old Testament in particular.

The contributors to this symposium are experts in their various fields, and I am tremendously grateful to them for their enthusiastic participation in this project while engaged in a busy professional life. The employees of Thomas Nelson Publishers have worked diligently to make this book attractive and useful, and in this connection I am particularly indebted to Mr. Paul Franklyn for the care and expertise lavished upon this book.

Mrs. Adrienne Taylor, Librarian of Wycliffe College, Toronto, and her assistant, Ms. Gayle Ford, have rendered cheerful and efficient service when technical assistance was needed. To them I extend deep and sincere thanks for their participation in my labors. Finally I must recognize with great gratitude the patience and skills of Ms. Beverley Black, who participated in the proofreading of this volume.

R. K. Harrison
General Editor

Period	*Dates* BC
Neolithic (New Stone Age)	8000-4000
Chalcolithic (Copper Age)	4000-3000
Bronze Age	
Early Bronze (EB)	3000-2000
EB I	3000-2800
EB II	2800-2500
EB III	2500-2200
EB IV	2200-2000
Middle Bronze (MB)	2000-1500
MB I	2000-1800
MB II	1800-1500
Late Bronze (LB)	1500-1200
LB I	1500-1400
LB II	1400-1200
Iron Age	From 1200
Iron I	1200-1000
Iron II	1000-600

This classification, which reflects the consensus of biblical archaeologists, is expressed in round figures and is meant to be approximate only. Individual contributors to this volume do not necessarily agree with it in all respects.

Major Cities of the Biblical World

ALEXANDRIA

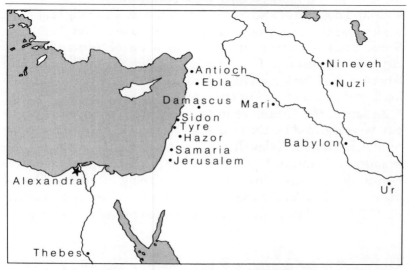

Alexandria bears the name of its founder, Alexander the Great, who chose the site for the city after his conquest of Persian-controlled Egypt in 331 BC. Alexander, allegedly influenced by a dream, chose a location eminently suited to a great city. Bounded by the Mediterranean Sea to the north and the Nile-fed Lake Mareotis to the south, the city had excellent access both to the interior of Egypt and to the entire Mediterranean world. On the Mediterranean were two harbors, separated by a mole, the Heptastadium ("seven stadia" = .8 mile). At the end of the mole was the island of Pharos with its impressive lighthouse. The geographer Strabo, who spent five years in Alexandria, gives a vivid description of the city in his *Geographica* (Book 17).

Description   Although a small Egyptian town (Rhakotis) had existed at the site since 1300 BC, Alexander's architect (Deinocrates) laid out the city afresh. According to legend barley sticks were used for the plans when chalk ran out. When birds devoured the sticks Alexander took it as a negative sign, but the Egyptian priests assured him it was propitious. Deinocrates followed the traditional Greek rectangular plan. The main street, the Canopic Way, lay parallel to the sea. It was two hundred feet wide and over three and one-half miles long. Crossing it at right angles was the major north-south street called *Sēma* "tomb" or *Sōma* "body"—named for the burial place of Alexander. The city was divided into five quarters, designated by the first five letters of the Greek alphabet. A canal linked the city to the Nile itself and was a source of fresh water for the city.

As late as the seventh century AD the Arab conquerors of the city were dazzled by the buildings of ancient Alexandria, none of which survives today. Indeed, our knowledge of ancient Alexandria is hampered by the fact that archaeological investigation is almost impossible, the city still being inhabited. One of the outstanding landmarks is the lighthouse at the northeastern tip of Pharos island, which was accounted one of the seven great

Lighthouse completed 279 BC

—— 2 ——

wonders of the ancient world. Four hundred feet high, the light reflected by its bronze mirrors was visible as far as four miles out to sea. A large complex of royal palaces, used by the Ptolemies until 30 BC and the Roman governors thereafter, faced the eastern harbor. Alexander's tomb was part of this complex. Of great cultural significance were the museum and library located near the palaces. Several important religious buildings reflected the varied population of the city. The Serapeion in the southwest section of the city was where the peculiarly Alexandrian god Serapis was worshipped. The Caesareum was dedicated (after the Roman conquest) to the cult of Caesar Augustus and later became the Christian Church of St. Michael. The central Jewish synagogue was large and impressive, with seventy-one golden chairs for the elders.

History   Shortly after its founding Alexandria became the capital of the Ptolemaic dynasty, initiated by one of Alexander's generals after the break-up of his short-lived empire. By ruling a country well-protected with natural barriers, the Ptolemies established a nation that focused on commerce and culture. Alexandria was the busiest port in the ancient world, exporting wheat to Rome and elsewhere (compare Acts 27:6, 28:11). The museum and library, established early in the third century BC, contained the greatest deposit of ancient literature in the world (almost 500,000 volumes) and attracted the greatest scholars of the day. Alexandria was the literary capital of the Greek world in the third century BC. The composition of poetry was especially significant; prose much less so. Here the Homeric poems received a definitive editing. Here Euclid, the "father of geometry," lived and worked. Eratosthenes devised an ingenious method for measuring the circumference of the earth, and sixteen centuries before Copernicus, Aristarchus suggested that the earth might circle the sun. As a crossroads city, made up of several different national groups *politeumata*—Greeks, Egyptians, and Jews—Alexandria embodied the synergism of the "Hellenistic" age. The city has been justly called the "spiritual center of the Hellenistic world."

Egypt and Alexandria with it fell under Roman control in 30 BC as a result of Octavian's defeat of Mark Antony and Cleopatra at the Battle of Actium. Octavian was permitted by the Roman Senate in 27 BC to assume the designation "Augustus" and became the first Roman "Emperor." As "the second city" of the Roman Empire, Alexandria was important for its culture and as "the granary of the Empire," the port from which Egyptian wheat was shipped. The population of the city in the time of Augustus (31 BC—AD 14) has been estimated as between 500,000 and 1,000,000, including slaves. Alexandria began to decline in cultural importance after the first century AD. A shift in the course of the Nile rendered Lake Mareotis unnavigable, further contributing to its decline. The city was conquered by the Arabs in AD 641 and was under the rule of various foreign governments for centuries. It is still today an important population center (El Iskandariya) of over 2,000,000.

Religion   Typical of the synergistic tendencies of the Hellenistic period, in which Greek and oriental influences mixed freely, was the worship of the most important god in Alexandria, Serapis. While the derivation of the religion is obscure, it combined Egyptian and Greek elements, and Serapis became the most important pagan god in Alexandria. The religion attained its greatest influence in the Roman period by spreading as far as Britain. Another development typical of the Hellenistic period was the deification of the Ptolemaic rulers. Beginning with Ptolemy II, each of the Ptolemies was worshiped under a cultic title ("Savior," "Benefactor"). Magic also played a prominent part in Alexandrian life.

An important religion in Alexandria was Judaism. Jews had been a part of Alexandria from its founding, and according to Josephus (*Contra Apion* 2.4) Alexander himself gave the Jews special privileges in the city. However, Josephus is almost certainly wrong in claiming that the Jews as a whole enjoyed the right to citizenship. Whether true or not, it is certain that Jews made up a substantial part of the city's population. They inhabited the fourth or "delta" quarter but spilled over into at least two others. Synagogues were located throughout the city. Strabo says that the Jews had their own *ethnarch* or "governor," and by the time of Augustus a *gerousia* or "senate." The Ptolemies exempted Jews from requirements that infringed on their religious beliefs, and many Jews served in high governmental positions.

The Jewish community also suffered its share of persecution. Josephus and the apocryphal book 3 Maccabees describe persecution under the Ptolemies, although they disagree on the chronology. The Jews' situation worsened under Roman rule, partly because the native population resented the aid that they gave to their Roman conquerors. A particularly difficult situation arose in AD 37-38, when the Roman governor Flaccus aided the Greek population in a savage persecution of Jews. A delegation of Jews, including the famous philosopher-theologian Philo, succeeded in persuading Emperor Claudius to restore their rights. Severe persecutions also arose at the time of the Roman-Jewish wars in AD 66-70 and 132-135. The latter repression led to a permanent decline in the Jewish population of the city.

The size of the Jewish population in Hellenistic Alexandria made it the most important center of Judaism outside Palestine. Martin Hengel speaks of "the remarkable and probably historically unique fusion of Jewish and Hellenistic culture in Alexandria from the third century BC" (*Judaism and Hellenism*, I, p. 66). Literary products of this environment included the apocryphal books Wisdom, Sirach, and 2 and 3 Maccabees; and the pseudepigraphal writings, Aristeas, the Sybilline Oracles, 4 Maccabees, 2 Enoch, and 3 Baruch. However, the most significant literary product of Alexandrian Judaism was the Septuagint, a Greek translation of the Old Testament. The Letter of Aristeas provides a lengthy but often legendary account of the origin of this translation. Probably the Pentateuch, at least, was completed in the reign of Ptolemy II Philadelphus (285-247 BC), with the other books being translated somewhat later. Undoubtedly intended to give Alexandrian Jews who had lost their Hebrew a comprehensible version of the Old Testament, the Septuagint was used by many New Testament authors and was the official Old Testament for much of the early church.

Another product of Alexandrian Judaism was the philosopher Philo. Deeply influenced by Platonic philosophy, Philo sought to explain the Jewish religion in philosophic terms and used allegory extensively in order to "explain" the Bible. The epistle to the Hebrews, though much more reticent than Philo, has been compared to this kind of approach.

Alexandria in the Bible While Alexandria is mentioned frequently in the Apocrypha and Pseudepigrapha, it plays a slight role in biblical accounts. Some schoalrs think that the book of Daniel may make mention of Alexandria in conjunction with references to the Ptolemies, but this is by no means clear. In the New Testament "Alexandrians" are mentioned along with other Hellenistic Jews who opposed Stephen (Acts 6:9). Apollos was an Alexandrian who became a significant evangelist and teacher after receiving instruction from Priscilla and Aquila (Acts 18:24). His eloquence and learning were undoubtedly the product of a good education in Hellenistic Alexandria. Finally, the ships that carried Paul from Myra to Malta (Acts 27:6) and from Malta to Puteoli (Acts 28:11) were Alexandrian. They were probably carrying grain from Egypt to the bakeries of Rome.

Early Christianity in Alexandria Tradition has it that John Mark, the author of the second gospel, was the first to bring the gospel to Alexandria (Eusebius, *H.E.* II. 16). The tradition is not very early, however, and it is probable that the first evangelists in Alexandria were ordinary Christians who had been converted on the Day of Pentecost in Jerusalem. Acts 2:10 specifically mentions Egyptians among those present. From uncertain origins the church in Alexandria came to be one of the most significant in the world. John Mark, whose reputed bones were moved from Alexandria to Venice in AD 828, was regarded as the first "bishop." In the second and third centuries orthodox and heretical teachers flourished in Alexandria. Among the latter were Valentinius and Basilides, who taught a "gnostic" Christianity. They were combatted by the famous "Catechetical School," whose most noteworthy leaders were Clement (*d.* 215) and Origen (*d.* 254). Both were heirs of the Alexandrian tradition in which philosophy infused theology. Later in the fourth century Alexandria again produced both a heretic and a defender of the faith; namely Arius and Athanasius, the persistent advocate of the deity of Christ. The Arab conquest, of course, brought an end to the significance of Alexandria for church history.

For further information on Alexandria see:

Bell, H. I. *Cults and Creeds in Graeco-Roman Egypt* (1953).

Davis, H. T. *Alexandria: The Golden City* (1957).
Forster, E. M. *Alexandria: A History and a Guide* (1961).
Jouguet, P. *La Vie Municipale dans l'Egypt Romaine* (1968).
Michalowski, K. *Aleksandria* (1970).
Stern, M. and S. Safrai, eds. *The Jewish People in the First Century*.

D. J. M.

ANTIOCH OF SYRIA

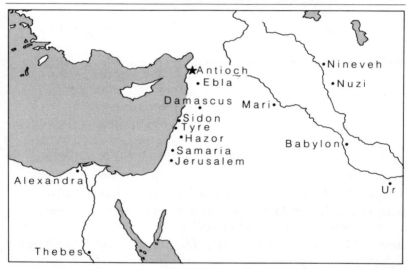

Antioch of Syria was founded about 300 BC by Seleucus I Nicator ("The Conqueror"), who named it after either his father or his son, both of whom bore the name Antiochus. It was situated at the foot of Mt. Silpius on the Orontes River, about three hundred miles north of Jerusalem and twenty miles east of the Mediterranean, at the joining of the Lebanon and Taurus mountain ranges where the Orontes breaks through and flows down to the sea. To distinguish it from fifteen other Asiatic cities built by Seleucus and also named Antioch, it was frequently called "Antioch-on-the-Orontes," "Antioch the Great," "Antioch the Beautiful," or "Antioch-by-Daphne" (alluding to its celebrated suburb five miles to the south). Because of its strategic location, political importance, and great beauty, it was referred to in antiquity as "Fair Crown of the Orient" or "The Queen of the East." During the first Christian century it was, after Rome and Alexandria, the third largest city of the Roman empire, with a population of over 500,000. In AD 540, after a catastrophic fire (AD 525) and two major earthquakes (AD 526, 528) in which over 360,000 of its people perished, Antioch was sacked by the Persians, who took most of the remaining young people to Mesopotamia as slaves. Those who remained suffered the horrible plague of 542. By the time the Arabs captured it in AD 637, Antioch was not much more than a frontier fortress. Today Antakiya (Antioch) is a sleepy, rather dingy town, part Turkish and part Arab, of about 35,000 inhabitants.

Antioch in Legend   Greek legend has it that Io, the daughter of the river-god Inachus, after being raped by Zeus, wandered to Mt. Silpius and died there in her grief. Later her devotees built a town at the western base of Mt. Silpius (on the east bank of the Orontes, which runs from north to south at Antioch), and this town became the core of the later city of Antioch. Another legend ascribes the choice of the site to Alexander the Great, who, after defeating Darius at the battle of Issus (333 BC), advanced over the Amanus mountains toward Phoenicia. At the spot where Antioch would later be built, Alexander drank from a spring and declared it to be as sweet as his mother's milk. There he wanted to build a city; but because of the exigencies of his military campaigns, its founding had to await the action of Seleucus, his general, a third of a century later.

Libanius, the famous Antiochene philosopher, orator, and man of letters, relates how Queen Semiramis of Assyria built a temple at Meroe, five miles east of Antioch, in honor of an Assyrian deity (probably Anaitis), whom the Greeks identify as Artemis. But this was probably a local tale designed to provide an illustrious origin for the cult of Artemis. Jewish tradition, seeking to establish the antiquity of the Jewish community at

—— 9 ——

Antioch, fixed the meeting of Nebuchadnezzar with the Great Sanhedrin at Daphne, the southern suburb of Antioch. And in the same spirit, the tractate Shekalim of the Jerusalem Talmud identifies Syrian Antioch as ancient Riblah "in the land of Hamath," where Jehoahaz was captive (2 Kings 23:33), Zedekiah was blinded, and his sons and nobles executed (Jer. 39:5-7), and from whence an eschatological remnant will return (Isa. 11:11).

Seleucid Antioch

After defeating his rival Antigonus at the battle of Ipsus in 301 BC and thereby winning full control of Syria for himself, Seleucus founded four "sister cities" in northwestern Syria: Antioch and its port city Seleucia Pieria; Apamea and its port city Laodicea-on-the-Sea. These cities were established to play a primary role in the subjugation of the conquered territory and were settled by Macedonians and Greeks to assure the transplantation of Greek culture onto Semitic soil. Seleucia Pieria, named for Seleucus himself, was built first and was originally meant to be the capital city of the Seleucids because of its highly defensible position. Before long, however, principally because of its better location on the trade routes, Antioch eclipsed Seleucia Pieria in importance, as it did also the other cities of the Seleukis (that is, the quadruplet of cities founded by Seleucus in northwestern Syria). Soon after Seleucus' death in 280 BC, his son, Antiochus I Soter (280-261 BC), established Antioch as the Seleucid royal city and capital.

Antioch was built by the architect Xenarius, who used elephants from Seleucus' army to mark the location of towers in the city wall and wheat to lay out the streets. The city was laid out in an oblong plan of about 555 acres (slightly less than a square mile) between the Orontes river to the west and the main trade route to the east, being set far enough away from Mt. Silpius (farther to the east) so as not to be inundated by sediment and gravel brought down from the mountain by the winter rains. Like many other Greek cities, Antioch was constructed on the Hippodamus plan, with streets crossing each other at right angles and buildings placed in the rectangles formed by the streets. The city was laid out to make the best use of the sun in both winter and summer, and so that the winds which blew up the Orontes valley from the sea could penetrate all its sections. The *agora* or "market" was situated along the left bank (east side) of the river and probably was about eight city blocks in size. A citadel for protection was located to the east at the top of Mt. Silpius.

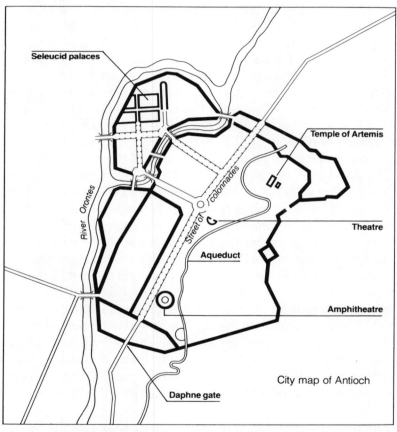

City map of Antioch

The original population of Antioch was made up of retired Macedonian soldiers of Seleucus' army, of Athenians who had been transferred from Antigonia and resettled at Antioch, of Jews who had served as mercenaries in the Seleucid army, and of slaves of diverse origins. In addition, there were native Syrians who were assigned a separate section in the city. Altogether, from various records and the excavations conducted during 1932-39, it seems fair to say that the free population of Antioch during its early Seleucid days numbered somewhere between 17,000 and 25,000—plus slaves and native Syrians, who were not counted.

Antiochus I enlarged Antioch to include a sizable second quarter east of the main trade route and up to the base of Mt. Silpius. He protected the new section from the wash down the mountain by diverting the waters around the city. After his death, the Ptolemies of Egypt controlled northern Syria and the city of Antioch for about two decades. Taking the city back again, Seleucus II Callinicus (246-226 BC) enlarged Antioch by building a third quarter on the large island in the middle of the Orontes northwest of the existing city (the island was completely wiped away by the earthquakes of the sixth century AD). The greed of Antiochus III (223-187 BC), however, brought him into conflict with Rome. He was defeated at the battle of Magnesia (190 BC) and lost all of his empire beyond the Taurus range to the Romans or to kingdoms allied with Rome (like Pergamum). This was the turning point in the history of the Seleucid empire, though not the end of the fame and fortune of Antioch.

Antiochus IV Epiphanes (176-163 BC) was the last of the great Seleucid rulers. Under his reign the broad slope of Mt. Silpius became the fourth and main quarter of the city, earning it the title "Tetrapolis" or "Fourth City." In this new section of the city Antiochus built a new senate house and several new temples. After Antiochus IV, however, bloody internal struggles for the throne exhausted the economy of the Seleucid empire and Antioch never regained its former splendor until the Romans came.

Roman Antioch

In 64 BC Pompey put an end to the Seleucid dynasty and annexed Syria to the Roman empire. Antioch, because of its location on the most important trade routes, served as the capital of the Roman province of Syria throughout its history as a Roman city, except for a brief period when it fell out of favor with Septimius Severus (AD 193-211). Under Rome the city gained new vigor. Soon it came to reflect in its life, thought, and physical appearance the quintessence of Roman splendor, power, and pettiness. Greek institutions continued to exist, but they were now under Roman control and gradually transformed to serve Roman ends. Even physically the city was changed from a Hellenistic to a Greco-Roman one.

In the civil war between Julius Caesar and the Roman Senate that began in 49 BC, Antioch sided with Caesar and rebuffed Pompey after his defeat at Pharsalus in 48 BC. In 47 BC Caesar visited Antioch and conferred on it freedom (presumably in terms that were greater than the "freedom" conferred by Pompey). He also rewarded the city by restoring its Greek Pantheon and by building a new theater, amphitheater, aqueduct, and public bath. To cap off his building projects at Antioch, he also ordered the construction of a splendid basilica, which he called after his own surname the Caesareum. The imperial favor shown by Caesar continued under other Roman emperors as well, with each succeeding emperor (there are a few exceptions) adding to the magnificence and beauty of the city. Particularly under Augustus (31 BC—AD 14) and Tiberius (AD 14-37)—with the cooperation of Herod the Great and Agrippa I—the city was transformed into one of the most splendid and imposing cities of the empire.

Probably the most noteworthy architectual feature of the time was the great colonnaded street that ran northeast to southwest along the line of an earlier Seleucid street and formed the main street of the Roman city. It was two miles long, about thirty-one feet wide, and had flanking porticoes that were each about thirty-two feet wide. Its more than thirty-two hundred columns supported the porticoes on each side and the vaulted stone roofs at each intersection, with these structures being highly ornamented. The surface of the road was paved with marble. Some of the porticoes led to the entrances of public buildings; some to homes of the wealthy. Others protected shoppers and a variety of merchants, whose booths were set up between the columns.

There was, in fact, no other city in the world where one could walk for two miles in such splendor under porticoes.

One of the major events begun at Antioch under Augustus was the founding of the local "Olympic" games, which in time became one of the most famous festivals of the Roman world. At first the games were held every four years for thirty days during the month of October and were not specifically called Olympic games. Later, after falling into disrepute through mis-management, they were reorganized by Claudius (AD 41-54) to include theatrical, dramatic, and musical events, in addition to athletic contests and races in the hippodrome. Under Claudius they were called the Olympic games (in continuity with the ear-lier Greek Olympic games) and held every five years; although later, because of wars, earthquakes, fires, or other public calam-ities, they were sometimes held at intervals of fifteen or twenty years.

Jews at Antioch
Jews were among the original settlers in the city founded by Seleucus I about 300 BC. Antioch's proximity to Palestine, its impor-tance as the administrative center of so much of the Orient, and its commercial prosperity made it at-tractive to many Jews. For most of the Seleucid period the Jews at Antioch seemed to have been free to follow their own customs and to carry on their affairs without governmental interference. Only during the reign of Antiochus IV Epiphanes, when repres-sions in Palestine seriously affected Jews in Syria as well, were the peace and tranquility of the Jewish population in Antioch broken. Under the Seleucid monarchs, in fact, the Jewish com-munity at Antioch grew and prospered.

Rome's capture of Antioch in 64 BC did nothing to diminish the legal and official status of Jews in the city. Rather, it proved highly beneficial to the Jewish community both economically and socially, at least for the next one hundred years. In this early period of Roman domination the Jewish community in the city reached its greatest numerical strength, numbering some-where around 65,000 or about one-seventh of the city's entire population. Few Jews, however, except some mercenaries upon discharge from the army and a few merchants, applied for and were granted citizenship, since that required the sacrifice of their Jewish religious and national identity. Thus as foreigners and a distinctive minority they lived in three or more separate settlements in and around the city—with probably one settlement being to the southwest of the city near Daphne; another, northeast of the city in the Plain of Antioch; a third in the city proper, with possibly smaller enclaves elsewhere.

The period of privilege and prosperity that Antiochene Jews enjoyed, however, came to an end toward the middle of the first century AD. In AD 40, mobs were organized in Antioch to attack the Jews; they burned their synagogues and killed many of them. This took place in the third year of the reign of Caligula (AD 37-41), who in the winter of AD 39-40 had ordered a statue of himself to be erected in the temple precincts at Jerusalem. So, while the details of this mob action at Antioch are obscure, it seems safe to posit that it should be seen in the context of Caligula's totally insane program of self-aggrandizement and antagonism against Jews (as was expressed also at Alexandria and Jerusalem), which ended when Claudius (AD 41-54) became emperor.

The greatest crisis, however, came during the Palestinian Jewish revolt against Rome in AD 66-70. Josephus tells us that although there were massacres of Jews throughout Syria in reprisal, the Jews of Antioch, Sidon, and Apamea were, at first, shielded to a large extent from the people's rage by the Roman authorities. But this did not last long, for shortly after Vespasian's arrival in Syria, a Jew named Antiochus, who was the son of the leader of the Jewish community and who evidently no longer thought of himself as a Jew, turned the pagan population of Antioch against the Jews with a story of how the Jews were planning to burn the city down to the ground in one night. As a result, an intense persecution of Jews broke out, with Jewish leaders burned to death in the theater, sabbath privileges revoked, demands made on Jews to sacrifice to pagan deities, and wholesale massacres. Added to all this, a fire of extensive dimensions broke out in Antioch during the winter of AD 69-70, which, of course, was blamed on the city's Jews and so became the occasion for further massacres and persecutions.

Jews at Antioch were further discredited by the imposition of the *fiscus judaicus* of Domitian (AD 81-96) and the decrees of Hadrian (AD 96-138) penalizing circumcision. They were also seriously affected by the active interests of Domitian, Hadrian, and their successors in prosecuting charges of "atheism" against all infidels and monotheists, which, of course, effectively put an end to Jewish proselytism and so severed the strongest tie between Jews and pagans. To shame the Jews further, Hadrian erected over a western gate of Antioch the Cherubim that had been taken from the Jerusalem Temple in AD 70. Thus while they continued to live in the city and their legal status remained officially unchanged, the civil status of Antiochene Jews after the Palestinian uprisings of AD 66-70 and 132-135 was considerably lowered, almost, in fact, to the point of insignificance. Thereafter when the pagans of Antioch needed a scapegoat for the disaffections, they turned on the Christians.

Christians at Antioch   Apart from Jerusalem, no city of the Roman empire played as large a part in the early life and fortunes of the Christian church as Antioch of Syria. The book of Acts tells us that it was Hellenistic Jewish Christians who, on fleeing Jerusalem, first brought the gospel to Antioch, preaching first only to Jews but soon including Gentiles as well. With the increase of believers at Antioch, the Jerusalem church sent Barnabas to check on the situation. It was through his efforts that the Christian community at Antioch was joined to the Christian community at Jerusalem, thereby preventing any possible alienation or split because of Antioch Christendom's rather unusual beginnings. Further, it was through Barnabas' efforts that Saul of Tarsus became involved in the ministry at Antioch.

First-century Antioch was a fertile place for various philosophies, cults, and religions. It was a city that prided itself on its toleration, with even its Jewish population more open to Gentiles than anywhere else in the Jewish Diaspora or Palestine. Yet many Antiochenes were looking for a more significant religious experience and more meaning to life than paganism offered. Many Gentiles, in fact, were associated in one way or another with the Jewish synagogues of the city, being impressed with the monotheism and ethics of Judaism. So when the Christian gospel came to Antioch, it was received not only by Jews but also by Gentiles who had been mentally and spiritually prepared by Judaism.

A great number of people at Antioch, Acts tells us, accepted the gospel message and committed themselves to Jesus. Since, however, this group was made up of both Jews and Gentiles, the city's officials had to find a name for them that would distinguish them from Jews and all the devotees of the various pagan religions of the city. So they nicknamed them Christians, which means "Christ Followers" or "People of Christ." And it is this name, rather than the earlier self-designation "Those of the Way," that stuck, simply because it was seen by the Christians themselves to be highly appropriate.

During a particularly severe famine that ravished Palestine in AD 45-47 (cf. Josephus, *Antiquities* 20. 51-53; possibly also *Antiquities* 3. 320-321)—with sporadic bad harvests and famine conditions occurring elsewhere in the empire throughout Claudius' reign (compare Seutonius, *Vita Claudius* 18. 2; also Tacitus, *Dio Cassius*, and *Orosius*)—the Christian community at Antioch, after only a year or so in existence, was strong enough and wealthy enough to send aid to Christians at Jerusalem in distress. Further, it was the community of Christians at Antioch that confirmed the call of God to send our missionaries to other Gentile cities, and so Antioch became the birthplace of foreign missions. Throughout Paul's missionary journeys, it was Antioch, in fact, that was the apostle's home base. In addition, it was the place where controversy between Jews and Gentiles first erupted within the Christian church, furnishing the immediate occasion for the first church council at Jerusalem.

Acts tells us nothing further about Antioch, for Luke's concern is with the forward movement of the Christian mission until it comes to Rome. That should not be taken, however, to imply that Antioch was no longer important as a Christian center. On the contrary, throughout the succeeding centuries Christianity played a vital role in the history of Antioch, and Antiochene Christianity was a dominant factor in the history of civilization within the Roman empire.

The meagerness of our sources, however, makes it impossible to reconstruct any continuous history of Christianity during the following centuries. We hear of a sect called the Nicolaitans, which supposedly arose from Nicolaus of Antioch (cf. Acts 6:5) and seems to have tried to reconcile Christian worship with certain pagan practices. We hear of Gnosticism, which was claimed to have been derived from Simon Magus of Samaria (compare Acts 8:9-24) and was brought to Antioch by Menander of Samaria, one of Simon's disciples. We also hear of Theophilus, a mid-second-century bishop, who attempted to work out some sort of synthesis between Christianity and Judaism, using in the process certain literal interpretations of the Old Testament and certain Jewish exegetical procedures for the New.

Most known of the second-century Christians at Antioch is Ignatius, the bishop of the church there, whose person and faith are familiar to us from his seven letters written while on his way to martyrdom at Rome. In December AD 115 a tremendous earthquake almost leveled Antioch. Both Trajan, the emperor, and Hadrian, who was then governor of Syria, were in the city at the time, and narrowly escaped with their lives. Many others, however, were killed, and Antioch and its suburb Daphne were extensively ruined. After the disaster, the populace turned on the Christians as scapegoats. Many Christians were killed, and Ignatius, their bishop, was sent under guard to Rome to be tried there and eventually (AD 117) eaten alive by wild beasts in the arena. Our knowledge of the period following Ignatius' death is scanty. For the most part we have only a bare list of bishops of the church at Antioch for the next 120 years or so.

Beginning with the third century, the fortunes of Antiochene Christianity take a decided turn for the better. The emperors Elagabalus (AD 218-22) and Severus Alexander (AD 222-35), who were both originally from Syria, were interested in the eastern religions and were tolerant of Christianity. In fact, Severus Alexander's mother, Julia Mamaea, who was deeply interested in religion and may even have been a Christian herself, sometime between AD 231-33, while living at Antioch, invited Origen, who was then at Caesarea, to come to her and instruct her in Christian doctrine. So Origen, accompanied by a military escort sent to assure his safety, arrived at Antioch and stayed in the city for some time. That such a leading figure in the government had invited Origen to the city must have given the Christians at Antioch great encouragement.

In AD 260 Paul of Samosata was elected bishop. His teaching stressed the unity of God and the manhood of Jesus, and so paved the way for the reception of Arianism at Antioch. To many of the clergy and faithful, however, Paul's doctrine, ecclesiastical conduct, and personal ethics were scandalous, and at the Council of Antioch in 268 his teaching was condemned as heretical and he was deposed as unworthy. Yet Arianism continued to thrive in the city, and much of the history of the Christian community at Antioch for the next century is connected with the controversy over the nature of Christ's divinity.

Under Diocletian (284-305), Christians at Antioch suffered intense persecution. Many were killed. The most famous martyr of this time was Lucian, a celebrated scholar whose critical edition of the Bible became dominant throughout the eastern part of the Roman empire. Later under the emperor Julian "The Philosopher" or "Apostate" (AD 361-63), in reaction to Constantinian policies and practices, a final, official Roman persecution of Christians broke out. But this came to a short end with the return of Christian emperors to the throne.

Most significant for Christians, of course, was the establishment of Christianity as the official religion of the empire by Constantine (AD 306-37). The capital of the empire was moved to Constantinople, and with that move Antioch became in large measure the mind and soul of the Roman state. To signal this change, Constantine built on Antioch's northwest island the magnificent, octagonal Great Church, which was called the Golden Church because of its gilded roof.

The later history of Christianity at Antioch is replete with the names of some of the greatest figures in church history. Basil the Great (330-79), for instance, the Cappadocian bishop of Caesarea, who opposed Arianism, studied at Antioch under the pagan philosopher Libanius and often visited the city. John Chrysostom (345-407), who was born there, was probably the most illustrious Antiochene church father. He also studied Greek literature and rhetoric under Libanius, but later gave his attention wholly to Scripture and Christian theology. His greatest success came at Antioch as a preacher ("John the Golden Mouth"), pastor, and statesman from 386-97. His literary output was enormous—chiefly sermons, essays, and letters. Then during the last decade of his life he was Archbishop of Constantinople, the capital city, where under the weight of administrative duties he seems to have withered and died.

Antioch of Syria has had a place and mission in history unlike that of any other city of the ancient world. Founded as an outpost of Greek civilization in Semitic lands, it was destined from the beginning to be always on the frontier of life and thought and to bring together widely diverse strands of culture and religion. Under the Seleucids, Antioch, as an offshoot of Athens, was a living link with the classical age of Greece, and this link grew stronger as time went by—culminating finally in the philosopher and orator Libanius. Under Rome the city by reason of its commercial prosperity and political power became a dominant factor in the history of civilization. Yet it was Christianity not Rome that was the real rival to the paganism of Antioch's old traditions and that laid the foundations for further intellectual and spiritual growth. Some of this it did by direct confrontation with Hellenism, as with John Chrysostom; some by accommodation with the worthier aspects of Hellenism, as with Basil the Great. In sum, it was during the first century AD that the Christian gospel went out from Antioch to the Gentile world. It is this gospel that then transformed the face of much of the world; it was during the fourth century AD that a new civilization was being formed in Antioch out of the living substance of the old. This heritage remains ours today.

The goddess Tyche

For further information on Antioch see:

Antioch-on-the-Orontes (Publications of the Committee for the Excavation of Antioch and its Vicinity), I: *The Excavtions of 1932*, ed. G. W. Elderkin (1934); II: *The Excavtions, 1933-1936*, ed. R. Stillwell (1938); III: *The Excavtions, 1937-1939*, ed. R. Stillwell (1941); IV, pt. 1: *Ceramics and Islamic Coins*, ed. F. O. Waage (1948); IV, pt. 2: *Greek, Roman, Byzantine and Crusaders' Coins*, ed. D. B. Waage (1952).

Brown, R. E. and J. P. Meier. *Antioch and Rome. New Testament Cradles of Catholic Christianity* (1982).

Cimok, F. *Antioch on the Orontes* (1980).

Downey, G. *A History of Antioch in Syria from Seleucus to the Arab Conquest* (1961).

Downey, G. *Ancient Antioch* (1963).

Kraeling, C. H. "The Jewish Community at Antioch." *Journal of Biblical Literature* 51 (1932), 130-160.

Liebeschuetz, J. H. W. G. *Antioch, City and Imperial Administration in the Later Roman Empire* (1972).

Meeks, W. A. and R. L. Wilken. *Jews and Christians in Antioch in the First Four Centuries of the Common Era* (1978).

R. N. L.

ATHENS

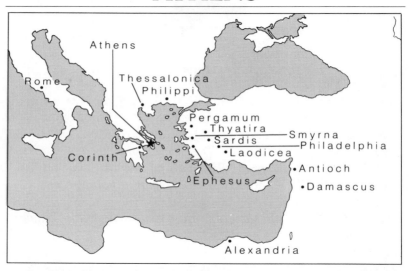

The place of Athens in biblical history does not begin to compare with its position in ancient history. Paul did not include Athens in his missionary itinerary but went primarily to wait for Silas and Timothy, who were trying to heal the wounds of the Berean church after the Jewish persecution there (Acts 17:16). Paul founded no church in Athens; indeed, it was his greatest failure and a source of deep hurt (1 Cor. 2:3). At the same time Athens was the major city in Attica and is still famed as a center of cultural and intellectual grandeur. Situated five miles from the Aegean Sea, Athens lay in the driest region of ancient Greece, with an average rainfall of sixteen inches, just suf-

ficient for its primary exports of olive oil and wine. In addition
there were excellent beds of clay for pottery and beds of marble,
silver, and lead for architecture and crafts.

Historical   The city was founded in the fourth mille-
Survey   nium BC and by the second millenium was
                   an important fortified citadel built on the
                   Acropolis. However, we know few details
before the sixth century BC, when Solon paved the way to Athenian democracy by establishing a constitution in which the
rights of individuals were protected. During this period the
predecessors of the famed architectural landmarks were constructed, including the old Bouleuterion or Senate house and the
older Temple of Apollo, the "father" of Athens.

Athens became one of the leading city-states in the fifth century BC. During the Persian War the city was destroyed (480-79
BC) but still played a decisive role in the defeat of the Persians,
due mainly to its maritime prowess. The city was soon rebuilt
and under Pericles (461-29 BC) entered its golden period. Pericles
constructed the Parthenon Propylea and Erechtheion on the
Acropolis as well as the Temples of Hephaestus and Ares (Roman Mars). The great sculptor Phidias and his school provided
a wide range of statues and other art works. Athens imported
philosophers, playwrights, and other artists who praised its
magnificence. It became the center of Hellenistic culture for the
next three centuries.

Politically Athens was not so fortunate, for its dominance
was comparatively short-lived. With the Peloponnesian War
and then the rise of Alexander, Athens lost first its influence and
then its freedom. Still, architecturally and intellectually the city
continued to grow. Throughout the Seleucid era other nations
and leaders showered gifts upon the city. The Dipylon Gate, the
Theater of Dionysus, the Temple of Apollo, and the Stadium
were erected in the fourth century, and the next two centuries
saw the construction of the Temple of Zeus, the Stoa of Attalus
and the Metroon. In 86 BC the Roman general Sulla sacked Athens and carried many of its treasures to Rome but left most of

the buildings relatively intact. By the first century AD Athens had totally lost its political importance and Corinth had taken over the economic reins of power, but the city retained its splendor and its educational status. The account of Pausanias, who devoted the first thirty chapters of his *Description of Greece* (159 AD) to Athens, describes a city still much the same as the one Paul visited.

Athens and Paul
Paul entered Athens from the major seaport of Piraeus via the Dipylon Gate and most likely walked down the wide thoroughfare southeast to the Agora or marketplace. We are told that Paul spent some time sightseeing (Acts 17:23). While the beauty of the city probably moved him aesthetically, his Jewish sensitivities were appalled by the flagrant idolatry. Paul would have crossed the Agora diagonally from the northeast via the Panathenean Way, so called because the annual procession honoring Athena followed this road on the way to the Parthenon. Paul would have first noticed on the right the Royal Stoa, a small edifice eight columns wide and the official seat of the king (archon) who had jurisdiction over the city's religious affairs. Here, too, the Council of Areopagus had its offices and occasionally met. Next to it was the Stoa of Zeus, with an enormous statue of Zeus, and several impressive paintings by the fourth-century BC master Euphanor, including the Meeting of the Twelve Gods and the battle against the Thebans at Mantineia. Across the northern section of the Agora was the famous "Painted Stoa," a most beautiful building with scenes depicting Athenian history: the Wars against the Trojans, the Persians, and the Amazons. This Stoa was also known as the seat of philosophers and Zeno, founder of the Stoic school, lectured here. Indeed, from this the "Stoics" derived their name as "men of the Stoa." Next to the road in the open square across from the Temple of Zeus was the Altar of the Twelve Gods, supposedly the very center of the city. All distances were calculated from this point.

As Paul walked further on the Panathenean Way, he would

pass next between the Temple of Ares and the Stoa of Attalus. The Temple of Ares had been moved during the reign of Augustus from its original setting outside the city to the very center of the Agora. As the temple had been dismantled each block had been carefully marked and these markings are still visible today. A series of statues depicting the gods and the Athenian heroes flanked the temple. Directly west and up a series of steps on a hill stood another temple which seemed a replica of the temple to the war God, namely the Temple of Hephaestus, god of the forge. Both temples were striking in appearance, constructed of white marble and Doric columns, thirteen on each side and six on the ends. In addition the Hephaestion was surrounded by a formal garden. With its view of the entire Agora, it indeed provided an impressive setting.

The magnificent Stoa of Attalus was nearly as long as the road itself, 382 feet in length and sixty-four feet wide. Its two stories were borne upon forty-five columns, Doric at the bottom and Ionic at the top. The lower story was lined with twenty-one shops, and in front of the structure stood the Bema, the podium from which city officials would address the public. The beautiful building has been reconstructed as the site of the Agora Museum.

To the west of the Bema and south of the Temple of Ares stood the Odeum or theater, built by Marcus Agrippa with comfortable seating for one thousand people in eighteen rows. This was a natural congregating place, with its view of everything to the north and the sides in the Agora, and from it people could watch the daily religious processions and colorful throngs as they stood in groups arguing philosophical points or sharing the latest gossip. The Athenians were famed for two things: their religious fervor, since they erected statues to all the gods and even to "unknown gods" (Acts 17:23; compare Pausanias, *Description of Greece* I, 1 and 4); their love of dialogue, searching always for "some new idea" (Acts 17:19).

As Paul looked further east across the Agora, he would see first the Temple of Apollos Patroon and then below it the Metroon. The temple was built by Euphranor and contained a statue of Apollo with a lyre, symbolizing the artisitic renown of the city. The Metroon was the first of three buildings which together formed the administrative center of the city. This building was the sanctuary of the mother of the gods and contained a small temple with a statue fashioned by Phidias. Primarily the state archives were housed there. Behind it was the Bouleuterion or senate building, where the city council of five hundred members conducted their business. It looked like a theater, consisting primarily of a large semicircular auditorium with raised tiers of seats. South of both was the Tholos or Prytanikon, a small circular building in which the prytanics or executive committee of the council met. It contained a dining room where the executives ate at city expense, and on a rotating basis several would stay overnight so that administrators were available to the people day and night.

The southern portion of the Agora was the commercial center, with an open market flanked by south, east, and middle stoas. The middle stoa was the largest in the Agora, 450 feet long with Doric columns along its length. The Heliaia, the major law court of Athens, lay at the west end of the commercial Agora. The Romans, however, found the space too constricting and built their own market place just east of the Greek Agora. With stoas on all sides, the interior courtyard measured 269 by 187 feet. Shops and arcades lined the facade, with entrances on the west and east sides. A large Tower of the Winds lay at the east end, 46 feet high and consisting of a large hydraulic clock and several sundials. On the far sides stood figures of the four winds.

Most impressive of all, of course, is the Acropolis itself, to which the Panathenaean Way led. It was the highest hill of Athens and the crown of her glory. Of course there is much more than the Parthenon, for all its magnificence. On the southern slope stood the Theater of Dionysus, where Greek drama had its origin. It contained seventy-eight tiers of seats with a capacity of 17,000 spectators. The orchestra was sixty feet in diameter with a raised stage. In addition there was a stoa 535 feet long and 85 feet wide. East of it was the Odeum of Pericles, 270 feet

Acropolis at Athens

long with a tier of seats and multitudinous columns. Southeast lay the Temple of Zeus, a magnificent structure with 104 Corinthian columns 50 feet high and $5^1/2$ feet thick at the bottom. The grandeur must have been breathtaking.

Yet the Acropolis itself still provided the most awe-inspiring sight. Paul would have entered from the west, passing through the beautiful Propylaea, a gateway of white marble built by Pericles and costing the equivalent of over thirty million dollars. At the right of the gate was a forty-five foot high monument, with a chariot and four horses atop a thirty foot rectangular marble slab. Just inside the gate was the huge statue of Athena, sculpted by Phidias, and the small temple dedicated to Athena and entitled "Wingless Victory," probably so named to keep "victory" from flying away from the city. To the left and right were the Erechtheion and the Parthenon, respectively. The former was a structure 78 by 42 feet, a temple to Athenia Polias and Poseidon Erechtheus. Its main feature was the Porch of the Maidens, with six women supporting the roof.

—— 27 ——

Porch of six maidens on Erechtheion

Parthenon

The Parthenon itself was one of the glories of the ancient world. It was a temple to Athena, patron goddess of the city. Pericles had it erected between 447 and 432 BC. It is 238 by 111 feet in size, with eight Doric columns on the ends and seventeen on the sides, each 34 feet high, six feet in diameter at the base. Two pediments 65 feet high stood at the ends, the eastern one depicting the birth of Athena and the western one depicting her contest with Poseidon for Attica. A Doric frieze of ninety-two panels stood atop the colonnade and encircled the Parthenon. These panels portrayed special scenes from mythology. Inside, another continuous Ionic frieze 525 feet long depicted the annual Panathenaic procession to the temple. In the east room was the statue to Athena Parthenos, forty feet high with her flesh formed from ivory and the rest made of gold. In her right hand Athena held a six foot high statue of victory. On Athena's breast was the head of Medusa; inlaid with ivory on her helmet is the image of the sphinx, and in her other hand is a spear.

From the above description one cannot help but be impressed by the staggering number of temples and idols. It is easy to see how Paul was both offended and drawn to the city. The high degree of religious fervor became the entry point to his message of salvation to the Athenians.

Paul before the Areopagus

When Paul began to debate daily with the Athenians, he undoubtedly provoked great interest, even though some dismissed him as a "seed-picker," that is, one without original ideas but who borrows the seeds or thoughts of others (Acts 17:18). Nevertheless, his proclamation of a God unknown to the Athenians led them to bring him before the court of the Areopagus. There are two opinions as to where he delivered his speech. The court or council itself was the most ancient institution in the city, and in the distant past had been the Senate. In the first century its primary function was to decide matters of religion, and particularly homicide. While its name indicates the traditional place where the council met in Roman times, the court often discharged its duties in the Royal Portico or Stoa in the

Mars Hill (Areopagus)

northwest section of the Agora. Since the court still convened in both places, it is most difficult to identify with certainty the actual site, whether the hill or the Stoa. The first is the traditional site, the second might better fit the geography, especially if the decision to take Paul before the court was hasty rather than planned, as many believe. Since the council met in both places it is impossible to know for certain, and there the matter must remain.

Paul's speech (Acts 17:22-31) is a model for understanding how context influences content, and should be examined briefly as it pertains to the history and culture of Athens. Athens' preoccupation with idols becomes Paul's point of contact as he uses their religiosity positively rather than negatively. Moreover, while his concepts are drawn from Judaism, his quotations are taken from the philosophers, particularly Epimenides of Crete (v. 28) and the Stoic poet Aratus of Cilicia (v. 28). One must note the absence of biblical quotations and the type of argumentation found in the Jewish speeches of Acts. The Athenians may also have recognized Euripides (fragment 968) in Paul's statement that God does not dwell in temples constructed by man, a point which bridges Jewish and Christian polemics (Acts 17:24). This message as much as any in Scripture shows how culturally relevant and intellectually aware the living Gospel must and can be. As the Athenians listened to Paul, their glance must have been drawn again and again to the architectural treasures and pagan temples surrounding them.

For further information on Athens see:

Broneer, O. "Athens: City of Idol Worship." *Biblical Archaeologist* 21 (1958), 1-28.

Bruce, F. F. "Pans and the Athenians." *Expository Times* 88 (1976-77), 8-12.

Finegan, J. "Athens," *Interpreter's Dictionary of the Bible* (1976), I, 307-09.

Hemer, C. J. "Paul at Athens: A Topographical Note." *New Testament Studies* 20 (1974), 341-50.

Mendague, A. T. "Paul and Athens." *Bible Today* 49 (1970), 14-23.

Rudprecht, A. "Athens." *Zondervan Pictorial Encyclopedia of the Bible* (1975), I, 403-406.

Thompson, A. A. and R. E. Wycherley. *The Agora of Athens* (1972).

G. R. O.

BABYLON

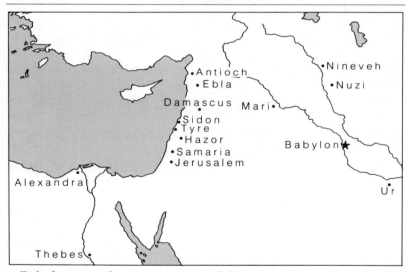

Babylon was the greatest city of the ancient Near East during the brilliant if short-lived Neo-Babylonian or Chaldean Empire (sixth century BC). Originally bisected by the Euphrates River, its ruins sprawling over two thousand acres now lie west of the present course of that river, fifty-four miles south of Baghdad and five miles north of Hillah.

Together with the region of "Babylonia," Babylon is mentioned over two hundred times in the Bible. In the New Testament era "Babylon" became a symbolic name for the great pagan city of that age, Rome.

The Hebrew name *bab-el* "gate of God" is derived from the

Akkadian *bāb-ili* or *bāb-ilāni* "gate of the gods." The comparable Sumerian name for the city was *ká-dingir-ra*, which may or may not be earlier than the Akkadian name. The name was transliterated into Persian as *Babirush* and into Greek as *Babylōn*. Another coded Hebrew name for Babylon was *Shēshak*, which appears in Jeremiah 25:26 and 51:41.

Foundations   According to Genesis 10:9-10 Babylon was founded by Nimrod along with the other great cities of Shinar (Mesopotamia): Erech (Uruk) and Accad (Agade). By a popular etymology or play on words the name was associated in Genesis 11:9 with the verb *balal* "be confused," in reference to the confusion of tongues at the Tower of Babel. There is also a comparable Sumerian story of the confusion of tongues. Early travelers associated the story with the ruins of the ziggurat at Birs Nimrud (ancient Borsippa), seven miles southwest of Babylon, but the story no doubt referred to the ziggurat (the staged temple tower) at Babylon itself.

The earliest textual references to Babylon come from the Akkadian era (twenty-third century BC) and from the Ur III period (twenty-second to twenty-first century BC). Though there is reason to believe that the city was founded at an even earlier date, archaeologists have not been able to confirm this because the high water table precludes digging below a certain depth. Any attempt to do so quickly turns the excavator's pit into a quagmire.

Early in the second millennium BC Mesopotamia was overrun by waves of Amorites ("Westerners" from Syria) who seized various cities. The First Dynasty of Babylon (late nineteenth century BC) was one of these Amorite dynasties. Its most illustrious ruler was Hammurabi, famed for his law code. Though this was not the earliest law code from the ancient Near East it is the most extensive one to be preserved. The law code, inscribed on a seven-foot high diorite stela, originally stood in the Esagila, Marduk's temple in Babylon. It was carried off to Susa by the Elamites, where it was discovered by the French in 1901-02.

Law Code of Hammurabi

The First Dynasty of Babylon was brought to a sudden and unexpected end by a lightning raid of the Hittites from Anatolia in 1595 BC. They carried off the statue of Marduk, the patron god of Babylon—the first of several ignominious journeys taken by the god in the course of Babylon's history.

After the Hittites withdrew, the Kassites from the Zagros Mountains to the east swept into Mesopotamia to dominate the area for four centuries until 1160 BC. We have the names of thirty-six Kassite kings. It was the ninth in this list, Agum II, who recovered the statue of Marduk from Hana, where it had been taken by the Hittites. In the middle of the fifteenth century Ulamburiash crushed the independent Sea Land at the head of the Persian Gulf to reunite Babylonia for the first time in two centuries.

Tukulti Ninurta I of Assyria attacked Babylon in 1250 BC, carrying off the statue of Marduk. It was sent back to Babylon sixty-six years later. But in 1160 the Elamites from Susa in southwestern Iran swept over Babylonia, carrying off as booty from Babylon the statue of Marduk and the Hammurabi Law Code. Marduk's statue was recovered by the energetic Babylonian ruler, Nebuchadnezzar I (1124-1103 BC).

—— 34 ——

Neo-Assyrian
Domination

The Assyrians to the north were to dominate Mesopotamia and much of the entire Near East during the ninth through the seventh centuries BC. The Assyrian king Shalmaneser III intervened in Babylon in 852. According to Herodotus, the fabled Assyrian queen Semiramis (Sammuramat, the mother of Ada-Nirari III [811-782 BC]) restored much of Babylon.

The great Assyrian king Tiglath-pileser III (745-27 BC) sent aid in 745 to Nabonassar, the pro-Assyrian governor of Babylon, against revolts by the Chaldeans and Arameans. He again intervened in 732 when Mukin-zeri, a Chaldean chieftain, seized Babylon. When Tiglath-pileser had himself installed as king over Babylon in 731, he became the first Assyrian king in five centuries to rule directly over Babylonia.

The Chaldeans (*Kaldu*), who occupied the Sea Land area north of the Persian Gulf, are first mentioned in Assyrian documents early in the first millennium BC. It was Merodach-baladan who succeeded in welding the various Chaldean tribes together. He first appeared in the last years of Tiglath-pileser III and then continued to trouble Assyrian kings in the reigns of Sargon II and Sennacherib.

Merodach-baladan seized Babylon in 721 upon the death of the Assyrian king Shalmaneser V. He was able to rule the city for a decade until Sargon II retook the city in 710. Some of the rebels from Babylon were deported to Samaria. With the accession of Sennacherib in 705, Merodach-baladan made another bid for power. It was probably on this occasion that he sent an ostensibly solicitous letter to Hezekiah (2 Kings 20:12ff.; Isa. 39:1-8), which was probably intended to sound out the Jewish king's interest in an anti-Assyrian coalition. After his invasion of the west in 701, Sennacherib marched his forces against southern Mesopotamia, driving Merodach-baladan into flight toward Elam.When the Elamites captured Sennacherib's son, who had been made king of Babylon, a Chaldean made himself king of Babylon. Sennacherib in 689 captured Babylon, devastated the city, and carried off the image of Marduk. The following Assyrian king, Esarhaddon, restored some of the damage to the city. One of his twin sons, Ashurbanipal, was made king of Assyria, and the other son, Shamash-shum-ukin, was made king of Babylonia. When Shamash-shum-ukin rebelled against his brother, Esarhaddon besieged the city for four years (651-48 BC). His brother perished in the flames which devastated the city.

Neo-Babylonian Empire The Chaldean Nabopolassar (626-05 BC) began the Neo-Babylonian era when he seized Babylon. Nabopolassar united with the Medes to overthrow the Assyrians, capturing Ashur in 614 and Nineveh in 612. After 607 Nabopolassar, because of old age and perhaps ill health, left the command of his army to his son, Nebuchadnezzar, who became king upon his father's death in 605.

Nebuchadnezzar (605-562), who was one of the greatest kings in antiquity, is mentioned almost a hundred times in the Old Testament. In 1956 D. J. Wiseman published the *Chaldean Chronicles*, which give us detailed information about the first ten years of the king's reign. In his very first year Nebuchadnezzar deported Daniel and his companions to Babylon (Dan. 1:1). As the Jews rebelled again, Nebuchadnezzar led the army against Judah in 598. He deported the eighteen-year old king, Jehoiachin, to Babylon. The Babylonian Chronicles laconically report: "He then captured its king and appointed a king of his own choice"—namely, Zedekiah, Jehoiachin's uncle (2 Kings 24:17). Nebuchadnezzar sent back to Babylon great treasures (2 Kings 24:13) and 10,000 captives (2 Kings 24:14). After a further rebellion, Nebuchadnezzar returned again in 586 to devastate Jerusalem, destroying the temple and carrying off its vessels to Babylon (2 Kings 25:13-17).

It was Nebuchadnezzar who transformed Babylon into the greatest city in the ancient world. Most of the buildings recovered by the excavators date to his reign. It was with some justification that he could boast, "Is not this the great Babylon I have built as the royal residence, by my mighty power and for the glory of my majesty" (Dan. 4:30).

Nebuchadnezzar was succeeded by a series of ephemeral rulers, including his son Evil-merodach, who was to rule from 562 to 560. According to 2 Kings 25:27-30 and Jeremiah 52:31-34 Evil-merodach released King Jehoiachin from imprisonment after thirty-six years of captivity in Babylon and treated him kindly.

When Evil-merodach was murdered, he was succeeded by Nebuchadnezzar's son-in-law, Neriglissar. He may be identified with the Nergal-sharezer, who accompanied Nebuchadnezzar to Jeusalem (Jer. 39:3) and who was entrusted with the care of Jeremiah (Jer. 39:13). During the early part of his reign he was involved in the restoration of the Esagila Temple and the repair of the canals around Babylon. After the death of Neriglissar in 556, his son Labashi-Marduk was able to reign only for nine months before being killed by Nabonidus, the last of the Neo-Babylonian kings.

Nabonidus (556-539 BC) is not mentioned in the Bible, but his son Belshazzar is depicted as the king of Babylon when it fell to the Persians in 539 (Daniel 5). Nabonidus hailed from the northern city of Harran, where Abraham tarried with his father Terah, and he was devoted to Harran's moon god, Sin. Nabonidus may have been married to a daughter of Nebuchadnezzar.

Nabonidus acknowledged that he had been elevated by the order of Marduk, even though he was "one who did not know Marduk." Nabonidus was concerned with restoring various temples including the Temple of Ishtar at Babylon. But above all he was concerned about the rebuilding of the Temple of Sin at Harran, which had been destroyed by the Medes in 610 BC.

This exaltation of Sin—"the king of the gods of heaven and earth"—over all the other gods, and even the suggestion of converting the temple of Marduk in Babylon into a temple of Sin, naturally offended the Babylonians. Inscriptions discovered at Harran in 1956 indicate that he believed Sin was punishing various cities with plague and famine because of their lack of respect for his patron god.

It was largely due to this tension that Nabonidus decided upon the drastic measure of moving his capital from Babylon to the oasis of Tema some five hundred miles away. He was to remain there for ten years (about 550 to 540 BC), leaving "kingship" in the hands of his son Belshazzar, which explains the leading role played by the latter in the book of Daniel.

As the Persian threat on the eastern frontier became acute, Nabonidus hastened to Babylon from his self-imposed exile in Arabia. He tried to rally resistance, but he was too unpopular. His attempt to collect the gods of the cities to the north of Babylon failed. Indeed, morale was so low that many of the Babylonians welcomed Cyrus as a liberator, who honored Marduk more than their own king, according to the propagandistic Cyrus Cylinder.

According to the Chaldean Chronicles Cyrus "did battle at Opis on the Tigris against the army of Akkad (that is, Babylonia)" in September, 539 BC. By October 10 the Persians were able to capture Sippar to the north of Babylon "without a battle." The Chronicles indicate that Gubaru, Cyrus' general, and his troops entered Babylon "without a battle" on October 12. This occurred even as Belshazzar, confident in the strength of Babylon's fortifications, was celebrating a feast with the sacrilegious use of the vessels from Jerusalem's temple (Daniel 5). According to classical sources (Herodotus I.191; Xenophon, *Cyropedia* VII,5.15) the Persian soldiers diverted the Euphrates and gained an entrance into the city's defences by following the river's course.

When Cyrus entered Babylon he found that the inhabitants resembled skeletons. He ordered his troops not to terrorize the people, and he instituted slum clearance: "I brought relief to their dilapidated housing." A fragment of the Cyrus Cylinder identified in 1970 informs us that Cyrus also restored Babylon's inner wall and moats.

Cyrus pleased the Babylonians by restoring to their cities the gods which had been removed by Nabonidus. Further, he had his son, Cambyses, observe the New Year's rite. This would have taken place on March 24, 538 BC (Nisan 1). On the fifth of Nisan, Cambyses would have been subjected to a symbolic humiliation before the high priest of Marduk. The priest would have pulled his ear and forced him to kneel. Then he would have had to say, "I have not sinned, O Lord of the Lands. I have not destroyed Babylon, nor damaged the Esagila, or neglected the temple rites."

Cyrus' decree in 538 (2 Chron. 36:22-23; Ezra 1 and 6), permitting the Jews in Babylonia to return to Judah and to rebuild their temple, was quite in accord with the Persian policy of toleration. The Persians not only returned the various temple vessels to the Jews but offered them aid in the rebuilding of their temple, as they did to the Babylonians, the Egyptians, and the Greeks.

While Cambyses (525-522 BC) was conquering Egypt, Gaumata (pseudo-Smerdis) usurped the Persian throne and held it for seven months until he was killed by Darius in 522 BC. As Darius relates in his famous Behistun inscription, he had to suppress numerous revolts. In Babylonia a dangerous revolt was led by Nidintu-Bel, who claimed to be "Nebuchadnezzar (III), the son of Nabonidus." He was defeated in two battles on December 13 and December 18, 522 BC. An Armenian called Arkha also claimed to be a "Nebuchadnezzar (IV), the son of Nabonidus." He was defeated on November 27, 521 BC.

After the capture of Babylon by the Persians, it became a favorite residence of the Achaemenid kings for at least part of the year. According to Xenophon (*Cyropedia* VIII, 6.22), "Cyrus himself made his home in the center of his domain, and in the winter season he spent seven months in Babylon, for there the climate is warm; in the spring he spent three months in Susa, and in the height of summer two months in Ecbatana."

Darius erected a small palace in Babylon just to the west of Nebuchadnezzar's palace. Its colonnaded forehall and rectangular hall with two rows of four columns bears a striking resemblance to the Achaemenid buildings at Pasargadae and Persepolis. Fragments of a copy of Darius's Behistun Inscription were found at Babylon. Under Darius' son, Xerxes (486-465 BC), the Babylonians rose in rebellion in 483. In 482 just before he embarked on his famous expedition against Greece, Xerxes captured the city, demolished its temples, and destroyed the statue of Marduk.

Shortly after his decisive victory over Darius III at Gaugamela near Arbela on October 1, 331 BC, Alexander marched triumphantly into Babylon. He gained the favor of the Babylonians by offering sacrifices to Marduk. For two months he put ten thousand of his soldiers at work clearing the debris left by Xerxes and rebuilding structures that had been destroyed. Josephus (*Contra Apion* I.192) recounts that the Jewish soldiers refused to take part in this project. After his capture of the Persian capitals and his penetration to the easternmost frontiers of the empire, Alexander returned to Babylon to die of a fever on June 13, 323 BC, having conquered much of the known world in a dozen years. One monument to the Greek presence in Babylon is a theater.

Seleucus I, one of Alexander's generals, fell heir to much of the eastern empire. He came to Babylon in 312 to establish the Seleucid Dynasty. The fate of Babylon was sealed when Seleucia, a new capital on the Tigris River, was founded in 305 by Seleucus I. Seleucus transferred most of the population of Babylon to the new city, and he used bricks from Babylon for the new construction.

A prime source of our knowledge comes from the *Babyloniaca* of Berossus, a Chaldean who left Babylon about this time to settle on the island of Cos in the Aegean. There he taught Greeks the secret of Chaldean astrology. In the mid-second century BC a certain Diogenes from Babylon became the head of the Stoic school at Athens.

The new Persian dynasty of the Parthians arose in 250 BC and endured until AD 225. The sixth Parthian ruler, Mithradates I, invaded Babylonia in 141 BC. After defeating Seleucid forces and the Hellenistic state of Characene, the Parthian general, Himerus, established himself as "king of Babylon" in 123 BC. He destroyed many of the temples in Babylon and sold many Babylonians into slavery. The Parthians established as their new capital the city of Ctesiphon, just across the Tigris from Seleucia.

In the New Testament era there was an active community of Jews in Babylonia, some of whom were present in Jerusalem during the day of Pentecost (Acts 2:9-11). The famous rabbi, Hillel, originally came from Babylon. But New Testament references (1 Pet. 5:13; Rev. 17:9, 18:2, 10, 21) are interpreted by most scholars as symbolic of Rome and not as literal references to Babylon.

The last dated cuneiform texts from Babylon date to AD 110. By 200 the site was largely in ruins as Old Testament prophecies had predicted (Isa. 13:19-22; Jer. 50:13, 23-26, 39; 51:24-26).

Herodotus, the "Father of History," visited Babylon in the mid-fifth century BC after the Greeks and Persians had signed a peace treaty. His accounts of Babylon (I. 178-87) were once questioned by scholars because he does exaggerate the total length of the walls and their height. But much that he reported has been confirmed by the excavations.

Excavations With the Islamic conquest of the area of Mesopotamia, pre-Islamic antiquities were neglected or deliberately defaced. The Jewish traveler from Spain, Benjamin of Tudelah (twelfth century AD), correctly associated the ruins near Hillah with Babylon, though he thought that the tower of Babel was located at Birs Nimrud. But since the reports of his travels were not published until centuries later, it remained to Pietro della Valle to reidentify the site in 1616. C. J. Rich did some surface surveys in 1811-12.

The travelers encountered a number of mounds which concealed the remains of ancient Babylon, covering a rectangular area about one thousand yards north to south, and six hundred yards west to east, or about twenty-one hundred acres.

1. *Babil* was a separate oblong *tell* a mile to the north of the main site, which covered the site of Nebuchadnezzar's summer palace.

2. *Qasr*, "Citadel" at the northern edge of the site was about seven hundred yards square. This covered the main palace area.

3. *Homera*, "Red Mound" to the east where the Greek theater was found. The excavators found debris which they attributed to the labors of Alexander's men.

4. *Sahn*, a depressed area, 550 yards long, to the south of Qasr which covered the site of the Esagila and the ziggurat.

Ruins of Babylon

5. *Merkes*, "Trade Center" to the east, as it was elevated, was the one area where Koldewey was able to find strata from the Old Babylonian Dynasty (eighteenth century BC) to the Parthian era.

6. *Amran ibn Ali* and *Jumjuma*, at the southern edge of the site.

7. The western area has not be excavated at all.

A. H. Layard, who had dug at Nimrud in 1845, did some limited work at Babylon in 1850. Jules Oppert recovered some materials from the site in 1852, but unfortunately these finds were lost when the boat carrying them sank in 1855. In 1875-76 people from the nearby villages, hunting among the ruins for building materials in the Amran-Jumjuma area, found clay jars with about three thousand inscribed tablets from the reign of Nabopolassar and his successors. In 1879 Hormuzd Rassam, who had assisted Layard, found at Jumjuma other important texts, including the famous Cyrus Cylinder. All told about thirty thousand texts have been discovered at Babylon, most dated to the Neo-Babylonian era but some as late as the Seleucid era.

The Deutsche Orientgesellschaft under the leadership of Robert Koldewey began the first of many seasons at Babylon in 1899. Koldewey had already dug in the Aegean, Italy, Sicily, and Syria. He was assisted by such eminent scholars as W. Andrae, B. Meissner, F. Weissbach, and F. Wetzel. Koldewey worked with a crew of 250 men, who had to be taught to clear rather than destroy the brick walls. They succeeded in clearing the Ishtar Gate and three other gates, the Processional Way, and the Qasr palaces. Excavations were finally halted in 1917 by the British occupation of the area. The 650 crates of bricks from the Ishtar Gate were finally shipped out of Iraq in 1926 for Berlin, where they were used in a reconstruction now displayed in the East Berlin Pergamum Museum. German excavators returned to Babylon in 1956 and worked for a number of seasons in the area of the Greek theater. Between 1955 and 1968 the Iraqi Department of Antiquities partially restored such areas as the Ishtar Gate, the processional way, the throne room, and the temple of Ninmah.

Ishtar Gate

——— 43 ———

An outer wall enclosed the summer palace a mile north and extended at a distance from the main city. The circuit of this wall was about eight miles rather than the fifty-six miles claimed by Herodotus. The main city was protected by a set of double walls: an inner wall twenty-one feet thick, then about twenty feet away, an outer wall about twelve feet thick. A hundred towers rose up to sixty feet high at sixty-foot intervals. Beyond these walls was a system of moats.

As Herodotus reported, Babylon was bisected by the Euphrates River. The western area was the New City, and was connected to the main city by a bridge about four hundred feet long. The excavators found that the bridge had been supported by eight piers made of bricks set in asphalt.

There were nine major gates which gave access to the city. The most spectacular of them, the Ishtar Gate, was flanked with towers forty feet high, decorated with alternating figures of the bulls of Hadad and the dragons or "walking serpents" of Marduk depicted in multi-colored glazed bricks. The sacred processional way, which was in some places sixty-six feet broad, led from the Ishtar Gate nearly a thousand yards to the Esagila Temple. The street was paved with red and white flagstones on a foundation of asphalt and brick. Some of the limestone paving stones bore the inscription, "I Nebuchadnezzar, king of Babylon, paved this road with mountain stone for the procession of Marduk, my Lord." The sidewalks were made of veined red breccia. The walls on either side of the processional street, which were found still standing to a height of forty feet, were decorated with hundreds of multi-colored bulls, lions, and dragons on a blue background. Each animal was over six feet long.

The major palace was located on the east bank of the river at the northern edge of the city to the southwest of the Ishtar Gate. It occupied a trapezoidal area, 985 feet west to east, and between 395 and 655 feet north and south, enclosing five major courts. The central court, 170 by 55 feet, was the most important as the king's throne room was located at its southern end. This room was decorated with enamelled bricks in the form of Proto-Aeolic columns, probably inspired by Greek artisans.

This court was probably the setting for Belshazzar's feast (Daniel 5). It could have accommodated a thousand persons.

To the west by the river was the original palace of Nabopolassar. Nebuchadnezzar boasted that he replaced the crude bricks of his father's palace with burnt brick. Morever he recorded: "Mighty cedars I caused to be laid down at length for its roofing. (Compare his dream in Daniel 4.) Door leaves of cedar overlaid with copper thresholds and sockets of bronze I placed in its doorways. Silver and gold and precious stones, all that can be imagined of costliness...I heaped up."

Just to the north of the main palace area was the "northern" palace. Nearby was an area which functioned as a kind of "museum" or storehouse for booty down to the Persian era. A mile further north at the edge of the ruins of Babylon lie the scanty remains of the "summer" palace at the site of the *Babil* mound. This palace was equipped with ventilation shafts to cool the building.

Literary sources (for example, Berossus in Josephus *Antiquities* X.226) credit Nebuchadnezzar with building the famed Hanging Gardens, esteemed as one of the Seven Wonders of the World. He built it to please his Median wife, who was homesick for the vegetation of her homeland. Koldewey discovered in the northeast corner of the palace area a space nine hundred by six hundred feet. He believed that two rows of seven chambers with barrel vaults, constructed of stone and brick, were the supports for the famed garden. A triple-shafted well may have been used for watering the plants. On the other hand, many scholars are sceptical of Koldewey's interpretation.

One reason for their scepticism is that it was in this very area that 300 important tablets were found. Though they were found earlier, they were not published until 1939 by Weidner. These date from 595-70 BC and record provisions of grain and oil given to numerous important captives, including Jehoiachin, the exiled king of Judah, and his five "sons." This is a dramatic confirmation of 2 Kings 25:27-30. As the Jehoiachin tablet is dated to 592, but five years after his exile, the king must have had one son a year or the term "sons" must not be interpreted literally.

Provisions are recorded also for captives from Egypt, Philistia, Phoenicia, Syria, Lydia, Cilicia, Elam, Persia, and Media.

Religious   The characteristic sacred structure in Meso-
Buildings   potamian cities was the ziggurat, a staged,
                       brick pyramid which served as an artificial
                       mountain platform for a temple. Herodo-
tus reported that Babylon's ziggurat had eight stages. A tablet translated by George Smith suggests that the stages were in different colors. Estimates of the total height of the ziggurat range from 165 feet up to 300 feet.

The Babylonian ziggurat was named *E-temen-an-ki* "Building of the Foundation of Heaven and Earth." The base of the ziggurat was three hundred feet square. Herodotus (I.181-83) described the temple of Marduk on top of the ziggurat as the place where the *hieros gamos* rite was practiced; the "sacred marriage" between the king and a cultic prostitute to ensure the fertility of the land.

We do not know when the earliest structure was erected. The ziggurat was damaged and restored on numerous occasions. After it had been damaged by Sennacherib, Nabopolassar repaired it and declared, "At that time Marduk commanded me to build the Tower of Babylon...its pinnacles should strain upwards to the skies." Nebuchadnezzar further restored the structure so that "it might rival heaven." The ziggurat was so destroyed by Xerxes that Alexander's army was not able to restore it after two months of labor.

Just to the south of the ziggurat was the Esagila "House with the Uplifted Head," the main temple of Marduk. It was first mentioned in the Ur III period (twenty-first century BC). The main shrine was a narrow rectangular structure, 33 by 260 feet. It was roofed with cedar beams and its walls were decorated with gold and precious stones. Herodotus (I.183) reports that there were two statues of Bel (Marduk), and that some seventeen tons of gold were used in their construction (compare Daniel 3). The god was provided with a throne and a bed. During the New Year's festival in the spring the king would grasp the hand of Marduk in a procession. Some scholars have detected a polemic against this *Akitu* festival in Isaiah 40-46.

About fifty temples are mentioned in documents, fifteen in the inscriptions of Nebuchadnezzar alone. Of these five have been excavated including the Esagila. Near the Ishtar Gate was the well preserved Temple of Ninmah, the goddess of the underworld, occupying an area 175 by 115 feet. Southeast of the main palace area was the Temple of Ishtar of Akkad in the area of Merkes, east of the processional way. At the south end of the processional way was a temple dedicated to Ninurta, the god of war, occupying an area 190 by 133 feet. This was originally built by Nabopolassar and then restored by Nebuchadnezzar. Just to the west was the temple of his consort Gula.

Texts also mention 180 open air shrines for Ishtar, three hundred daises for the Igigi gods, and twelve hundred daises for the Anunnaki gods. Jeremiah 50:38 had accused the Babylonians of being given over to idolatry: "It is a land of graven images, and they are mad upon idols." The excavators found over six thousand figurines in Babylon. But as the Jewish prophets proclaimed, none of these was able to save the city from God's judgment.

For further information on Babylon see:

Allen, K. W. "The Rebuilding and Destruction of Babylon." *Bibliotheca Sacra* 133 (1976), 19-27.

Black, J. A. "The Near Year Ceremonies in Ancient Babylon." *Religion* 11 (1980), 39-60.

Böhl, F. M. T. *King Hammurabi of Babylon in the Setting of His Time* (1946).

Erlandsson, S. *The Burden of Babylon* (1970).

Koldewey, R. *The Excavations at Babylon* (1914).

LaRue, G. A. *Babylon and the Bible* (1969).

Oates, J. *Babylon* (1979).

Parrot, A. *Babylon and the Old Testament* (1956).

———— . *Nineveh and Babylon* (1961).

Thomas, D. W. *The Greatness That Was Babylon* (1962).
Unger, E. *Babylon* (1970 reprint of 1931 ed.).
Yamauchi, E. *Greece and Babylon* (1967).

E. Y.

CHAPTER FIVE

BETHEL

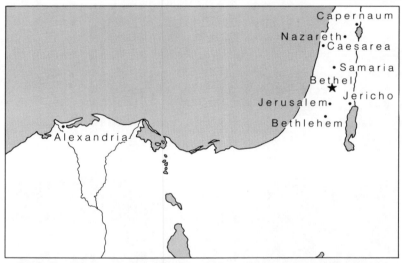

Bethel, the city most frequently mentioned in the Bible, Jerusalem alone excepted, was situated in the central hill country of Palestine, on the border between Israel and Judah. The highest point of the site usually identified as Bethel is three thousand feet above sea level, about 350 feet higher than Jerusalem, and 4219 feet above the Dead Sea. Near the top of the mountains along the north-south watershed ridge is an abundance of excellent springs which made natural camp sites for nomads and their flocks. The country is ideal for nuts and fruits.

A north-south highway ran along the ridge of the mountains, going south from Shechem, bypassing Shiloh and on to Bethel and then Gibeah (Judg. 21:19, compare 20:31). This was crossed by another road that went westward from Jericho up to Bethel and on to the Mediterranean, one branch to Philistia and the other to the Plain of Sharon. The road from Jericho to Bethel was so important that it served as the boundary between the tribes of Ephraim and Benjamin (Josh. 16:1-2, 18:13.) This was the route used by Joshua when he first cut through the land to divide and conquer.

Name It was Jacob who named the site Bethel ("house of God"). The older name of that city was Luz (Gen. 28:19, Judg. 1:23).

Sometimes Bethel is identified with Luz, as in Genesis 35:6: "So Jacob came to Luz..., that is, Bethel." Yet Joshua 16:2 distinguishes the two—Joseph's boundary went westward "from Bethel to Luz" and Joshua 18:13 states something of a compromise formula, describing the boundary that goes "toward Luz to the slope of Luz southward which is Bethel" (cf. RSV).

Reconstructed eighth-century BC home

What Jacob named was the sacred spot on which he dreamed about the angelic ladder. It was likely the altar site used by Abraham on the high ground east of the city, between Luz and Ai (Gen. 12:8, 13:3; the name "Bethel," unknown till Jacob named the place, would then have been put in the Abraham account in retrospect by the compiler of Genesis). Jacob named the spot again in Genesis 35:15. The first time, he had been a lone traveler passing through. Who would have known of his new name for the spot? To change the usage of a name is very difficult; it does not happen overnight. And so the new name would have gone unused in that locality. On the second visit his family traveled with him; therefore he had occasion to inform them of his name. Still, on his death-bed Jacob yet calls the spot by its native name: Luz (Gen. 48:3). Both names appear in Judges 1:23; thereafter the term that persists is Bethel.

History   Bethel receives first mention in the patriarchal narrative (Genesis 12). On the mountain between Bethel and Ai, Abraham set up camp and built an altar to Yahweh, as he journeyed through Canaan for the first time. A brief trip to Egypt, where he tried to pass off his wife as his sister, incurred Pharaoh's displeasure and landed him back at Bethel and back to restored fellowship with Yahweh (13:3ff.).

Bethel rises to prominence in the Jacob narrative. On his first night away, escaping from his brother's murderous intentions under the ruse of wife-hunting, Jacob's uneasy sleep was interrupted with a dream of stairs, angels, heaven, and reassurance from God. He set on end his stone pillow to mark the spot, and he called it the "house of God" (Gen. 28:10ff.).

Then in Canaan, as a married man with growing sons and a daughter, the family met with rape, and retaliated with a treacherous murder of all the males of Shechem. Amidst fears of a counter attack, Jacob listened to God's direction, "Arise, go up to Bethel" (35:1), and they made a new start (35:2-4). Young Joseph, between age six and seventeen, probably welcomed the prospect of a move with his father to the site, having been told again and again the story of the ladder to heaven. Here Rebekah's nurse was buried, and here were Joseph's last memories of his mother (35:16). Later, when he and his father were reunited in Egypt, tradition has it that the old man's reaction was, "Yea, true is the vision which I saw at Bethel" (Jubilees 45:4).

Joshua's conquest took the army initially up the road from Jericho to Ai, just on the other side of the hill before coming to Bethel (Josh. 7:2). Between the two towns he set an ambush with five thousand soldiers. However, Joshua and the main part of the army set up camp in the valley north of Ai, in sight of the town's inhabitants. The men of Bethel joined their neighbors in pursuit of the Israelite soldiers, leaving Ai an easy open prey to the ambush (Joshua 8). Eventually both the kings of Ai and Bethel were defeated (Josh. 12:9, 16), and Bethel came into Israelite hands.

When dividing up the land among the tribes, Bethel became the southern boundary point for Joseph's settlement (Josh. 16:1). Yet the town itself is listed among the cities of Benjamin (18:22). It seems to have been lost to the Canaanites in the Judges period, and reconquered by the "house of Joseph" who thereafter kept it. In the recapture they slaughtered the entire population save one man and his family, who had shown them the entrance into the city (Judg. 1:22ff.; compare 1 Chron. 7:28). Shortly after, Bethel became the center of worship, at least for a time, for the ark of the covenant was there (Judg. 20:27). There Israel assembled to ask Yahweh which tribe should lead in revenge of some Benjaminite's impropriety to a visitor's concubine. There, a couple of miles south down the road, was the palm under which Deborah sat to give her judgment to those who came up for counsel (Judg. 4:5). There at Bethel, Samuel made one of his annual circuit stops (1 Sam. 7:16). This was a town in Saul's home area, a town where people came to worship (1 Sam. 10:3, 26). In the surrounding hills Saul had his first exposure as military captain (1 Sam. 13:2). The town fathers were among those whom David courted with his victory spoils (1 Sam. 30:27).

If Bethel enjoyed a respectful status during the days of a

united monarchy, it seemed destined indeed for a bright and prosperous future economically, if not spiritually, when Jeroboam I established its religious superiority for the northern kingdom. On a main north-south road, he could intercept all worshipers headed for Jerusalem, and so effectively break their ties with that cultic center. He needed new clergy to attend his golden calf worship (1 Kings 12:31f.), and this meant a new population influx. With the sanctuary in full operation, and with the king's special blessing, the outlook was very promising. The new cult did not go altogether unchallenged, however, for a visiting prophet from down south in Judah announced that the priests' bones would one day desecrate Jeroboam's altar (1 Kings 13). Bethel remained in Jeroboam's hands for approximately ten years and then was lost to the south when Abijah (Rehoboam's son) captured Bethel and other cities (2 Chronicles 13).

Elijah used the opportunity to establish one of his schools of the prophets in the city of the golden calf. Elijah visited the school with his associate, Elisha, just before his death. They journeyed from the Gilgal school near the Jordan, up to the college at Bethel, and back down to the one at Jericho. As the new headmaster, Elisha shortly returned, only to be met and mocked by a group of hecklers. The latter were fatally silenced by two she-bears (2 Kings 2)! Apparently the calf cult and the prophetic school did not enjoy a happy association in the town.

When Jehu became the northern king and effected his purge of Ahab and Jezebel's family, Bethel seems to be back under northern jurisdiction, for Jehu razed the house of Baal but allowed the calves at Dan and Bethel to stand (2 Kings 10). By the time of Jeroboam II, Bethel is called a royal sanctuary (Amos 7:13). Amos, prophet of Yahweh, and Amaziah, priest of Bethel, were in outright conflict. The prophet was sent out of town, but not before doom had been pronounced on the priest and the whole town (3:14, 5:5f., 7:17f.). Bethel, the seat of sin (4.4), was far from a "house of God." Hosea, in scornful reluctance to use its name, calls it Beth-aven, "house of iniquity" (Hos. 10:5, 8; compare 10:15 and Josh. 7:2). His voice joins with Amos to foretell destruction. Mothers will be dashed in pieces with their children, thorns and thistles will grow on the altars, and the calf-idol will be carried off to Assyria. Assyria marched in and took over in 722 BC. Bethel was then partly occupied by Babylonian colonists planted by the Assyrians (2 Kings 17:24-28). Apparently the shrine retained a strong influence into the exile, for the Assyrian king allowed a priest to return there to teach the customs of the god of the land, and thereby ward off the attack by lions. So Bethel continued as a center of religious syncretism.

It was King Josiah who, after cleaning up Jerusalem, continued the sweep northward into Samaria, focusing particularly on Bethel. He broke down Jeroboam's longstanding high place and altar, ground the stones to dust, and burned the Asherah. Then he defiled the altar with human bones disinterred from the mountain graves, in accord with the prophecy of two hundred years past (2 Kings 23:14ff.). And Bethel's shame was subsequently used as a warning to neighboring Moab (Jer. 48:13).

After the exile, Ezra's census lists the men of Bethel and Ai at 223 (Ezra 2:28; compare Neh. 7:32). Bethel is the northernmost town listed with the Benjaminites in Nehemiah 11:31ff., but its inhabitants are not listed at all among the people rebuilding the walls of Jerusalem. Amos had said, "Bethel shall come to nought" (5:5). The prophets generally leave it at that, and the New Testament ignores the place. It is named as one of the last towns captured by Vespasian before he left Palestine to become emperor of Rome. There he established a Roman garrison (Josephus, *Jewish Wars* 4, 9.9). By the fourth century AD it was called a large village, twelve Roman miles north of Jerusalem on the road to Neapolis (the new town just west of Shechem—Eusebius and Jerome). Thereafter it goes unmentioned for fourteen hundred years.

Archaeology   Identification of Bethel with the modern town of Beitin has been under challenge. The association of the two has been made since the nineteenth century. The phonetic relation of Beitin to Beitil is entirely normal in Arabic; compare Yesrā'ēl/Isrā' in, Yešmāl'ēl/Išmā'īn.

Ruins outside Beiten

Four archeological expeditions have been made to Beitin:
1934, 1954, 1957, 1960. Kelso worked with Albright on the first,
led the other three, and became spokesman for them all. Nearly
four acres were available to the excavators, with the modern
town at the south end. The earliest sherds were found to date
from 2200 BC. Beitin peaked in the Hyksos period (*ca.* 1720-
1550). Around 1240-1235 there was evidently a terrific conflagration—one of the thickest ash levels reported in
Palestine—leaving five feet of debris. Whereas the city before
the burning contained some of the finest homes in pre-Hellenis-
tic times, afterward they were of the crudest contruction. Canaanite cult objects disappeared. Kelso identifies this as a
cultural break from feudalism to a "democracy of scarcity," and
links it to a thirteenth century conquest under Joshua. The four
archaeological campaigns at Beitin have failed to locate Jeroboam's calf sanctuary. This was a major aim of the excavations,
but much of the city has not been touched, and some is inacces-
sible because of the present buildings. A Canaanite sanctuary
was found on the low ridge northeast of Beitin. But as Kauf-
mann has observed, Abraham would hardly have erected an al-

tar to Yahweh in the same place. No major manufacturing industry was found. One olive oil factory was unearthed from the Late Bronze period. The city was torched by the Babylonians *ca.* 550 BC. Settlers of Nehemiah's time lived in crude houses constructed of stones from the old city wall. Byzantines (*ca.* AD 500) discovered the older Bronze Age city wall and used it as a major quarry to furnish stone for their new defences. The spot remained in ruins until a century ago when a small Arab clan reinhabited it.

The identification of Bethel with Beitin has been challenged by Livingston. His reasons are listed as follows:

1. *Geographically.* Beitin was not on a main crossroad (nor even on the main northerly Roman road from Jerusalem to Caesarea via Neapolis). An abnormal northerly bend to the border is called for. Ai has not been discovered east of Beitin, where it should be according to the Bible. The distance from Jerusalem is too far (compare Eusebius and Jerome).

2. *Topographically.* There is a small valley between Beitin and et-Tell (Gen. 12:8 speaks of a mountain between Bethel and Ai).

3. *Archaeologically.* The Bible does not say Bethel was burned by Joshua (but compare the five feet of ashes Kelso consigns to Joshua's conquest). There is no archaeological evidence identifying Beitin as Bethel. Beitin shows no occupation for 1500-1400 BC (compare Joshua's conquest) nor 2200-2000 BC (compare Abraham's and possibly Jacob's visits to the site, though see above with reference to the first pottery sherds found).

Livingston suggests rather that Bethel be identified with Bireh. He notes that Bireh has a similar meaning to Luz: "stronghold, fortified place." He advances four items that argue for Bireh. First, it is at a natural crossroads. Secondly, it is on an east-west geographical dividing line, with a plain to the north and another south, but deep valleys running to the east and west. Thus it would be a natural place for Jeroboam's sanctuary that served as a roadblock to potential worshipers heading south to Jerusalem. Thirdly, he argues that Bireh is the correct number of Roman miles (twelve) north of Jerusalem. And fourthly, there is a mountain east of Bireh instead of a valley. Ai

Roman well at Bethel

then would be a ruin one and one-half miles to the south east.

To date there has not been archaeological work to establish Livingston's hypothesis. Because of the dubiety of the situation, the histories of Bethel and Beitin are not combined, leaving that decision to further evidence.

For further information on Bethel see:

Dumbrell, W. J. "Role of Bethel in the Biblical Narratives from Jacob to Jeroboam 1." *The Australian Journal of Biblical Archaeology* 2 (1974-75), 65-76.

Kelso, J. L. "Excavations at Bethel." *Biblical Archaeologist* 19 (1956), 36-43.

———. "The Excavation of Bethel." *Annual of the American Schools of Oriental Research* (1968).

Livingston, D. "Location of Biblical Bethel and Ai Reconsidered." *Westminster Theological Journal* 33 (1970), 20-44.

MacKay, C. "From Luz to Bethel." *Evangelical Quarterly* 34 (1962), 8-15.

D. H.

BETHLEHEM

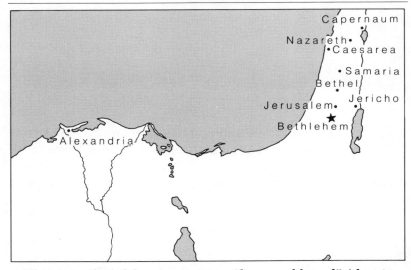

The name *beth-lehem* may mean "house of bread" (that is, a place of food) or possibly "the place of Lahamu" (that is, the shrine of an Assyrian deity). From an early period Bethlehem was the name of a town in the hill-country of Judah, and in its long history was the home of king David and also the birthplace of Jesus.

It is located some five miles southwest of Jerusalem near the main highway linking Jerusalem to Hebron and the Negeb. The village is well placed geographically, thus lending itself as an important military garrison historically. Little is known about the origins of the settlement.

The first historical reference to Bethlehem was found in the the Amarna letters of the fourteenth century BC where the prince of Jerusalem complains that "Bit-lahmi" [Beth-lehem] has betrayed him.

Genesis 35:19 indicates that the tomb of Rachel was in the vicinity of Ephrath or Bethlehem. The name variation is probably an attempt to distinguish Bethlehem of Judah (or Bethlehem Ephrath) from Bethlehem in northern Israel—Bethlehem of Zebulun. Tradition points out the site of Rachel's tomb near where the road to Bethlehem leaves the main highway.

Important Bethlehem citizens included the Levite who became the priest of Micah (Judg. 17:7-13), as well as the concubine of the Levite from Ephraim. Her death precipitated a war between all of the tribes of Israel and the tribe of Benjamin (Judges 19-20). Bethlehem was also the setting for most of the book of Ruth (Ruth 1:1-2, 19, 22; 2:4; 4:11). However, the most famous citizen of Bethlehem was king David (1 Sam. 17:12, 15; 20:6, 28). The city was the site of his anointing by Samuel and the sacrificial episode in the story (1 Sam. 16:1-13) suggests that Bethlehem may have been a sacrificial worship center for ancient Israel.

By the end of Saul's reign Bethlehem had become a Philistine garrison. 2 Samuel 23:13-18 as well as 1 Chronicles 11:16-18 record a famous story of "three mighty men" of David who were so devoted to their leader that they broke through the Philistine defenses and drew water from the well of Bethlehem in order to respond to David's lament that he would like water from Bethlehem's well. He was so overwhelmed by their courage and devotion that he refused to drink the water but poured it out as an offering to the Lord. Tradition still points out the well.

Bethlehem was fortified by Rehoboam in the late tenth century BC (2 Chron. 11:6), but its citizens were captured by the Babylonians in 587 BC and deported to Babylon. Some of the citizens that remained were involved in the assassination of Nebuchadnezzar's Judaean governor, Gedaliah (Jeremiah 40-41). Before fleeing to Egypt the assassins regrouped at Geruth Chimham, a caravan inn near Bethlehem and a well-known starting place for journeys to Egypt. At the time of Cyrus' decree that allowed the exiles to return to their homeland, both Ezra (2:21) and Nehemiah (7:26) record that more than one hundred male Bethlehemites returned to their town.

In the prophetic writings of Micah 5:2 (Heb. 5:1) the writer refers to it as Bethlehem Ephrathah—"from you shall come forth for me one who is to be the ruler in Israel." Christians would later view this text as a prediction of Jesus' birth at Bethlehem.

Jews lived in Bethlehem until the second century of the Christian era. However, the war of Simeon Bar Kokhba brought a Roman garrison to the town and the Jewish population ceased to play an important role. A gentile citizenship eventually grew, and a temple to Adonis was subsequently erected at the edge of the city (Jerome, *Epistle 58:3 to Paulinus*).

The gospel traditions record that Jesus was born in Bethlehem (Matt. 2:1-16; Luke 2:4-15; John 7:42). It is probable that early Christians venerated a birth place in Bethlehem. However, the Roman occupation of the town, especially during the Bar Kokhba war of the mid-second century AD resulted in the loss of the actual birth site.

In AD 325 Helena, the mother of the Roman emperor Constantine, erected a church over a series of caves that second century

Terraced hills around Bethlehem

Church of Nativity

tradition had held was the place of Jesus' birth. This building was destroyed in a Samaritan revolt against Byzantine rule in AD 529. Justinian I, the Byzantine emperor (AD 527-565) built a new and larger church on the same site and this same structure still stands today although it had undergone extensive alterations especially during the Middle Ages. It is called the Church of Nativity in modern day Bethlehem. The grotto of the nativity is carved out of rock and it is lined with marble in a cave structure beneath a crypt. An interesting tradition about the Church of Nativity concerns a scene on the facade of the building directly over the entrance. The scene depicts the birth story and the worship of the kings from the east. Because the kings are portrayed in oriental dress, the Persians are said to have spared the church when they captured Bethlehem in the war of AD 614.

Jerome, the fourth-century church father and biblical scholar, settled in Bethlehem and built a monastery for study and residence. In preparing his Latin translation of the Bible he established the basis for the Vulgate version. He died in Bethlehem in AD 420.

During the early Arab period Bethlehem suffered no damage although it came under Arab control. The city came under Christian control once again in the twelfth century to the Norman crusader, Tancred. Both Baldwin I and II (1100-18; 1118-31), crusader kings of Jerusalem, were crowned in the Church of Nativity in Bethlehem. The crusaders built a fort in the city, but it was destroyed in 1489 during fighting between Christian forces from Bethlehem and Muslims from Hebron.

In the modern era Bethlehem had a predominantly Christian population. However, following the 1967 war the population base shifted by the influx of Arab refugees, with the result that the citizenship is equally divided between Muslims and Christians. Bethlehem maintains close ties with Jerusalem because of their physical proximity, especially in the areas of trade and tourism. The main attraction of modern Bethlehem, apart from the busy marketplaces, is the Church of Nativity maintained by the Greek Orthodox and the Roman Catholic churches. The city and the church form a major center of pilgrimage especially during Christmas celebrations (Protestant/Catholic—December 24/25; Orthodox—January 6/7; Armenian—January 19/20).

Bethlehem was also the name of a settlement in northern Israel. Bethlehem of Zebulun was a town in the area where the tenth tribe of Zebulun settled (Josh. 19:15). It was the home and burial site of Ibzan, one of the judges of Israel (Judg. 12:8, 10). The ancient town is usually identified with the modern Beit Laham, a town located some seven miles northwest of Nazareth.

For further information on Bethlehem see:

Cornfeld, G. *Archaeology of the Bible: Book by Book* (1977).
Crowfoot, J. W. *Early Churches in Palestine* (1941).
Hamilton, R. W. *Guide to Bethlehem* (1939).

W. O. M.

CAESAREA MARITIMA

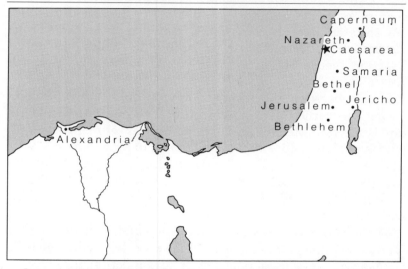

Caesarea (*Kaisàreia*), one of the largest cities of Judaea, is distinguished from the lesser-known Caesarea Philippi usually by the epithet "the one on the coast (*hē epíthalassē*), or *Maritima*, sometimes by the surname *Augusta*, or it is called "Kesri/Kisri." Only seventy-five miles by road northwest of Jerusalem (fifty-five miles direct) on the Plain of Sharon, Caesarea was a center of Hellenism in the midst of the Jewish people.

Foundation   Caesarea was a new city built by Herod the Great at the site of Straton's Tower (*Strátōnos púrgos* or *Stratonis turris*). Begun *circa* 22 BC, the city took approximately twelve years to build. It was dedicated *circa* 10 BC. After Antony's and Cleopatra's suicides, Herod had visited, welcomed, and aided the potential new Roman Caesar, Octavian Augustus (mentioned in Luke 2:1). In appreciation, following the Battle of Actium around 30 BC, Augustus had given to Herod several cities including Straton's Tower. In return Herod named the city after Caesar Augustus. The name "Straton" probably implies that originally the fort and later the fortified town were founded by one of the Straton (or Abdastart) Kings of Sidon in the fourth century BC, either Straton I (*ca.* 375-61) or Straton II (*ca.* 343-32). "Stratos" may also be a Greek rendering of the name of the Phoenician goddess Astarte or Aphrodite, which also mean "warrior," hence Straton's Tower would be literally "Astarte's Tower."

Traders between Phoenicia and Egypt would stop at Straton's Tower. The earliest person to mention the name in extant literature is a certain Zenon, an Egyptian official serving Ptolemy II who landed there for supplies on his way to Jerusalem in 259 BC. The town is also mentioned by Artemidorus (*ca.* 100 BC), Strabo (*Geography*, XVI, 2.27), Pliny (*Natural History*, V.14), Tacitus (*The Histories*, II.78), Philo (*The Embassy to Gaius*, XXXVIII), and Josephus.

The territory was originally Canaanite and Philistine. Under David it became part of Israel until the exile, allotted to the tribe of Manasseh. The Hasmonean ruler Alexander Jannaeus reconquered a number of cities on the coast of Syria including Straton's Tower (*ca.* 104 BC). He usually forced Jewish customs on the inhabitants. The tower had been held by a local ruler called Zoilus. When Cneius Pompey conquered Judaea along with other cities (*ca.* 63 BC), he set free Straton's Tower from the Jews and annexed it to the province of Syria.

Description of the City   Caesarea was renowned for its beauty and its large, well-protected harbor. Herod chose to build at the site a major city since a large port was needed to serve Jerusalem and the larger country. The harbors at Joppa and Dora were too small, too far away from each other, and had too much sand driven into them by the wind to satisfy Herod. Consequently, Caesarea grew rapidly and remained a major city for centuries.

The harbor, *Portus Augusti*, was as big as the famous Pyreum harbor at Athens. The circular first breakwater was built with large stones of about fifty feet in length, eighteen in breadth, and nine in depth. This first breakwater was two hundred feet wide so as to impede the largest waves. The entrance to the harbor faced north since the north wind brought the clearest weather. The second breakwater had upon it a wall with several impressive towers and arches. The largest tower was named after Nero Claudius Drusus, the son-in-law of Caesar Augustus. Sailors disembarked in these arches or inlets. A landing-place encircled the harbor. Josephus describes it as "a very pleasant place to promenade for those who wished to do so" (*Antiquities* XV. 4.6 [337]). When Paul left Jerusalem for Tarsus he left by way of the port at Caesarea. After his second missionary journey in Asia he returned to Antioch by way of Caesarea (Acts 9:30; 18:22).

Magnificent buildings made of white marble were built by Herod all along the harbor. In the middle of these buildings was a hill, which supported a temple to Caesar with two large statues. It could be seen a great way off by persons sailing toward the city. Priests of the imperial cult *Sebastophants*, annually elected citizens and tended the sacrifices in the temple. Near

Pilate's theater dedication stone

Roman aqueduct at Caesarea

the sea were a theater and a large amphitheater, which are being excavated and rebuilt. The dedication stone from the Roman theater is the only surviving monument that bears the name of Pontius Pilate. The aqueduct at Caesarea had several legionary inscriptions, including that of the tenth legion dating from Hadrian's time (AD 130). Caesarea's sewer system was particularly ingenious. The sea would flow into underground passages and wash all the debris clean. (See *Antiquities* XV. 9.6 and *War* I. 21.5-8 for a detailed description of the city.) Graveyards were located at the eastern and probably, as well, the western sides of the city (Mishnah, *'Oholot* 18.9) The Jews had at least one synagogue at Caesarea. Its walls have been recovered.

Herod also constructed a palace or praetorium. The prefect or procurator of Judaea, a customs collector and the imperial finance officer for the province, resided in Caesarea. Many military troops were stationed at Caesarea permanently or temporarily. Procurator Pilate's army was stationed there during the summer. (The winter quarters were in Jerusalem.) The Roman fifth and tenth legions wintered in Caesarea. Josephus describes the weather as "genial in winter as it is suffocatingly hot in summer, from its situation in the plain and on the coast" (*War* III. 9.1). A military cohort (five to six hundred men) of Roman citizens, such as Cornelius, was stationed there (Acts 10). The Samaritans (Sebastenians) and Caesareans themselves had a squadron or corps (five hundred to one thousand men) of cavalry officially known as the *Sebasteni* stationed at Caesarea.

The city was on the great seacoast road between Tyre and Egypt. Five major roads led into Caesarea. It was bordered by the Zerga or Crocodile River (Nahal Tanninim) and Mount Carmel to the north and the Mefjir or Alexander River (Nahal Hadera) and a forest to the south. The territory around Caesarea was fertile and known for its pomegranates, grain, and its purple industry. Athletic contests were held every five years in Caesarea. The horse and foot races in the hippodrome were world famous.

Caesarea had approximately fifty thousand inhabitants around AD 60, at least twenty thousand of whom were Jews. Most of the native inhabitants were Hellenized Syrians. Romans, Phoenician, Greek merchants, and Galileans were also heavily represented in the population. Thus Caesarea was a commercial, military, and governmental center.

New Testament Events   Caesarea was in Archelaus' domain in 4 BC—AD 6. Although Jerusalem was always their most famous city and dear to the Jewish people, after AD 6 Caesarea became the Roman capital of the Jewish nation for over six hundred years. Tacitus reflects this tension in *The Histories* by calling both Caesarea and Jerusalem the capital of Judaea (ii.78; v.8). The Roman prefect or procurator such as Pontius Pilate (AD 26-36) resided in the praetorium in Caesarea. An inscription bearing his name was found in the theater. When the Jews complained about Pilate's shields in Jerusalem, he tranferred them to Caesarea to be set up in the Temple of Augustus.

After Stephen was killed (*ca.* 34), a great persecution arose against the church in Jerusalem, and it was scattered throughout the region of Judaea and Samaria. Philip, one of the seven disciples appointed to serve the widows in Jerusalem, preached in the villages of Samaria until he came to Caesarea (Acts 8:40).

Cornelius, a centurion of the Italian Cohort, resided at Caesarea. Since he prayed constantly to God and gave alms liberally, an angel appeared to him and commanded him to bring Simon Peter to Caesarea. Peter was at the nearby port of Joppa, over thirty miles and a full day's journey away. Peter and several Christians from Joppa met Cornelius and his family and close friends. Cornelius was the first Gentile with whom Peter had eaten. After Peter's sermon, Luke records the first instance in Acts where the Holy Spirit was poured out on the Gentiles who consequently were baptized (Acts 10:1—11:18).

In AD 41 King Herod Agrippa I was given jurisdiction over Judaea, Samaria, and Caesarea by the Emperor Claudius. Agrippa resided in Caesarea as well as in Jerusalem. Samples of his coins minted at Caesarea have been found. He had statues of his daughters Berenice, Mariamne, and Drusilla erected there. In AD 44 when he celebrated spectacles in Caesar's honor with many officials and persons of high rank, he died the second day of the celebration. He appeared to the crowd to look like a god because of his attire, but he died according to Luke because he did not instead give God the glory (Acts 12:1-23; compare *Antiquities* XIX, 8.2). At his death the Gentile people of Caesarea and Samaria, including the large number of people on military service, removed the statues of the daughters and celebrated rather than mourned Agrippa's death. Although the squadron of Caesareans and Samaritans were to be transferred by the new procurator Cuspius Fadus, instead, they were left in Caesarea fueling the Jewish discontent.

After Paul's third missionary journey, Luke, Timothy, Aristarchus, Tychicus, Gaius, and other Christians returned with Paul to Jerusalem (*ca.* 57) by way of Caesarea. They stayed for many days with Philip the evangelist, who still resided at Caesarea with his four daughters, who were prophetesses. At that time the prophet Agabus came from Judea to warn Paul of his impending imprisonment. Some of the disciples from Caesarea accompained Paul and his associates to Jerusalem (Acts 21:8-16), where Paul was imprisoned.

In a short time, the Roman tribune Claudius Lysias returned Paul to Caesarea with seventy horsemen (two hundred soldiers and two hundred spearmen accompanying them half the way) to governor Felix in Caesarea, to prevent him from being killed by the more than forty Jewish conspirators.

Paul was guarded in Herod's praetorium at Caesarea during the last two years of procurator Antonius Felix's governship (*ca.* 58-59). After Felix heard the high priest Ananias and Tertullus, he kept Paul in custody but with some liberty, allowing Paul's friends to attend to his needs. For two years the freedman Felix and Drusilla, his Jewish wife, daughter of Agrippa I, often sent for Paul to converse with him, at the same time hoping he would give them bribe money.

While Paul was imprisoned at Caesarea the Syrians and Jews were arguing, to the point of street riots, about their equality of citizenship (*isopoliteía*). The Jews claimed precedence since Herod had founded the city. The Syrians argued that the city was theirs. Once Felix quelled the Jews by force and had their houses plundered by soldiers.

At the end of his governorship, Felix left Paul in prison as a favor to the Jews. Paul appealed to Caesar before the new procurator Porcius Festus. King Herod Agrippa II and his sister Berenice arrived at Caesarea to welcome Festus. The military tribunes and prominent persons of the city along with Agrippa and Berenice heard Paul. Although he could have been released, Paul with some other prisoners was entrusted to the centurion Julius of the Augustan cohort. Luke and Aristarchus accompanied Paul on a ship embarking from Caesarea during his journey to Rome (*ca.* autumn 59; Acts 23:12—27:2).

After AD 60 Emperor Nero deprived the Jews of or possibly refused them equal citizenship with the Syrians and declared the "Hellenes" masters of the city. According to Josephus, the dissatisfaction of the Jews at Caesarea was one of the factors that caused the beginning of the great war in AD 66, which culminated in the fall of Jerusalem.

In AD 66 the customs collector at Caesarea was John, a wealthy and respected Jew. In the same year procurator Gessius Florus sent out two cohorts from Caesarea forcing a welcome from the Jews in Jerusalem, and instead creating more havoc. The Syrians ended up massacring in one hour's time on the Sabbath the entire Jewish population—twenty thousand persons. [See Josephus *Wars* II, 13-18 and *Antiquities* XX, 8.] Vespasian and Titus then used Caesarea as a center of operations for the Roman army during the war of AD 66-72 against the Jews. The Roman legions were stationed at Caesarea until needed. After the war Titus left his plunder at Caesarea and there incarcerated his prisoners of war. When Flavius Silva had conquered Masada he, too, returned to Caesarea.

After Vespasian was acclaimed emperor in AD 69, he turned the city into a Roman colony. Officially it was now called "colonia prima Flavia Augusta Caesarensis." The emperor Titus extended Caesarea's privileges, conferring on it the legal status of *ius Italicum*, the highest privilege a provincial municipality could obtain. As all Roman colonies in Italy, Caesarea was made exempt from provincial taxes (*tributum soli*), as well as property taxes (*tributum capitis*).

Early Christian Events   Both the Christians and the Jews established famous schools of higher learning in Caesarea. A rabbinic academy was founded there *ca.* 250 by Rabbi Hosha'ya. One of its prominent scholars was Rabbi Abbahu who is often quoted in the Talmud. The oldest section of the Babylonian Talmud, on civil law, is attributed to the Caesarean rabbis. Even in the third century Caesarea was a synecdoche for the Roman Empire, as also Edom was in Rabbinic literature the prototype of Imperial Rome. Rabbi Abbahu said: "[It is written], 'Ekron shall be rooted up'; this is Kisri [Caesarea] the daughter of Edom, which is situated among the sands, and which was a thorn in the side of Israel in the days of the Greeks. When the House of the Hasmoneans grew powerful and conquered them, they called it 'the capture of the Tower of Shir' " (*Babylonian Talmud*, Megillah

6a). One variant reads "Tower of Shed," which literally means "Tower of Demons"; perhaps an illusion to the worship of Astarte by the original Syrian inhabitants.

Origen lived in Caesarea for twenty years (231-50). Pamphilius (*d.* 309) created a library second only to that of Alexandria. His pupil Eusebius (260-340) who became bishop of Caesarea (*ca.* 314) is known as the first church historian. Origen and Eusebius employed certain Bible texts which have come to be known today as the Caesarean text type (for example, family Koridethi).

In 640 the city fell to the Muslims. When Baldwin I of the First Crusade captured Caesarea from the Muslims in 1101, he discovered a green glass bowl which he took to be the Holy Grail. Today it is on display at the Cathedral of San Lorenzo in Genoa, Italy. The city was destroyed by Sultan Malik al-Ashraf in 1291. Muslims from Bosnia (Yugoslavia) inhabited the site between 1878-1948. Remains of Straton's Tower, Herod's City, and the later Byzantine and Crusader cities survive.

For further information on Caesarea Maritima see:

Avi-Yonah, M., ed. *Encyclopedia of Archaeological Excavations in the Holy Land.* Vol. I (1975).
Fritsch, C.T., ed. *The Joint Expedition to Caesarea Maritima.* Vol. I: *Studies in the History of Caesarea Maritima* (1975).
Kadman, L. *The Coins of Caesarea Maritima* (1957).
Levine, L. I. *Caesarea Under Roman Rule* (1975).
_____.*Roman Caesarea: An Archaeological-Topographical Study* (1975).

A. B. S.

CHAPTER EIGHT

CAPERNAUM

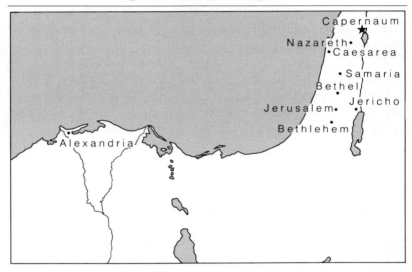

The little town of Capernaum may have been of minor significance in the minds of most first-century Jews, but those who
came to trust in Jesus were to remember it as "his own city"
(Matt. 4:13; 9:1). For it was in Capernaum that he made his
headquarters as he traveled around Galilee and beyond, preaching and teaching. Here he chose his first disciples and preached
in the synagogue; here many people found new health and new
hope because of their encounter with Jesus. Our English name
"Capernaum" comes from the Greek form of the Hebrew name
Kefar Nahum, meaning "Village of Nahum." This Nahum, otherwise unknown to us, may have originally owned the land where

the village first grew up. He should not be confused, as often happened in the Middle Ages, with the Old Testament prophet by the same name. As far as we can tell from ancient sources, the town was first founded in the second century BC.

Location   Where exactly was Capernaum? In modern times two sites that are about two and one-half miles apart have vied for the honor of being identified as Jesus' city: Khirbet Minyeh and Tell Hum, as they are called today in Arabic. Both ruins are northwest of the Sea of Galilee, but Khirbet Minyeh is slightly inland, whereas Tell Hum, whose name is reminiscent of *Kefar Nahum*, lies immediately on the lakeshore, stretching from west to east between the lake on its southern edge, and on its northern edge the hills rising steeply from the Jordan Rift toward Upper Galilee. Perhaps partly because Khirbet Minyeh has never been excavated, it is Tell Hum which has established itself as the modern choice, and which will now be described as Capernaum.

Although a small town compared with a walled city like Jerusalem, Capernaum was very favorably situated as far as natural resources and trade were concerned. The first-century Jewish historian Josephus said that Galilee "is everywhere so rich in soil and pasturage and produces such variety of trees, that even the most indolent are tempted by these facilities to devote themselves to agriculture." We cannot totally discount his words as the exaggeration of national pride when we see what grows near Capernaum today. Just a couple of miles to the southwest is the Plain of Gennesaret, blessed with unusual fertility due to its near-tropical climate and rich alluvial soil. The basalt hills which form the town's northern border absorb so much solar energy that farmers can bring their ripened produce to market days and weeks before others. Abundant rain, streams which flow all year round, long hot summers and warm winters (even in January the mean temperature is 57 degrees F.) make the area capable of supporting just about every plant that grows anywhere else in Israel: date palms, olive, fig, and walnut trees,

Winepress at Capernaum

vineyards, wheat, wildflowers so profuse that they create bright "wall-to-wall" carpets, and in our century even bananas! If Jesus spoke of the glorious colors of the lilies of the field, or of sowing seed, or oil presses, or hand-turned grain mills, or sheep herds to illustrate his teaching, his listerners in and around Capernaum did not need much imagination to get his point. They saw these things every day; indeed many of them earned their livelihood from their own agriculture or from the transportation of produce. For Capernaum was not only an agricultural center. It was involved in international trade, since it was situated on the major road between Damascus and Egypt; and in domestic trade, since it was linked by road and water with a string of towns and cities on the shores of the Sea of Galilee, also called the Lake of Gennesaret.

This beautiful harp-shaped lake, almost thirteen miles long and eight miles at its broadest, with its surface about seven hundred feet below sea level, was a blessing tinged with peril for the inhabitants of Capernaum. Many people earned their living by fishing from its plentiful supplies, yet they knew from experience that the steep hills surrounding this low basin tend to trap violent wind and rain storms which can very suddenly endanger sailors' lives. Capernaum had its own little port for fishing boats, and excavators find fish hooks in abundance throughout the site. This is the lake to which we owe so many of the best-loved symbols of Christian faith: the miraculous catches of fish when seasoned fishermen had given up hope; Jesus' disciples as fishermen who began "fishing" for human beings; Jesus as the one who had authority to tread the waves or to rebuke a storm so fierce that professional sailors feared for their lives.

The site of Tell Hum is now owned, protected, and under excavation by two different groups. The Franciscans control the western half, which was occupied from one or two centuries before Jesus until it was destroyed in the seventh century AD, and the Greek Orthodox control the eastern half, where the town was re-established in the seventh century. It is the western, or Franciscan, half that mainly concerns us, because this is the town that Jesus and his disciples knew.

A very rough estimate might put the size of the first-century town at 150,000 square yards with a population of between five thousand and sixty-five hundred people. Capernaum's population is thought to have been mostly or exclusively Jewish, in contrast, for instance, to the city of Tiberias that had recently been founded about ten miles down the western shore of the lake by Herod Antipas and was a much more cosmopolitan center with a mixed population. Thus Capernaum was larger and more strategically located than a village such as Nazareth where Jesus grew up, yet was much smaller and probably more homogeneous in population than a city such as Jerusalem where Jesus was to die. It is generally thought that the references to a Roman centurion (Matt. 8:5; Luke 7:2) and a tax collector (Matt. 9:9; Luke 2:14) in Capernaum mean that the town housed a garrison of soldiers and a customs station. The presence of both would be explained if Capernaum were the first town within Herod Antipas' territory after one crossed the border, probably the Jordan River three miles to the northeast, from Herod Philip's territory, necessitating provision for import taxes and security, and underlining the importance of Capernaum's location.

The town was laid out in fairly regular blocks divided by east-west and north-south streets, each block consisting of three or four houses sharing common walls. Such a layout indicates a central administration responsible for town planning, although we know nothing specific about the nature of the town government. The houses were black and were relatively poorly and simply built. The local basalt stones were used as nature had shaped them, without being worked, and were held together with small pebbles and perhaps some mud. Such walls were not strong enough to hold more than one story, but the roofs, probably of wood covered with straw and mud, were flat and gave space for some activities. Each house held a large patriarchal family, so there was little privacy. The rooms were organized around one or two unroofed courtyards, one of which served as the common kitchen, with oven and grinding stones, and also had the stairs up to the roof. A second would provide space for animals and home industry. This design illuminates the story of the four men who could not get through the crowd inside the house to Jesus but yet could let their paralyzed friend down through a hole they made in the roof (Mark 2:1ff.). Jesus' parable of the woman lighting a lamp and sweeping her house looking for the lost coin (Luke 15:8-10) would have struck a chord with women whose floors consisted of uneven black stones rather roughly put together on top of a dirt surface, and whose small, high windows let in little light.

It was people such as those who lived in these crowded houses and hot climate, with a relatively simple lifestyle and modest standard of living, earning their living from fishing, agriculture, trade, and related industries, who were Jesus' early listeners and followers. Yet we should not make the mistake of thinking that they were poverty-stricken or isolated from the world. If they had few luxuries, still food and jobs were plentiful in this busy town. If the population was mostly Jewish, still they had contacts with gentile cities near the lake such as Tiberias and with the larger world through the trade route that linked Damascus with Alexandria. If they perhaps spoke mostly Aramaic and Hebrew in their own homes and in their synagogues, they no doubt could speak Greek, and even some Latin, to communicate with travelers, merchants, and soldiers.

The excavations that are still in progress at Capernaum have produced some finds that perplex and tantalize those who are trying to put together a coherent picture of the population and history of the town during Jesus' life and during the first few centuries of Christianity. What most strikes a visitor to Capernaum today are the partially-reconstructed remains of a large synagogue that was built much later than the first century. Underneath this splendid edifice have been found architectual remains from Jesus' day, which have been interpreted as belonging to a public building because the thick walls were built of stones cut to uniform size and followed a plan similar to the later synagogue. If so, one argument goes, it would be a prime candidate

Synagogue ruins at Capernaum

for a first-century synagogue, since the Jews, and indeed many peoples of the ancient world, preferred to rebuild new synagogues and other holy places on the same site where earlier ones had stood. It is then frequently assumed that this is the synagogue mentioned in the Gospels where Jesus preached and healed on the sabbath (Mark 1:21ff.; 3:1ff.). All of this may be true, but it is worth remembering that a town with a population of five thousand Jews would have needed more than one synagogue! To mention only two out of a range of possibilities, this could have been a specially-built synagogue and yet never have been visited by Jesus; or, on the other hand, it could have been a private home used as a synagogue, and precisely the one referred to in Mark 1. Rather than attempting to determine the very spot where specific events occurred, it is usually more valuable to learn as much as possible about the way of life of a given town in a given period so that we may better understand the biblical narratives.

The function of synagogues in the first century, as well as we can make it out, was to provide a place where the local community could assemble for a wide variety of purposes, including study. An inscription found from first-century Jerusalem refers to a synagogue having been built there for "the reading of the law and for the teaching of the Commandments" and to an associated hostel for travelers. There have been discovered several other candidates for remains of synagogue buildings of the first century: at Herodium and Masada in Judea, at Magdala very close to Capernaum, and at Gamlah in Gaulanitis (now the Golan Heights). It is fascinating to compare the plans of all these structures, and yet it is also necessary to recall that such architectural remains are not labeled, and that their interpretation is left to us, who are sometimes too eager to make positive identifications without sufficient evidence. Even if these five were synagogue buildings, it does not follow that every synagogue (the word is Greek, and simply means assembly) was a specially-built public edifice. If Americans in the 1970s saw the possibilities of meeting in "house churches," may not the relatively poorer people of first-century Capernaum have met in "house synagogues"? On a related matter, the report that the centurion in Capernaum had built a synagogue (Luke 7:2-5) must be carefully interpreted: are we to think that the commander of one hundred soliders was wealthy enough to finance the construction of an entire public building? Or are we perhaps to understand that he contributed to some feature of a building or its renovation, such as a column or a floor (see below), and that this generous gift was gradually in the memories of grateful recipients transferred to an entire building? Second, are we to suppose that the centurion's synagogue was necessarily the one in which Jesus taught? Again, it is more helpful to learn all we can about life in the first century than to try to locate each biblical narrative.

House Church   Another tantalizing ruin is the fifth-century church just one block away from the synagogue and consisting of two concentric octagons and five sides of a third. Other churches were built in an octagonal shape to mark sites in Palestine that were sacred in Christian memory, such as in Bethlehem and Jerusalem. It appears that this site was sacred as well. Beneath this fine church have been found the ruins of a simpler, rectangular building, interpreted as a church, from the fourth century, which in turn was built around the largest room of one of the houses of the block, a block such as has been described above, first built in the century before Christ. Why was this one room of a private dwelling singled out to become the center of a church? The excavators are satisfied that the lowest level was Peter's house (Matt. 8:14; Mark 1:9; Luke 4:38) in which Jesus lived, and that the large room was used as a public place of worship by the local Jewish-Christian community already from the second half of the first century, until with the coming of the Byzantine Empire Christians were wealthy and powerful enough to construct church buildings in the fourth and fifth centuries. If this is true, then Capernaum preserves perhaps the oldest Christian sanctuary yet discovered, already from a few decades after Jesus' stay in the town.

The excavators base their conclusions on evidence such as: (a) this one room having received three new plastered floors, and perhaps plastered walls and ceiling, during the first century, whereas private houses had simple stone floors and walls, as we have seen, (b) an absence of domestic pottery beginning at the same time, (c) fragments of 131 graffiti in Greek, Aramaic, Syriac, Latin, and Hebrew, written on the plastered walls of this room during the second and third centuries, some addressed to Jesus or Christ, some to Peter, and (d) reports of pilgrims beginning late in the fourth century that they visited the "house church" of Peter. While this is extremely intriguing, it is well to be cautious. Even the plastering, unusual as it is, is open to other interpretations. Some of the graffiti fragments are capable of being deciphered differently, and others of being interpreted differently. For instance, does the name *Peter* necessarily mean the writer was addressing a prayer to Peter—and that because he had lived on this very spot!—or might he not have been writing his own name, as graffiti writers so often do today? It might be more safe to say that by the fifth century people in Capernaum thought that they knew where Peter had lived, and to recall that we have no sure knowledge of where Jesus stayed. Is it just as likely to imagine, for example, that he might have lived in the home of the tax collector who became his disciple? As to the later decades of the first century, the fact that Matthew 11:23f. and Luke 10:15 preserve a curse against Capernaum for rejecting Jesus may indicate that when those Gospels were written there were few or no followers of Jesus in that town, which would be especially ironic because it had been Jesus' "own city." It is possible that the graffiti were written only by visitors to the town, not by those who lived in Capernaum itself. Perhaps we have access not to a place of Christian worship by a community, but rather to a place of pigrimage in an otherwise hostile environment.

None of these possibilities makes the finds less significant. They only remind us that we are far removed from the situation and must be cautious in our interpretation of the evidence. If indeed there was a Christian community in Capernaum worshiping in this home, then we have physical remains from a very early house church, and can imagine modest Christians worshiping in a simple place, a home just like their own home but with a more finished floor. If the lack of domestic pottery mentioned above is accepted as an argument for use as a house church, it would presumably also indicate that such worship would not have involved eating a common meal. On the other hand, if indeed the graffiti were only from pilgrims, then we still have physical remains of the very early development of the idea of pilgrimage, of travel to places perceived as sacred because of the Lord's having been there, and of a sense that this was the Holy Land.

Another mystery is the relationship between the later church and the synagogue, the ruins of which still dominate the site. This synagogue fills an entire block and consists of a basilica and courtyard built on an artificial platform raised above the rest of the city, and made of beautiful, finely-cut white limestone which stands out from the rough black native stones used in the other buildings. On the basis of stylistic and historical considerations, it has been called the finest remaining example of early synagogue architecture, and has been dated to the second or third century AD. Yet on the basis of coins and pottery found under sealed layers of its foundation, the current excavators date it to the fourth, or most recently, to the third quarter of the fifth, century. As for the octagonal church, it may have been a church for the worship of a local community, but on the other hand its distinctive shape may indicate that it was solely a memorial structure, a shrine put up for the sake of Christian pilgrims.

On the other hand, if the synagogue was built in the fourth or fifth century and if the fifth–century church was the place of worship of a local community, then it may have been that for almost two hundred years in Capernaum there were Jews and Christians living close together and worshiping in large, ostentatious sanctuaries just one short block apart. Despite the Byzantine ban on the construction of synagogues, this particular Jewish community would have managed to build a magnificent edifice proudly displaying its Jewishness to the town. If indeed these two communities found a mode of peaceful coexistence in the days when Christians were using their secular power to put down the Jews, it would constitute one of the brighter moments in the disturbed history of Christian-Jewish relations.

For further information on Capernaum see:

Gutmann, J. *The Synagogue: Studies in Origins, Archaeology and Architecture* (1975), 72-76.

Levine, L.I., ed. *Ancient Synagogues Revealed* (1981).

Meyers, E. M. and J. F. Strange. *Archaeology, the Rabbis, and Early Christianity* (1981).

Sapir, B. D. N. *Capernaum: History and Legacy, Art and Architecture* (1967).

Shanks, H. *Judaism in Stone: The Archaeology of Ancient Synagogues* (1979).

Strange, J. F. and H. Shanks. "Has the House Where Jesus Stayed in Capernaum Been Found?" *Biblical Archaeology Review* 8 (1982), 26-37.

———— . "Synagogue Where Jesus Preached Found At Capernaum." *Biblical Archaeology Review* 9 (1983), 24-31.

Tzaferis, V. "New Archaological Evidence on Capernaum." *Biblical Archaeologist* 46(1983), 198-204.

J. E. S.

CORINTH

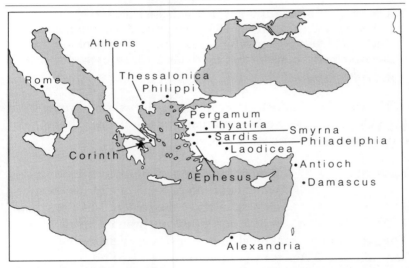

Situated at the southwest extremity of the narrow isthmus that connects the southern part of the Greek peninsula to the mainland, Corinth was the hub of a complex that included one and a quarter miles to the north, Lechaeum on the Gulf of Corinth, and six and a quarter miles to the east, Cenchreae on the Saronic Gulf. Its strategic location explains its importance. The voyage around the tip of the peninsula was long and dangerous. The channel between Cape Maleae, the southernmost tip of the Peloponnesus, and the island of Cythera was infamous for treacherous winds, giving rise to the proverb, "When you double [Cape] Maleae, forget your home." The risks were so great that shipowners preferred to have the cargoes of larger vessels unloaded and transported across the isthmus, a distance of less than five miles where other ships would be waiting. Light boats could be hauled from one sea to the other on moveable trolleys across the *diolkos*, a paved road joining the Corinthian and Saronic gulfs. Nearly all trade and travel from the east and the west moved overland from sea to sea through Corinth. Strabo, who visited Corinth in 29 BC, summed up the significance of the city:

> It is situated on the Isthmus and is master of two harbors, of which the one [Cenchreae] leads straight to Asia, and the other [Lechaeum] to Italy, and it makes easy the exchange of merchandise from both countries that are so distant from each other (*Geography 8.6.20*).

The fact that Corinth also controlled the overland route from the Peloponnesus and the mainland made it one of the great crossroads of the ancient world.

History   Despite a long and illustrious past during which Corinth became one of the most celebrated cities of the eastern Mediterranean, it did not enjoy an uninterrupted history. The arrival of a Roman delegation in 147 BC demanding the dissolution of the Achaean League, of which Corinth was a member, made war with Rome inevitable. The League was decisively defeated in 146 BC, and in reprisal Corinth was sacked by the Roman consul Lucius Mummius. Its citizens were executed or sold into slavery, the city was set on fire and razed to the ground, and its territory was designated as public land of Rome (Strabo, *Geography*, 8.6.23; Pausanias, *Description of Greece*, 2.1.2; Dio Cassius, *Roman History*, 21 [Zonaras, 9.31]).

Corinth had been reduced to ruins, though not entirely abandoned, for approximately a century when Julius Caesar announced his intention to found a Roman colony on the site. The decision was clearly dictated by economic considerations, for Caesar recognized the significant economic potential of the site of Corinth. The first colonists arrived in 44 BC, shortly before Caesar's death and consisted primarily of Italian freedmen. The majority were undoubtedly small shopkeepers, craftsmen, teachers, and secretaries, who were recruited because they comprised the technical core that is necessary for a new city.

Influences The colony, known officially as *Colonia Laus Julia Corinthiensis*, quickly began to flourish through the enterprise of the colonists. It experienced phenomenal growth and prosperity under Augustus and his successors, and within two generations regained its reputation as a thriving commercial center. Political influence accompanied the surge of economic power. In 27 BC Corinth was made the capital of the province of Achaia and the administrative seat of the Roman proconsul for southern and central Greece (Apuleius, *Metamorphoses* 10.18; compare Acts 18:12).

Although the new colony possessed the topographical characteristics of the old Greek city, it bore little formal relationship to its predecessor. Corinth was rebuilt along the lines of a Roman city. Its organizational structure and civil administration were Roman. Latin was established as the official language of the colony, and through the end of the first century AD nearly all of the datable inscriptions are in Latin rather than Greek. The Roman character of the city in the middle of the first century AD is further reflected in the many Latin names attested in the New Testament (Acts 18:7-8; Rom. 16:21-23; 1 Cor. 16:17). Although

Erastus—Romans 16:23

there were Greeks among the mixed population of Corinth, and Greek may well have been spoken in the marketplace and along the docks, it is impossible to think of the Corinth of Paul's day as in any way distinctively Greek.

Few cities enjoyed a more impressive setting than Corinth. It was situated ona plateau dominated by a rugged crag of gray limestone with sheer cliffs, the Acrocorinth. Towering 1887 feet above sea level, the acropolis served as the citadel of the city. The city itself sloped down from Acrocorinth toward the sea in the direction of Lechaeum.

The immediate vicinity of the city was not fertile but rifted and rough. Thin soil covered jagged limestone, and the plateau suffered from erosion. To the west of Corinth, however, in the coastal plain cut by the Nemean River, the land was very fertile, and Corinth served as the principal market of the region.

Paul in Corinth　　In reconstructing what would have been visible to Paul and his colleagues when they entered Corinth, we are fortunate to be able to weigh the literary evidence against the findings of archaeology. The primary literary source is Pausanias, who visited Corinth not long after AD 165. He prepared a guidebook to the city in which he identified for visitors its principal buildings and monuments. The excavations which have been conducted on the site since 1896 permit us to determine which of the structures he mentions were actually in existence at the middle of the first century AD. They indicate that there had been extensive rebuilding under Augustus (31 BC—AD 14), Tiberius (AD 14-37), and Claudius (AD 41-54), and that when Paul entered Corinth in AD 50 the reconstruction of the city along Roman lines was still in progress.

If Paul followed the land route from Athens to Corinth he would have crossed the *diolkos* at Schoenus. The boisterous throng of laborers along this road would have been the Apostle's first exposure to the strategic importance of Corinth. The immense volume of trade crossing the isthmus generated both employment and transit taxes, the major source of revenue for the city.

The road then led straight to Isthmia, the sacred precinct of Poseidon, whose temple was the focal point of the Isthmian games. After the Olympic contests held every four years, the games celebrated biennially at Isthmia in the spring were the most splended and best attended of the four great national festivals of Greece. With the destruction of Corinth in 146 BC the site of the games had been transferred to Sicyon, west of Corinth. Inscriptions confirm that Corinth regained control of the games by the beginning of the first century AD, and the contests were restored to the Isthmian sanctuary. During this period the stadium was remodeled, but the theater remained in ruins. A simple wall surrounded the temple of Poseidon, dating from the fifth century BC. Outside the south wall of the sanctuary was an enclosed sacrificial pit associated with the cult of Palaemon, the legendary child in whose honor the games were founded.

From Isthmia the road continued southwest to Cromna, where it was joined by the main road from Cenchreae. It then climbed uphill for six and a quarter miles through a series of little plateaus, finally entering the city by the Cenchreaean Gate. At this time the city walls were in a ruined state. They had been torn down in 146 BC, but the gates had been preserved to indicate the extent of the city, the largest in all Greece. The length of the perimeter wall had been nearly six and a quarter miles and enclosed an area of about two and a half square miles.

Passing through the Cenchreaean Gate, Paul's first impression would have been of the striking contrast offered to eastern cities he had known, such as Jerusalem or Antioch. In the cities of the east, walled areas were crowded with urban structures. In Corinth there were vast open spaces because the wall followed the edge of the plateau, even though it was outside the developed area. A younger contemporary of Paul who visited Corinth, Dio Chrysostom, could refer to the amphitheater, which was inside the perimeter wall, as being "outside the city in a glen" (*Discourses* 31.121).

Making his way toward the city, Paul would have climbed through the wooded gentle slopes of a Cypress grove at the base of Acrocorinth, known as Craneum. The elevation of the area

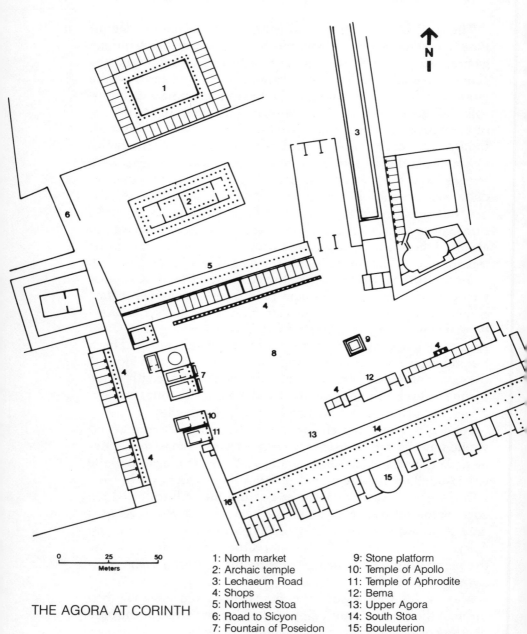

THE AGORA AT CORINTH

0 25 50
Meters

1: North market
2: Archaic temple
3: Lechaeum Road
4: Shops
5: Northwest Stoa
6: Road to Sicyon
7: Fountain of Poseidon
8: Lower Agora

9: Stone platform
10: Temple of Apollo
11: Temple of Aphrodite
12: Bema
13: Upper Agora
14: South Stoa
15: Bouleuterion
16: Road to Acrocorinth

and the spacious park-like quality of the suburb made this section the choicest residential and recreational quarter of the city.

Coming to the developed section of the city, Paul would have been impressed by the sheer size of the central square, which was one of the largest in the Roman empire. He may have approached it by the street at the southwest corner of the Agora, as did Pausanias when he visited the city.

The central square was divided into two levels by an incomplete line of buildings. The elevation of the southern section, which was roughly six and a half feet highter than the northern portion, identified it as the Upper Agora. It was reserved primarily for civic and adminstrative functions, while the Lower Agora, which covered twice as large an area, served the commercial concerns of the city.

A colossal colonnaded pavilion known as the South Stoa was

Ancient Corinth

one of the few structures to have survived the destruction of 146 BC. Approximately 173 yards in length, it was one of the largest buildings in ancient Greece. It had formerly housed small shops and taverns, but in the early first century AD the shops in the center and in the eastern end were converted into administrative offices. The elliptical chamber in the center was the Bouleuterion, in which the city council met. The Fountain House provided a cool place for the four elected magistrates to gather. Beyond the steps leading up to the South Basilica were offices for the officials charged with the organization and administration of the Isthmian Games. Arriving at the end of the South Stoa, Paul would have turned left in front of a building erected shortly after the founding of the Roman colony in 44 BC. It appears to have been the public records office. A stairway at the corner brought the Apostle down into the Lower Agora.

The Julian Basilica, to his right, was identical in design to the South Basilica behind the South Stoa. Both had been erected under Tiberius (*ca.* AD 40) and appear to have served as commercial centers for the display and sale of a variety of goods. A large central arch flanked by two smaller arches marked the head of the ramp from the Lechaeum Road. On one side of the gateway was the famous Fountain of Peirene, the city's primary water supply; the reservoir, fed by subterranean waters, had a capacity of over eighty-one thousand gallons. In Paul's day water could be drawn from at least fifteen spouts. On the other side was a basilica that may have served as a law court.

The Lechaeum Road was constructed of well-fitted slabs of hard limestone, with a raised walk on each side. Shops lined the road near the archway, and just off the road was the Peribolos of Apollo, a large paved court surrounded by columns and containing a statue of Apollo, which was the oldest market in the colony. The restoration of the "meatmarket...and a fishmarket" in this area in the time of Augustus is attested by a badly broken Latin inscription. The presence of the large Jewish community in Corinth (Philo, *Embassy to Gaius* 281; Acts 18:4, 12-15) is reflected by a broken lintel with the crude inscription, "[Syna-]gogue of the Hebr[ews]," found on the Lechaeum Roadside of the archway. This may be the site of the oldest synagogue in the city.

Paul would soon have found himself in front of a large, elevated platform covered with sculptured marble in the middle of the shops that bisected the Lower Agora. This was the Bema, or speaker's rostrum, from which public proclamations were read and the magistrates addressed the city. Those who appeared before them in a judicial setting (compare Acts 18:12-17) stood on a square stone platform just beside an altar.

The west side of the Lower Agora offered an indication of the extent to which religion permeated life in the Roman colony. Temples dedicated to Fortune, Apollo, and Aphrodite were erected in close proximity to each other under Augustus. Here also was a fountain dedicated to Poseidon. On the base of one of the marble dolphins was the name of the donor, Gneaus Babbius Philinus, a Corinthian magistrate under both Augustus and Tiberius, and the dedication, "Sacred to Neptune." Beside it stood a small monument which was the gift of the same person.

The steps leading up to the west terrace would have brought Paul back to the point from which he had begun. Here the road led south to Acrocorinth or north to Sicyon. If he had followed the road that zigzagged up the steep slopes of Acrocorinth he would have passed a series of small temples, only one of which has been excavated. High on a terrace above the ancient road lies the temple dedicated to Demeter and Kore. Dating from the seventh and sixth centuries BC, it had been restored in the early days of the Roman colony in the conviction that an abundant food supply depended upon proper devotion to these twin goddesses of fertility.

On the summit Paul would have located a small Temple of Aphrodite. It contained a statue of the goddess armed with weapons. The site of this temple on the higher, eastern peak of the Acrocorinth is consistent with the common association of the city with the goddess of love on coins of the imperial period. The reputation of Corinth as center of vice *par excellence*, which was perpetuated by Strabo in reference to the pre-146 BC city (*Geography* 8.6.20), was diligently cultivated by the Athenians.

By the middle of the first century AD, however, sexual mores at Corinth were probably no worse than in any other great maritime center in the Mediterranean basin (compare Cicero, *On the Republic*, 2.7.9). Just south of the temple of Aphrodite the spring of Upper Peirene burst forth near the edge of the cliff.

The most impressive structure dating from the pre-146 BC city was the Archaic Temple supported by thirty-five huge monolithic columns. The largest sanctuary in Corinth, it dated from the sixth century BC and may have been dedicated to Athena. It had been restored by the Romans in the early part of the first century AD, when the area around the temple was paved with limestone slabs. Just north of the hill on which the Archaic Temple stood was the North Market, which had been completed shortly before Paul arrived in Corinth. It consisted of a series of shops around a huge courtyard. Paul would have passed the new entrance to the Archaic Temple, made necessary by the construction of the Northwest Stoa and the adjoining basilica. From there he could walk to the theater, which could seat fourteen thousand persons. Built in the fifth century BC, it had been repaired by the Romans late in the reign of Augustus when a multistoried stage wall was erected.

To the east of the theater a gray limestone pavement was laid before the middle of the first century AD. Let into the stone was an inscription in bronze which read: "[ ] Erastus in return for his aedileship laid (the pavement) at his own expense." Two aediles were elected annually as commissioners of public works. The reference is almost certainly to the city treasurer who became a Christian during Paul's residence in Corinth (Rom. 16:23; compare Acts 19:22; 2 Tim. 4:20).

After crossing this pavement Paul would have left the Sicyon Road, which at this point turned due west. Continuing north he would have discovered just inside the perimeter wall one of the more pleasant quarters of Corinth; as a recreational area it compared favorably with Craneum. Here was located a spacious courtyard containing a large swimming pool fed by a spring which Pausanias called "Lerna." The construction of this facility had been begun before 146 BC, but it was richly repaired with marble and frescoes during the early period of the Roman colony.

The same water supply served the Temple of Asclepius, the Hellenistic god of healing, located about 162 yards to the northeast. The sanctuary, which had been erected in the fourth century BC, had been damaged when the city was sacked in 146 BC. It was restored and brought back into use by the colonists who arrived in 44 BC, and the number of baked clay votive offerings discovered in the vicinity attest its popularity. Eventually dining facilities were added to the sanctuary, although it is uncertain whether they were functioning by the middle of the first century AD (compare 1 Cor. 8:10; 10:21). In each of three dining rooms couches around the walls could accommodate eleven person. A square slab in the center of each, cracked and blackened by fire, demonstrates that cooking was done in the dining room.

The life-line of Corinth was its two harbors, Lechaeum and Cenchreae. Of the two, Lechaeum, on the Gulf of Corinth, was far larger, possessing an inner harbor of 325,000 square feet and an outer one of 1,170,000 square feet. The harbor was serviced by four and a half miles of docks and warehouses. Little is known of Lechaeum because it has not been excavated, but according to Strabo, who was there in 29 BC, there were not many houses. An impression of the intense volume of the traffic that passed through the harbor is conveyed by Plutarch who observed "the whole length of the street even to the water's edge was one mass of dust and confusion on account of the vast crowds of vehicles and people" (*Moralia* 146E).

One result of Paul's residence in Corinth was the establishment of a Christian community in Cenchreae (Rom. 16:1). Work on the harbor must have begun soon after the foundation of the colony in 44 BC because the port facilities had to be completely rebuilt. The two sea moles, which were completed in the early first century BC, enclosed an area of 97,000 square feet, sufficient for small merchant vessels (compare Acts 18:18). The large building on the north mole, which Pausanias identified as a Temple of Aphrodite, may actually have been the residence of a wealthy citizen when Paul visited the city. On the south mole there were at least four blocks of warehouses that fronted the wharf against which ships stern-docked. Early in the first century AD two of the rooms in one of the blocks were modified to create a sanctuary for Isis.

A survey of buildings and inscriptions conveys an adequate impression of official Corinth, but fails to reflect the actual flavor of the city or the experience of its social classes. By the middle of the first century AD Corinth's only aristocracy was one of wealth, while its sole tradition was the pursuit of profit and pleasure. The Corinthian ideal appears to be expressed in the declaration of one of its young men:

> I am living as appropriate to a man of breeding. I have a mistress who is very attractive. I have never wronged anyone. I drink Achaian wine, and in every respect I attempt to satisfy myself, since my private resources are sufficient for these purposes" (Athenaeus, *The Deipnosophists* 4.167e).

This attitude, of course, is reflective of the privileged few who constituted the new wealthy class. A different impression is conveyed by the biting comment of Alciphron:

> I did not enter Corinth after all, for I learned in a short time the sordidness of the rich there and the misery of the poor (*Life of Parasites* 324).

It was primarily among the miserable poor that Paul found a positive response to his preaching (compare 1 Cor. 1:26-29; 6:9-11; 7:21).

From Paul's point of view, Corinth was admirably suited as a base for the Christian mission. In the absence of a general postal service, it was a great advantage to be resident in a thriving commercial and shipping center from which transportation and communication were available to any point in the Empire. From Corinth Paul was able to contact his churches by letter and messenger. The constant movement of travelers, merchants, and pilgrims through Corinth made it possible for the Apostle to influence persons from every part of the Roman world.

For further information on Corinth see:

Broneer, O. "The Apostle Paul and the Isthmian Games." *Biblical Archaeologist* 25 (1962), 1-31.
———. "Corinth: Center of St. Paul's Missionary Work in Greece." *Biblical Archaeologist* 14 (1951), 78-96.
Corinth. A Brief History of the City and A Guide to the Excavations (1969).
Frazer, J. G. *Pausanias's Description of Greece.* Translated with a commentary; Vol. 3 (1913).
Hawthorne, J. G. "Cenchreae: Port of Corinth." *Archaeology* 18 (1965), 191-200.
Lang, M. *Cure and Cult in Ancient Corinth. A Guide to the Asklepieion* (1977).
Murphy-O'Connor, J. *St. Paul's Corinth. Texts and Archaeology* (1983)
O'Neil, J. G. *Ancient Corinth* (1930).
Theissen, G. *The Social Setting of Pauline Christianity: Essays on Corinth.* Ed. and transl. by J. Schutz (1982).
Wiseman, D. J. *The Land of the Ancient Corinthians* (1978).

W. L. L.

CHAPTER TEN

DAMASCUS

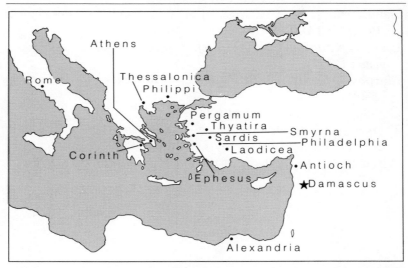

For thousands of years Damascus has been one of the important cities of the lands east of the Mediterranean Sea. During the several centuries when the Hebrew people had kings as their rulers, Damascus was the capital of a country that was sometimes a friend but more often an enemy.

Name In the Hebrew Old Testament, the spelling of this city's name is *dammeseq*, but the earliest references to the city are on the clay tablets (2400-2250 BC) from the archives of Ebla. The name was spelled *dimashqi* at that time. The earliest

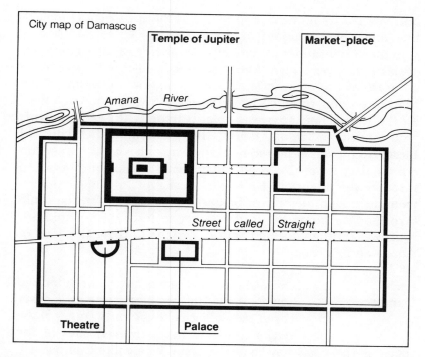

City map of Damascus

Temple of Jupiter

Market-place

Amana   River

Street called Straight

Theatre

Palace

Egyptian reference to the city is in an inscription attributed to the Pharaoh Thutmose III in the fifteenth century BC. The transcription of the Egyptian name for the city is *timasqu*. The next important reference is in a letter of the Amarna achives from a king Akissi of Qatna to Pharaoh Amenophis IV of the fourteenth century BC. Akissi calls the city *timaashgi*. The Assyrians spelled the name of the city variously as *imerishu, dimashgi,* or *shaimerishu,* but the Arabic spelling is *dimashqu.*

**Geographical
Environment**

The city is located a few miles northeast of Mount Hermon in a fertile oasis surrounded on the south, east, and north by desert. Several streams flow by the city which provide an abundance of water for vegetables, grains, and fruit trees for a sizeable population. The streams are the Amana (modern El-Barada) and the Pharpar (modern El-Awaj);

both are fed by numerous springs and the spring snow-melt of the Anti-Lebanon mountain range.

In the ancient times the city also sat astride several major caravan routes over which the inhabitants traded with peoples in all areas of the ancient Near East. A major route came from Mari, providing products from the entire Mesopotamian Valley. To the west, Damascus was able to trade with sea merchants who landed at Tripoli, Beirut, Tyre, Sidon, and Accho. Of these, Accho was easiest to reach by way of a road across northern Galilee. From this road the caravans could journey south through the Plain of Esdraelon to Egypt. Another branch wound through the hills of Samaria to Jerusalem, or one could take the way along the Jordan River to Jericho. A significant route was through the highlands east of the Jordan to the Gulf of Aqaba and Arabia.

**Early
Damascus**

Because Damascus has always been located on the same site, archaeologists have never been able to excavate the early stages of the city's development. However, sites at the edges of the oasis have yielded some Chalcolithic and Early Bronze Age artifacts. The cuneiform tablets of the Ebla archives (2400-2250 BC) mention Damascus as one of the cities in Ebla's trading network. This is the first evidence that the city actually existed during the third millenium BC. Nothing about its size or its inhabitants is available from these ancient tablets.

One might expect that a reference to Damascus would occur on the tablets in the large archives of Mari (1800-1700 BC) located on the south bank of the Euphrates River not far from Damascus. So far the city's name is absent from these clay tablets. The same is true of the clay tablets of the archives of Nippur located in the lower Mesopotamian valley. Surely Damascus continued to function as a trading center, led by Amorites who dominated the area.

Inscriptions from the Twelfth Dynasty of Egypt do not mention Damascus, but they do mention the presence of the armies of the Egyptians in the land of Canaan. Also, Egyptian artifacts such as seals, statuettes, and other royal items have been found in the ruins of the nearby cities of Byblos and Ras Shamra. The Execration Texts seem to rest on the reality of Egyptian control of lands east of the Mediterranean Sea.

The name of the city is present in two narratives of the patriarchs in the book of Genesis. Most scholars place the time of Abraham and his family in the Middle-Bronze Age (2100-1550 BC).

The first narrative is in Genesis 14. Kings from the east had invaded the land of Canaan and carried off Abraham's nephew Lot and much booty. Abraham led a force of several hundred men and defeated the invaders near Damascus (14:15), delivering Lot from his plight.

The second narrative is in Genesis 15 and tells the story of Abraham's desire to obtain a wife for Isaac from relatives at Harran. Abraham sent Eliezer, a native of Damascus, on the mission (15:2).

The aggressive Eighteenth Dynasty of Egypt spread its control into the land of Canaan and areas to the north, especially under the leadership of Thutmose III and Amenhotep II. Damascus was captured and made an important part of Egypt's city-state network of power.

Due to the rising power of the Mitanni Empire to the east of the Euphrates River, Egypt's control of Damascus was seriously challenged but not successfully. It was the push of Hittite power from the north led by Shuppiluliuma that wrested Damascus from the Egyptians, though not for long. The Egyptians were still strong in the region, and the contest between these two powers swept back and forth across ancient Syria for a century and a half. The records are not clear, but Damascus seems to have been at times controlled by the Hittites and at times by the Egyptians. The end of the struggle came with the destruction of the Hittite Empire by invaders from the west during the last half of thirteenth century BC.

The disappearance of the Hittites and the retreat of the Egyptians gave opportunity for the Arameans to move in from the desert and take control of Damascus and surrounding territory.

For the next three centuries, free of foreign pressures, the new-comers were able to amass wealth and strength which enabled them to become a formidable nation.

Relations with Israel   While the Israelites were settling the land of Canaan, the Aramaeans were quietly con-solidating their mercantile and military power to the north. They made no effort to stop the movement of Hebrew tribes, especially Dan, into the northern regions of Galilee. Instead they developed into city-states which finally came under the leadership of Hadadezer, head of the city-state of Zobah, with headquarters at Damascus.

The first violent contact between the Aramaeans and Israel is recorded in 2 Samuel 8:3-13. King David defeated Hadadezer and put a garrison in Damascus. This seems to be a summary of the account found in 2 Samuel 10:6-19. David had attacked the Ammonites who enlisted the help of the Syrians of Beth Rehob, of Zoba, of Maacah, and of Ish-Tob. David won the battle, but Hadadezer found more allies and launched another attack with the same result. From then on Damascus was solidly under the control of David and Solomon.

Rezon rose to power by leading a successful revolt that gave him control of Damascus and seriously weakened Solomon's power in areas north of Galilee. The division of the tribes of Is-rael into nations early in the reign of Solomon's son Rehoboam gave to the Syrians in Damascus their golden opportunity. For almost two centuries they were to be the implacable enemy of the two kingdoms, Israel and Judah.

The first violent contact was with Israel's king Baasha (1 Kings 15:16-21). The instigator of the affair was King Asa of Ju-dah who paid "Ben-Hadad the son of Tabrimmon, the son of Hezion, king of Syria (v. 8)" to attack Baasha. The cost of this act was great and long lasting, for it gave an opening that al-lowed Ben-Hadad I to demonstrate his military power and strongly influence the course of events in the two Israelite king-doms. Damascus had become the power center that dominated the flow of commerce across the northern part of Galilee and soon made a treaty with the northern kingdom of Israel to the disadvantage of Judah.

Before that treaty was made, Ben-Hadad I had to deal with the rise of Omri to power in Israel. Omri strengthened his position by building a new capital at Samaria. He cemented relationships with Ethbaal, king of Sidon, by agreeing to the marriage of the Sidonian princess, Jezebel, with the crown prince of Israel, Ahab. This act tended to curtail the trading power of Damascus. The rise of Assyrian aggression to the north also kept the king of Damascus from enlarging his conquests in Galilee.

Street Called
Straight in Damascus

In Ahab's reign, Ben-Hadad I thought he saw an opportunity to strike against the Israelite king and sent a force against the almost impregnable fortress at Samaria, but he was defeated with great slaughter (1 Kings 20:1-22). Ben-Hadad I tried to attack Ahab again with the same bloody result (1 Kings 20:23-30). The king of Damascus sued for peace and a treaty was forged between them (1 Kings 20:31-34). The next year Damascus joined Ahab and his army with other Syrian allies at Karkar in an attempt to stop Ashurnasirpal II. This battle, which ended in an Assyrian victory, is recorded on the Monolith Inscription of Shalmaneser.

All went well until King Ahab decided to make an alliance with king Jehoshaphat of Judah. Ahab wanted to regain the city of Ramoth-Gilead from the Syrians, but he was warned by the prophet Micaiah that the project would result in his death. Ahab ignored the warning and died as a result of wounds he suffered in the battle (1 Kings 22:1-40).

Ben-Hadad was unable to take advantage of Ahab's death, and a revolt of the Moabites against the northern kingdom of Israel, because the Assyrians under Shalmaneser III were pressing hard from the north. Ben-Hadad of Damascus twice led a coalition of Syrian states against Shalmaneser, who claimed he defeated Ben-Hadad both times. The defeats must not have been decisive, for Shalmaneser III did not at that time push to Damascus to bring it under his control. Instead, Ben-Hadad renewed his attacks on the northern kingdom of Israel and surrounded the capital city of Samaria. Guided by the counsel of the prophet Elisha, King Joram (Jehoram) held steady. Yahweh intervened by causing the Syrians to hear noises of chariots and horses. They thought the Egyptians were coming and fled the scene (2 Kings 6:8—7:16).

The biblical records relate how Elisha revealed to Hazael, an officer in Ben-Hadad's court, that the Syrian would become king over Syria and then invade Israel. Hazael hastened the fulfillment of the prophecy by murduring Ben-Hadad at the palace in Damascus (2 Kings 8:7-15).

Joram of Israel, with King Ahaziah of Judah, joined in an attack against the Syrian forces that held the Israelite city of Ramoth Gilead. King Hazael of Damascus and his soldiers succeeded during this battle in wounding Joram, who returned to Jezreel to recover. He was killed in the revolt led by Jehu, a general in the Israelite army (2 Kings 8:28; 9:21-26).

Jehu's act of doing homage and paying tribute to Shalmaneser III may have been the cause of Hazael's savage attack on territories controlled by Jehu east of the River Jordan as far south as the River Arnon (2 Kings 10:32). The death of Jehu seemed to open new roads along the coast, for Hazael pushed his advance to the gates of Gath. After taking the city, Hazael moved toward Jerusalem, but King Jehoash paid the invader with gold and silver. This mollified the king of Damascus enough that he returned to his capital (2 Kings 12:17-18). However, Hazael continued to oppress the Israelites until the end of his reign (2 Kings 13:3-7; 22-24).

In the sixteenth year of the reign of Tiglath-pileser III, that ruler was able to surround Damascus and destroy crops, but could not capture the city.

The son of Hazael, Ben-Hadad II, was not able to keep Israel under control, for King Jehoash of Israel, in a series of three attacks, recovered the territory east of the River Jordan (2 Kings 13:24-25). Jeroboam II was even more successful; he was able to extend his control to the north over Hamath and Damascus (2 Kings 14:25-28).

During the period after the death of Jeroboam II, Damascus regained its power under the leadership of Rezin. Because Tiglath-pileser III, king of Assyria, was pushing across the Euphrates River into northern Syria, Rezin decided to build a coalition to stop the drive. He turned to Pekah and with him tried to force King Ahaz of Judah to join. Ahaz refused, though Rezin and Pekah sent an army against him.

Contrary to the advice of the prophet Isaiah, Ahaz decided to put into action a plan of his own, a plan that had disastrous consequences. Ahaz sent officials with much gold and silver to induce the Assyrian to harass the northern borders of Syria and thus force Rezin to pull back his soldiers to Damascus. Tiglath-pileser did more than harass Rezin; he led his army to the gates of Damascus and captured it in 732 BC. King Rezin was killed and many citizens of the city were taken into captivity. Northern Israel was also attacked and Pekah killed (2 Kings 15:29-30, 37; 16:5-9). As a result, Damascus lost its autonomy, and for many centuries the city was to experience the oppressive control of a series of foreign rulers.

Post-exilic
Damascus
Damascus did not remain a victim of Assyrian power without a struggle. Twice, in 727 and in 720 BC, the city led a revolt against Assyria but to no avail. Tiglath-pileser III smashed the first revolt and Sargon II the second, removing many more people to other parts of the empire. Damascus was formed into an Assyrian province and ruled by representatives of the Assyrian throne until the demise of that empire in 612 BC.

The Babylonian empire absorbed Damascus and its province into its hegemony, and the city seemed to function as a prosperous trading center governed by an appointee of the emperor. There seemed to be little change when the Persians conquered the Babylonians in 539 BC, except that the governors were Persian satraps.

Greco-Roman
Damascus
After Alexander the Great defeated the Persians at Issus in 333 BC, he sent his general, Parmenio, to capture Damascus and loot the Persian treasury there. Basically, the provincial divisions of the previous three empires were retained except that Damascus, along with other cities, was organized according to the pattern of Greek city-states.

During the period following Alexander's death in 323 BC, Damascus became a pawn in the struggle between several of his top generals. Antigonus commissioned his general, Demetrius, to attack the Greek armies in Babylon in 311 BC. He used Damascus as his staging area for this strike to the east.

Ptolemy, the Greek ruler of Egypt, coveted the Palestinian area. He successfully brought under his control all of Palestine and placed a garrison at Damascus. Antiochus I took the city by surprise in 274 BC, and from then on it was a possession of the Seleucid division of the Greek empire. The Seleucid rulers, however, did not make Damascus their administrative center. Instead they built a new city on the northeast tip of the Mediterranean Sea and called it Antioch.

Damascus came to prominence again during the revolt of the Maccabees which began in 168 BC. Bacchides, a general stationed at Damascus, was sent by Demetrius I in 161 BC to bring the Jews under control. However, Jonathan was able in 150 BC to take advantage of a struggle for power between several Seleucid leaders and take control of Damascus. Demetrius II tried to destroy Jonathan's army at Hazor in 144 BC, but he was defeated.

Tryphon, a rival of Demetrius II, also feared Jonathan, but Tryphon chased Jonathan from Damascus and managed to entrap the Maccabean at Ptolemais (Accho), and took him prisoner in 143 BC. Tryphon finally killed Jonathan the next year at Bascama before returning to Damascus.

The contest between Seleucid leaders continued until a decisive battle near Damascus between Demetrius II and Alexander II (Zabinas) in 126 BC. Alexander won the battle and ruled for three years.

Damascus became the capital of the Seleucid rulers Demetrius III and Antiochus XII early in the first century BC, but the city asked Aretas III, the Nabataean king in 85 BC, to help repel the Ituraeans. He soon made Damascus part of his kingdom and erased as much Greek influence in the city as possible.

The Roman general Pompey captured Damascus in 64 BC. It became part of the Roman province of Syria as well as the staging center for Pompey's advance on Judea. Antony gave the city to Cleopatra, who held it until Octavian captured it for Rome. The Parthians invaded Syria in 40 BC and launched an attack on Galilee from Damascus which was led by Barzapharnes. After this thrust, which went as far south as Jerusalem, the Parthians withdrew from Palestine to their homeland beyond the Euphrates river.

During the early phases of Roman control of Syria, Jews from Judea moved to several cities in the eastern part of the empire, including Damascus. Here they established several synagogues to which Christians came preaching the gospel and winning many Jews to their messiah. Saul, a zealous devotee of his faith, obtained permission to go to Damascus to stop the Christian activity in the Jewish communities. It was near Damascus that he saw the Lord in a vision. The Lord rebuked him and told him to go to Damascus and await further instructions. Blinded by the vision, Saul was led to Damascus and was visited by Ananias, through whom Saul's sight was restored and he was baptized. Saul preached Christ in the synagogues, but he had to flee the city by night because some sought to kill him (Acts 9:1-25).

There is no further reference to Damascus in the New Testament, but it was not long before it became a center of the Christian movement and remained so until the city was captured by the Islamic armies in AD 639. Damascus, capital of Syria, has remained an important city in the Arabic world until the present day.

For further information on Damascus see:

Negev, A. *Archaeological Encyclopedia of the Holy Land*. s.v. "Damascus" (1972).
Pearlman, M. *The Maccabees* (1973).
Unger, M. F. *Israel and the Aramaeans of Damascus* (1957).

G. H. L.

EBLA

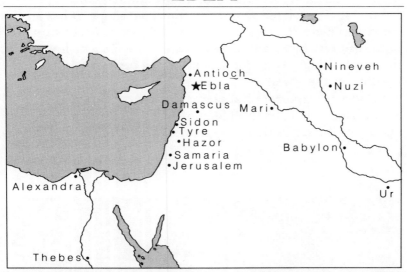

Ancient Ebla, the modern uninhabited mound called Tell Mardikh, has been acclaimed in newspapers, magazines, and scholarly journals as a major archaeological find of modern times. It is increasing our understanding of the ancient Near East in a remarkable way. For Bible students, the Ebla excavations are illuminating the history and culture of ancient Syria-Palestine, the context in which the Hebrews and the Hebrew Scriptures (the Old Testament) are to be understood.

Discovery
of Ebla

In 1963 the University of Rome sent a young scholar, Paolo Matthiae, to northern Syria to choose a tell, the excavation of which would elucidate urban culture in the second millenium BC. In consultation with the Department of Antiquities in Damascus, Matthiae chose Tell Mardikh. Its size (140 acres) and strategic location (about thirty-four miles south of Aleppo, close to the ancient caravan route to Hama and Damascus) suggested its importance. It was to prove elucidating not only for the second millennium but more so for the third millennium BC. In 1964 the Italian Archaeological Mission to Syria was constituted, with Matthiae as its director. Excavations began immediately and have continued annually to the present.

The 140 acre tell has a rounded trapezoid shape. It has an elevated perimeter (the walls), an elevated center (the acropolis), both fifty feet high, and between them the circular lower city, thirteen feet high. Four depressions in the perimeter indicate the position of the gates.

In 1968 an important statue was unearthed, dating to *ca.* 1900 BC, bearing a twenty-six line cuneiform inscription. Giovanni Pettinato, the expedition's epigrapher, identified the language as

Artistic impression of Ebla, from *Science Year, The World Book Science Annual* © 1977. Field Enterprises Educational Corporation. By permission of World Book.

Akkadian. The inscription declared the statue to have been dedicated by Ibbit-Lim, king of Ebla, to the goddess Eshtar. It appeared that Tell Mardikh was ancient Ebla, but further confirmation was needed.

Then in 1975, in Royal Palace G, the excavators unearthed the main state archives, dating to *ca.* 2400-2250 BC and containing thousands of tablets and fragments—1000 in room L.2712 and 14,500 in L.2769. More were found in 1976—600 in L.2769, 450 in L.2875 and 500 in L.2764. About 17,000 tablets, fragments, and chips had been discovered, representing 4,000 to 5,000 original tablets, of which about 1,700 have been published.

Tablets   The tablets of the state archives were inscribed with the cuneiform script. The majority were written in the Eblaite language, although 80 percent of the signs used were Sumerian logograms (word signs) intended to represent and be read as Eblaite words. Pettinato and Matthiae identified the Eblaite language as the oldest known example of Northwest Semitic. They called it Palaeo-Canaanite because of its supposed similarity with other branches of Canaanite; namely, Phoenician, Ugaritic, and Hebrew. A minority of texts was written entirely in Sumerian.

The majority of texts describe economic and commercial transactions. Others were word lists (compare Solomon's lists in 1 Kings 4:33)—lists of professions, animals, birds, fish, geographical names, and objects of stone, metal and wood, vocabulary lists of Eblaite words, as well as bilingual dictionary lists of Eblaite and Sumerian words. There was a handful of historical texts such as state letters, edicts, and international treaties; one was a commercial treaty between Ebla and Assur; another documented a successful military campaign against Mari on the middle Euphrates; a further marriage treaty text documented the marriage of an Eblaite princess to the ruler of the city of Emar. Among the literary texts were myths, epic tales, hymns, incantations, and collections of proverbs. On the basis of these tablets Tell Mardikh was identified conclusively as Ebla.

History   Enough information has been unearthed for us to outline the successive levels of the city's history. Level I (*ca.* 3500-2900 BC) was a small village centered on the acropolis. By the end of Level II A (*ca.* 2900-2400 BC) Ebla became a town as it expanded to the lower city.

In Level II B (*ca.* 2400-2250 BC) Ebla became a thriving city, as documented by the tablets of the state archives. Royal Palace G, situated at the southwest slope of the acropolis, had a large audience courtyard flanked on the north and east by the colonnaded facade of the palace itself, and opening on the south and west onto the lower city. The courtyard, with its throne-dias, no doubt functioned as a meeting place for state administrators with emissaries and commercial businessmen. Ebla of Level II B1 became the capital of a kingdom with wide-ranging commercial and political influence, extending east across the Euphrates into northcentral Mesopotamia, west to the Mediterranean as far as Cyprus, north into east central Anatolia, and south into Palestine.

A succession of five kings, belonging to Level II B1, ruling altogether about fifty years, can be reconstructed from the texts—Igrish-Khalam, Irkab-Damu, Ar-Ennum, Ebrium, and Ibbi-Sipish. Igrish-Khalam and Irkab-Damu began expanding Ebla's political and commercial influence. Irkab-Damu made a treaty with Zizi, king of Hamazi in northern Iran, resulting in the provision of mercenary troops for Ebla. The next king, Ar-Ennum, organized a military campaign against Iblul-Il of Mari who had extended his control over Assur and over Ebla's commercial colony near Emar on the Upper Euphrates. Ebla was victorious, but her victory was short-lived because Sargon I of Akkad reclaimed Mari. With the election of Ebrium as king of Ebla, four times in a row, the city recovered its pre-eminent position, aided by the fact that Sargon faced internal and external threats in Akkad. Ebrium established political marriages between Eblaite princesses and rulers of other important cities. He made a bilateral treaty with Assur concerning the founding of a commercial center in Anatolia. Ebrium's son, Ibbi-Sipish, succeeded as

—— 110 ——

ruler, re-exerting Ebla's control over Mari. However, Sargon's grandson, Naram-Sin, who was now king of Akkad and had overcome Akkad's problems, launched a campaign into Syria *ca.*2250 BC, destroying Ebla in the process.

Ebla was rebuilt in Level II B2 (*ca.*2250-2000 BC). Palace G, however, was not rebuilt but was replaced by a monumental approach to a Temple D. The city became important once again but was apparently overshadowed by the neighboring city of Urshu. Ebla was destroyed a second time (*ca.*2000 BC) by unknown forces, which were possibly related to the disorders created by Amorites who were penetrating Syria around that time.

Levels III A (*ca.*2000-1800 BC) and III B (*ca.*1800-1600 BC) evidence a new culture, due to the absorption of Amorites, which parallels the emergence of Amorite kingdoms throughout Palestine, Syria, and Mesopotamia. The names of two of Ebla's kings contemporary with Level III A are known from the Ibbit-Lim statue (dated *ca.* 1900 BC). The inscription on the statue refers to king Ibbit-Lim as son of Igrish-Khepa. Presumably his father preceded him as king. By the beginning of Level III B (*ca.* 1800 BC) the kingdom of Ebla was probably absorbed into the neighboring kingdom of Yamkhad (Aleppo). The city of Levels III A-B was reconstructed on the ground plan of the previous city with some changes. New rampart-style walls with four well-fortified monumental city gates were built. A number of temples (D, Bl, and N), a sanctuary (B2), a fortress (M), and a city gate (A) have been excavated, as well as two palaces (Q and E). Most significant is the Western Palace or Building Q (from Levels III A and B), with a royal necropolis (from Level III B) extending underneath its central area. Nine tombs have been discovered in natural caves in the rock on which the palace was built. Three of them, the "Tomb of the Princess" (*ca.*1800 BC), the "Tomb of the Lord of the Goats" (*ca.*1750 BC), and the "Tomb of the Cisterns" (*ca.*1700 BC) consisted of a complex of caves artificially connected to each other. Though pillaged around 1600 BC, they still contained skeletons, many vessels of pottery and stone, a bronze axe, an Egyptian ceremonial mace, two limestone maces, as well as much jewelry.

Matthiae suggests that the Western Palace, with its necropolis, together with Temple B1 and Sanctuary B2 formed a single complex devoted to the worship of royal ancestors to guarantee the city's prosperity. Such a cult, he maintains, was comparable to the cult of the *rp'um* known from later Ugarit (fourteenth century BC). The biblical word *repha'im* may be related etymologically to *rp'um*. However, the Bible uses the term *repha'im* in a transformed sense to refer either to the dead inhabitants or "shades" of the netherworld (Isa. 14:9; 26:19; Ps. 88:10; Prov. 9:18; Job 26:5) or in an ethnic sense to the Palestinian inhabitants or "giants" prior to the Israelites' arrival (Deut. 2:11, 20; 3:11; 2 Sam. 21:16, 18, 20, 22; 1 Chron. 20:4, 6, 8).

Ebla was finally destroyed *ca.* 1600 BC by one of the Hittite kings, either Hattusilis I or Mursilis I, during their campaigns against the kingdom of Yamkhad. A couple of tablets, dated just prior to 1600 BC and found in the northwest part of the Western Palace, mention an Indilimgur in a date-formula. He may have been one of the last kings of Ebla prior to its destruction.

Ebla's Golden Age　　*The City and Its Government.* At the height of its power Ebla had a population of 260,000 (according to tablet TM.75, G.336). This figure no doubt included Ebla and those environs which she directly controlled.

The acropolis was devoted to the state's central administrative complex. This complex had four "palaces": the Palace of the King, probably the royal residence; the Main Palace, possibly concerned with the municipal government of Ebla itself; the Stables, perhaps concerned with Ebla's commercial affairs; and the Palace of Service (?), possibly concerned with public works and city maintenance.

The head of state was the "King" (Eblaite *maliku*), elected from an aristocracy every seven years but not necessarily from the royal family. The royal family, especially the queen, princes, and queen mother, were prominent in the state administration. The power of the king and royal family was balanced by a

Council of Elders (Eblaite *abbu*). Initially royal power was neither absolute nor hereditary. However, the last two kings, Ebrium and Ibbi-Sipish, established the dynastic principle of hereditary succession.

Under the king was the "lord" (Eblaite *adanu*), head of the civil service. Under the *adanu* were fourteen "governors," two in charge of the Lower City and twelve in charge of the entire state territory. Under the fourteen "governors" were seven thousand civil servants, who were undoubtedly located not only in Ebla itself but also throughout the villages and vassal cities of the kingdom of Ebla. Another forty-seven hundred civil servants were employed directly by the central administrative complex.

The Lower City was divided into four quarters. It functioned largely as a residential area of small houses and narrow streets, together with some temples and sanctuaries. Each quarter was associated with a city gate and each gate with one of the chief gods of Ebla—Dagan, Rasap, Sipish, and Baal.

The Economy. Ebla's economic base was threefold—agriculture, livestock, and industry. The major crops were grains (barley and wheat), grapes, and olives for their oil. Other crops were malt for beer brewing, figs, pomegranates, and flax for the textile industry. Cattle were raised—small cattle (sheep and lambs, for their wool and for sacrificial offerings, as well as goats and pigs) and large cattle (oxen and cows, as work animals and as sacrificial offerings).

Industry was the largest source of Ebla's great wealth. The major industry was that of textile manufacture, which produced woolen, linen, and damask fabrics. The metal industry worked with gold, silver, and bronze to craft weapons, tools, jewelry, and ornamental objects; copper and tin were used to produce bronze alloys. Carpenters produced first class furniture. Workers in precious stones produced objects of carnelian and lapis-lazuli. Much of the raw material was imported, crafted, and exported for a profit. Silver and gold were the international mediums of exchange. Ebla was very prosperous and its international, commercial influence spread throughout the ancient Near East.

The School System. Ebla must have had a well-organized school system for the training of scribes. The head was called the "expert," a teacher was called "one who knows the tablets," and a scribe was called "one who inscribes the tablet." Many of the word lists, bilingual dictionaries, lists of verb paradigms, and literary texts would have been used in the school as reference works and as texts for practice-copying by scribes in training.

Religion. Eblaite religion was polytheistic. About five hundred deities are known from the texts. Semitic-Canaanite gods predominate, but many Sumerian and a number of Hurrian gods are also mentioned. The supreme god was Dagan, god of vegetation, often referred to as "Lord," as in "Lord of the land" and "Lord of the gods." A city gate was named after him, as was the first month of the new calendar. He was worshiped at Ebla under a number of forms associated with various local cities. A reference to the "Lord of Kanana" *(dBe ka-na-na-im)* possibly refers to "Dagan of Canaan." Dagan is known from later tradition at Ugarit. The Bible attests a Philistine god Dagon (1 Chron. 10:10) worshiped in Gaza (Judg. 16:23) and in Ashdod (1 Sam. 5:2), as well as two places called Beth-Dagon, one in the Shephelah of Judah (Josh. 15:41) and one on the border of Asher (Josh. 19:27).

Other important deities, occurring in the new calendar or used to name the city gates, were Rasap (Sumerian Nergal; Resheph in Ugaritic and in Hab. 3:5), god of pestilence and of the netherworld after whom another city gate was named; Sipish (Sumerian Utu, Ugaritic Shapash, Akkadian Shamash), the sun-god, after whom a further city gate was named; Baal, well-known at Ebla in theophoric personal names, after whom a fourth city gate was named, and who was the dominant god at later Ugarit and in Canaan of biblical times; Eshtar (the Sumerian/Akkadian goddess Inanna/Ishtar), mother-goddess of love and war; Ada (Akkadian Adad), the storm god, the later Ugaritic and Canaanite Hadad (equated there, but not at Ebla, with Baal), and known in the Bible from theophoric personal names such as Hadad-ezer (2 Sam. 8:3-12), king of Zobah in Syria, and Ben-Hadad, king of Damascus (1 Kings 20:1, 2, 5,

—— 114 ——

passim); and Kamish, the later Chemosh, chief god of Moab (Numb. 21:29; 1 Kings 11:7, 33; 2 Kings 23:13; Jer. 48:46); as well as two Hurrian gods Ashtabi and Adamma.

Other deities were Balatu, "lady," the consort of Dagan; the fertility goddess Ashtarte, the later Canaanite Ashtarath, known in the Bible as Ashtoreth (1 Kings 11:5, 33; 2 Kings 23:13), and in her many local forms as the Ashtaroth (Hebrew plural; cf. Judg. 2:13; 10:6; 1 Sam. 7:4); the mother-goddess, Ashera, who appears at Ugarit as Athirat and in the Bible as the Canaanite consort of Baal (Judg. 3:7; 1 Kings 15:13; 18:19; 2 Kings 21:7); Malik, referred to in the Bible as Molech/Milcom, the chief god of the Ammonites (1 Kings 11:5, 7, 33; 2 Kings 23:10, 13; Jer. 49:1, 3); and Tiamat, known from the Babylonian creation myth Enuma Elish, who was the goddess of the primeval ocean, with whose name the Hebrew word *tehom* ("deep" in Gen. 1:2) is etymologically related but without maintaining the pagan mythological associations. As the above implies, a kind of syncretism was practiced at Ebla; Sumerian and Hurrian deities were worshiped alongside the dominant Semitic-Canaanite deities.

The Ebla texts provide few details concerning cultic rituals, appurtenances, and personnel. There were sacrifices of sheep and oxen; offerings of loaves, beer, oil, wine; gifts of gold and silver objects, and of costly cloths. One type of priest was called *pashishu*, "anointed one," who could be male or female; two types of priestesses are known, called *ashiratu* and *ishartu*. There were many temples and chapels, though none has been excavated contemporary with Ebla's golden age. Among the temples from Levels III A-B (*ca.* 2000-1600 BC) one (Great Temple D on the acropolis) exhibits a tripartite plan on a longitudinal axis—comparable but not identical to the basic plan of the later Solomonic temple in Jerusalem (1 Kings 6:1-22; 2 Chron. 3:1-9). Feasts were observed in celebration of various gods and occasions. There is evidence of a possible yearly procession in which Dagan, represented by his statue, went out to the surrounding cities and villages to keep them in contact with Ebla's chief deity and his cult.

There was at Ebla a popular, personal religion in contrast to the official religion of the established deities and their cults. The names of a number of personal deities appear in personal names. The most popular of such deities are Damu, Malik, Ya, and Il. Also mentioned in the texts is "the god of the king" (Sumerian *dingir-en*) and "the god of my father" (*dingir-a-mu*). The latter are reminiscent of the personal God of the patriarchs; the so-called "God of the fathers," the God of Abraham, the God of Isaac, and the God of Jacob (Gen. 24:12; 26:24; 28:13; 31:5, 42: 32:9; 46:1, 3: 49:25; 50:17; Exod. 3:6; 18:4; Deut. 6:3).

There were prophets at Ebla, called *mahhu* or *nabi'utum*. The *mahhu*-prophet is known from later Mari (*ca.* eighteenth century BC) on the Middle Euphrates. *Nabi'utum* is related to the Hebrew word for prophet *nabi'* in the Old Testament. The study of prophecy at Ebla will become important for providing a broader ancient Near Eastern context against which to understand Old Testament prophecy.

Biblical Significance   In assessing the significance of Ebla for Old Testament study caution needs to be exercised. The Ebla texts are not easy to read. Since their discovery in 1974-75, the interpretation of key texts has often had to be revised and previous hasty conclusions abandoned. For example: (1) The assertion that all five cities of the plain (Sodom, Gomorrah, Admah, Zeboiim, and Bela; that is Zoar, in Gen. 14:2) are referred to in the same order on a single tablet from Ebla was founded on what are now known to be erroneous readings of more than one tablet. (2) The assertion that the first king of Assyria, Dudiya (up to now considered legendary and known from the Assyrian King List, compiled many centuries later), is referred to in a treaty tablet from Ebla is open to question. The actual name was written NI-a-UD-DU. The capitalized syllables are of uncertain reading. The name Dudiya can only be arrived at by reading the signs backwards (!) as Du-ud-a-ya (the sign NI can be read ya). The name could also be read NI-a-e (e is the usual reading of UD-DU). (3) That the Eblaite language is "Palaeo-Canaanite" has been challenged by I. J. Gelb, who contends that it is closer to

Akkadian than to "Canaanite." (4) Some have asserted that Yahweh, the God of ancient Israel, was worshiped at Ebla under an
abbreviated name Ya or Yau. The evidence adduced comes from
personal names containing the element *ia*, interchangeable with
the element *il* ("El" or "god"); for example *en-na-ia/en-na-il, ish-
ra-ia/ish-ra-il*, and especially *shu-mi-a-u* and *dia-ra-mu* (in which
the d is the divine indicator). However, *ia* may simply represent
a shortened, pet name (compare our Monty for Montgomery
and, from Mari, the Amorite name Zimriya for Zimri-Dagan)
or it could be read as *i, li*, or *ni*. The name *dia-ra-mu* could be
read as *il-i-ra-mu* or *ilu-ni-ra-mu*. The evidence is inconclusive,
and even if *ia* represents a deity there is no evidence that it is
Yahweh the God of the Old Testament.

The pursuit of parallels in order to demonstrate a direct,
unique relationship between the Old Testament (and its people)
and Ebla is hazardous. Parallels do exist, however. Old Testament personal names occur in the Ebla texts; for example
Abramu (Abraham), Ishmail (Ishmael), Ennaia (Hanania),
Ishrail (Israel), Daudum (David), and Mikaya (Micaiah). No
one would argue, however, that these are the same persons as
those in the Old Testament. The most noteworthy personal
name is Ebrum/Ebrium, one of the kings of Ebla. Ebrum is comparable to Eber, the ancestor of Abraham and the Hebrews
(Gen. 10:21), and Ebrium to the Hebrew word *'ibri* "a Hebrew."
Old Testament city names occur in the Ebla texts; for example
Hazor, Megiddo, Lachish, Nahor, Gaza, Harran, Damascus,
and Jerusalem. The occurrence of a city called Ur in the region
of Haran is most interesting in view of the biblical tradition that
Abraham came from "Ur of the Chaldean" (Gen. 11:31). The
preceding pages of this chapter have indicated a number of other
cultural and religious parallels. These parallels are general, not
specific, and show no direct, unique relationship between Ebla
and the Old Testament.

The real significance of the Ebla finds for Old Testament
study is the fact that they are enlarging our understanding or
the ancient Near East, and especially of Syria-Palestine, in a remarkable way. As the history, culture, and religion of Ebla is

studied in depth and described more accurately in the coming decades, grounds for asserting the antiquity and historicity of the contents of the Old Testament, especially the patriarchal traditions, will be enlarged. Also, the Old Testament will be seen more clearly as a living, historical document, conditioned by but also reacting against the Canaanite culture and religion in the midst of which it developed under divine inspiration. In the meantime we must be patient and cautious, aware of the tentativeness of present conclusions.

For further information on Ebla see:

Bermant, C. and M. Weitzman. *Ebla, A Revelation in Archaeology* (1979).
Kitchen, K. A. *The Bible in Its World* (1977).
Mattiae, P. *Orientalia* 44 (1975), 337-360.
Pettinato, G. *Monographs on the Ancient Near East*, vols. I-VI (1977).

M. J. H.

HAZOR

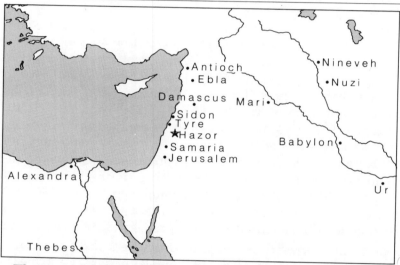

The mound of Hazor marks the location of one of the two or three largest Canaanite and Israelite cities of Old Testament times. The modern Hebrew name of the ancient site is *Tēl Ḥasor;* the Arabs call it *Tell el-Qedah.* Its ancient Greek name was *Asōr,* its Hebrew name *Ḥāsor,* and its Akkadian name *Hasūra.* The Hebrew word probably means "enclosure" and perhaps refers to the lower and larger portion of the mound.

Location   Hazor is located in the Huleh plain at the foot of the eastern ridge of the upper Galilee mountains. It is about nine miles due north of the Sea of Galilee and about four miles southwest of former Lake Huleh (recently drained by the Israelis for the purpose of land reclamation). In ancient times it dominated the various branches of the *Via Maris*. Two areas are distinguishable at Hazor: (1) a bottle-shaped tell oriented in a west-east direction, measuring about 130 feet in height and containing about twenty-five acres; (2) north of the tell is a rectangular plateau or "enclosure," containing about 185 acres, protected on the west by a huge *terre pisée* (beaten-earth) wall and on the other three sides by nature. It was thus well fortified.

Literary References
The earliest literary references to Hazor occur in Egyptian execration texts of the nineteenth to eighteenth centuries BC, which list as one of the potential enemies of Egypt in her external provinces "the ruler of Hazor, *Getji*." Two of the eighteenth-century Mari letters (*ARM* VI:23:23 and VI:78:5, 10, 14-15) cite Hazor as the only city in its area worth mentioning (in both letters it is referred to together with the important city of Qatna in north central Syria). Egyptian lists of conquered cities mention Hazor as having been taken during the reigns of Thutmose III (*ca.* 1490-1436 BC), Amunhotep II (*ca.* 1438-1412 BC), and Seti I (*ca.* 1303-1290 BC), although the conquest of Amunhotep II may have been more propagandistic than actual. Four of the fourteenth-century Amarna letters also contain references to Hazor: (1) in a letter of Abimilki of Tyre (*EA* 148:41); (2) and (3) in letters from Hazor itself (*EA* 227:3, 20; 228:4, 15-16, 23)—one letter is especially interesting in that it mentions "Hazor together with its cities," thus underscoring the importance of Hazor (compare Josh. 19:35-38); (4) in a letter of the king of Ashtaroth. The thirteenth-century Papyrus Anastasi I, a satirical Egyptian letter written by a royal official to an apprentice scribe, mentions Hazor in connection with certain military and topographical problems.

We come to the biblical references to Hazor and learn of its strategic importance. Joshua 11:1-15 describes the defeat by Joshua's army of a coalition headed by "Jabin [I?] king of Hazor" (11:1), one of "the cities built on their mounds" (11:13).

Hazor is also mentioned in the list that recapitulates Joshua's conquests (12:19) and in the roster of Naphtali's inheritance (19:36).

Judges 4 relates the story of the deliverance of Israel from the oppression of "Jabin [II?] king of Canaan, who reigned in Hazor" (4:2), by Deborah and Barak. In 4:17 Jabin is called simply "the king of Hazor," a reference that once again attests to the importance of the city. (Judges 5, the Song of Deborah, is a poetic account of the same deliverance.) 1 Samuel 12:9 refers to the same event, the Hebrew text alluding to "the army of Hazor" and the Septuagint version rendering "the army of Jabin king of Hazor."

Hazor is further mentioned in 1 Kings 9:15 in connection with certain Solomonic rebuilding operations that included the other prominent cities of Megiddo, Gezer, and Jerusalem. The latest reference to Hazor in the Old Testament is 2 Kings 15:29, where it is mentioned together with other cities in Naphtali as having fallen to Tiglath-pileser (III) of Assyria, probably when the latter destroyed Damascus in 732 BC.

From the one Apocryphal reference to Hazor (1 Macc. 11:67) we learn that Jonathan successfully fought the forces of the Seleucid king, Demtrius (II), in "the plain of Hazor" (147 BC). This battle is referred to later by Josephus (*Antiquities* XIII.5.7) as having taken place in "the plain that is called Asor." *Antiquities* V.5.1. helped modern explorers to locate the site of ancient Hazor by noting its general geographical position: "Hazor, a city that was situated above Lake Semachonitis" (Lake Huleh).

Excavations   The literary references to Hazor and modern excavations at the site have combined to help trace its history from the earliest times. It was inhabited from *ca.* 2700-150 BC in a succession of twenty-two separate occupations, reaching its golden age as one of the greatest cities of Canaan during the Middle and Late Bronze ages with an estimated population of forty thousand. During the third millennium only the mound area was occupied; but during the so-called "Hyksos" period the

Tell el-Qedah (Hazor)

lower city was built, and Hazor flourished during most of the second millennium, tempting conquest by various Egyptian pharaohs. The Israelites under Joshua destroyed it. From Solomon's time forward it experienced something of a revival but on the mound or upper city only. The Assyrians destroyed it in the late eighth century, and thereafter it was crowned by a sequence of Assyrian, Persian, and Greek citadels until about 150 BC, after which it ceased to be inhabited.

J. L. Porter suggested in 1875 that *Tell el-Qedah* was probably Hazor, but John Garstang was the first modern investigator to so identify it. He made preliminary soundings at the site in 1928. Under the direction of Yigael Yadin, the James A. de Rothschild Expedition sponsored a series of four campaigns at Hazor, beginning in 1955 and ending in 1958, in what was to be the first serious excavation in Palestine north of the Sea of Galilee. During each of the four seasons work was undertaken on both the upper mound and the lower enclosure. In the following review of the excavations, the number in parentheses following the area letters refer to the campaigns during which significant areas were worked.

Area A (1,2,3,4) was opened up in the center of the upper mound. Stratum I contained a small late eighth- to early seventh-century settlement that arose after the destruction of Hazor by Tiglath-pileser III (probably in 732 BC). Stratum II, a destruction layer of ashes, dates from *ca.* 750-700 BC and represents the Tiglath-pileser siege and capture. In Stratum III was found ninth- to eighth-century pottery, including also a beautiful bone handle of a scepter or mirror and an ivory cosmetic palette among the smaller objects. Also discovered in the stratum was the so-called "House of Makhbiram" dating from the time of Jeroboam II, the walls of which had been heavily damaged by an earthquake (compare Amos 1:1?). In the house were found the first two Hebrew inscriptions from the times of the kings of Israel to be discovered in Galilee. One reads *lmkbrm* ("belonging to Makhbiram") and the other *yrb'[m?] bn 'lm[ ]* ("Jeroboam[?] the son of Elm[...]"). Stratas IV and V contained a large public building, perhaps a storehouse, of the time of Ahab and his successors. Built on a thick burnt layer—the destruction of Ben-Hadad of Damascus?—its remains include two rows of nine monolithic columns each. Although an earthquake separated Strata V and VI, those two strata contained, south of the pillared building, the elaborate residence of a well-to-do Israelite. Fifty feet square, it included in its southeast corner a large court in which were found well-dressed stone pillars. Remains of the Solomonic casemate wall of the city were found in Stratum VII. Below the pillared "storehouse" of Ahab were discovered structures of Strata IX, X (Solomonic) and XI (Late Bronze II). The evident gap between the Late Bronze II and the Solomonic occupations is attributed by some to Joshua's conquest. The Stratum X, Solomonic remains include the gate belonging to the casemate city wall of Stratum VII. The gate is located in the northern part of the dig and contains three chambers on each side like those at Megiddo and Gezer (compare 1 Kings 9:15). The earlier strata (XI-XX) reflected the grandeur of the Amarna period (fifteenth and fourteenth centuries BC) containing several well-built Middle Bronze Age walls and significant pottery deposits. The lowest level (Stratum XXI) was established on bedrock.

Area B (1,2,3,4) was opened up at the western tip of the mound in its most defended part. (Each area was given its own provisional stratum numbers, so no correlation between the stratum numbers of the various areas should be sought.) Stratum I contained ruins of a Hellenistic citadel, Stratum II of a Persian citadel, and Stratum III of an Assyrian citadel. The imposing ninth-century Israelite citadel of Stratum VIII was apparently built by Ahab. It included a fort and a living annex, and its corners were strengthened with ashlar stones. Evidence of an earthquake was found in its ruins, which contained also numerous small objects such as a partly broken Samaria-style ivory box, a cultic incense ladle, and two wine-jar inscriptions, one reading *lpqḥ* ("belonging to Pekah") and the other *smdr* (a kind of wine; compare Song of Sol. 2:13). Its builders had used the Solomonic casemate wall of Strata IX and X. The citadel of Ahab was destroyed by Tiglath-pileser III (probably in 732 BC), as Stratum V reveals. The inhabitants of Stratum V built their own wall on top of the structure and surrounding it. In front of the entrance to Ahab's citadel and above the plastered floor of Stratum VII were found two proto-Aeolic (or Ionic) capitals serving as a shelter for a clay oven. They were originally column-tops belonging to the citadel itself. In Stratum XI was discovered the paved area of an idolatrous Israelite cult place of the pre-Solomonic period (Iron I). Stratum XII represents a poor Israelite settlement of the twelfth century.

Area G (3), on the eastern slope of the mound, revealed further Israelite fortifications. The entire eastern terrace was surrounded by a double wall with two huge towers. In the center of the terrace was a huge rectangular silo sixteen feet deep. On the west of the terrace was a large city wall, running from north to south across the slope and preserved to a height of eight and one-half feet, dating from the time of Ahab (Stratum VIII). Nearby, Strata VII through V revealed a residence with an intact ashlar staircase. Under the Israelite wall on the northern and eastern slopes of the eastern terrace was a huge Middle Bronze II double wall, both stonemade, the westernmost of which was a *glacis*.

Ahab's pillared building

Turning now to the vast lower enclosure at Hazor, we begin with Area C (1,2), located at the enclosure's southwest corner near the beaten-earth wall mentioned earlier. At the foot of the wall were two late fourteenth- to thirteenth-century Canaanite temples containing sculpture under Hittite influence but obviously of local Canaanite manufacture. Elsewhere in the area were found house floors littered with thirteenth-century Mycenaean pottery. Near the sanctuary area were discovered storerooms containing large jars. A potter's workshop nearby contained a complete potter's wheel *in situ* as well as a clay cultic mask. In the potter's storeroom was a bronze cultic standard plated with silver. Stratum II was of the fourteenth century; Stratum III (seventeenth to sixteenth centuries) was destroyed by fire, perhaps by either Amunhotep II or Thutmose III. Below the floors were found scores of infant burials in jars.

The latest buildings of Areas D (1) and E (1) were of the thirteenth century; the earliest were of the "Hyksos" period. Numerous water cisterns were found in these areas. In Area D was discovered a small jar fragment bearing two letters (...*lt*...) in the proto-Sinaitic alphabet.

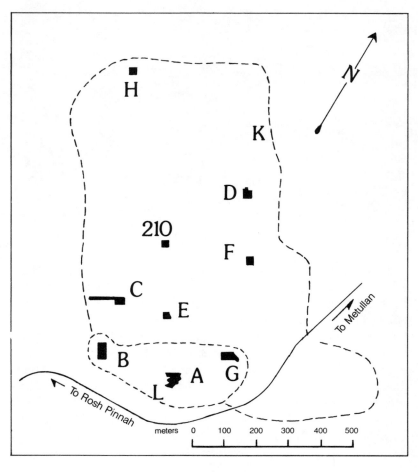

Area F (2,3) was opened in a different section of the thirteenth-century Canaanite city. Stratum I contained part of a large Late Bronze (fourteenth to thirteenth centuries) Canaanite temple. A huge five-ton altar of an earlier period was found in its court. Also discovered were a basalt offering table and a platform of small rough stones. The court was flanked on two sides by a series of large rooms, in one of which was found a basalt sculpture of a seated figure. A Late Bronze II burial cave was also uncovered, containing about five hundred vessels, including imported Mycenaean and Cypriote ware. Strata III and IV (Middle Bronze II) included an intricate complex of underground tunnels hewn in the rock. Among them were three enormous caves, the largest being 55 x 10 x 10 feet. Although empty when found, they doubtless served as the necropolis for the tell acropolis during the Middle Bronze period.

Area 210 (3) consisted of a small exploratory trench in the center of the enclosure revealing evidence of habitation from *ca.* 1700 to 1200 BC.

Area H (3, 4) was opened at the northernmost tip of the enclosure. Discovered here was a remarkable series of four Canaanite temples, one atop the other. Temple Ia (Late Bronze II, second half of thirteenth century) was 81 x 55 feet and consisted of three chambers: porch, main hall, and holy of holies, thus forming a kind of prototype of Solomon's temple. In the holy of holies was found a series of ritual implements, including an incense altar, offering tables, and vessels of various kinds. Also found was a basalt sculpture of a seated figure, better preserved than that discovered in Area F; a broken basalt statue of the temple's god bearing a crossed sun-disc on its breast; and, in the vicinity, a statue base depicting a bull. The remains of Temple Ib (fourteenth century) included a basalt lion orthostat found in the debris of the porch. Temple II (Late Bronze I, fifteenth century) consisted of only one room built under, and of the same size and dimensions as, the holy of holies of Temple I. To its south was a monumental gateway. In a heap of pottery near the altar was found a cuneiform liver model. Temple III (Middle Bronze II, seventeenth century) was similar in size to Temple II.

The basalt ashlar steps in front probably led up to a kind of platform.

Area K (4) is at the northeast edge of the enclosure. It revealed a Late Bronze (*ca.* 1550-1250) gate of huge ashlar stones. The exterior walls, still standing to a height of nine feet, remain from a destruction by violent conflagration. Also found in the area was a Middle Bronze (eighteenth to seventeenth centuries) gate, in front of and beneath which is a mammoth revetment wall twelve feet high.

One of the greatest surprises encountered by the excavators at Hazor turned out to be its water supply system, discovered by Yadin and his associates after a hiatus of ten years. Having earlier noticed a deep depression at the southern end of the mound, and having suspected the presence of a water tunnel there, they opened up Area L in 1968. The results of their subsequent months of labor were spectacular indeed: a vertical shaft one hundred feet in depth, supported by retaining walls and measuring 62 x 50 feet at its upper end, and a sloping tunnel, fourteen feet high and fourteen feet wide, beginning at the bottom of the shaft and extending for about eighty-one feet to a pool situated at the natural water level. This impressive water system, dating to the ninth century BC and one of the largest of its kind, is worthy of a city that, during the days of Joshua, was "the head of all those kingdoms" (Josh. 11:10).

A tablet discovered accidentally at the site by an American tourist in 1962 contained an Akkadian account of a legal suit brought before the king at some period between 1800 and 1600 BC. It is of interest because it indicates the way in which Middle Bronze Age Canaanite life was under Babylonian cultural influence.

For further information on Hazor see:

Malamat, A. "Hazor, 'The Head of All Those Kingdoms.' " *Journal of Biblical Literature* 79 (1960), 12-19.

Yadin, Y. *Hazor: The Rediscovery of a Great Citadel of the Bible* (1975).

————— .*et. al. Hazor.* 4 Vols. (1958-1964).

————— . "Hazor." *Encyclopedia of Archaeological Excavations in the Holy Land.* ed. M. Avi-Yonah (1976), 2. 474-95.

R. Y.

CHAPTER THIRTEEN

JERICHO

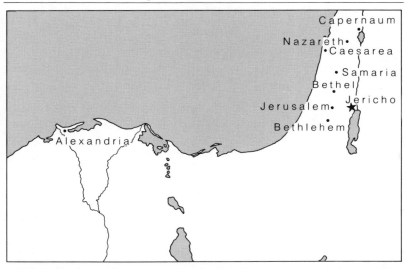

The city of Jericho receives frequent mention in the biblical narratives before Joshua (Numb. 22:1, 26:3, 31:12, 33:48, 50; 34:15; 35:1; Deut. 32:49) and is alluded to as the "city of palm trees" (Deut. 34:3; 2 Chron. 28:15; compare Judg. 1:16). However, its prominence is derived from the remarkable narratives surrounding its capture: Joshua 2-6. It is subsequently apportioned to Benjamin (Josh. 18:21).

Joshua 2-6 is enclosed by narratives concerning the reception of the Israelite spies by Rahab (Joshua 2), who was the first gentile convert and the ancestress of David, and her rescue with her family (Josh. 6:25). These narratives thus hint at the ultimate use to which the promised land was put. Jericho was the paradigm for the manner in which the promised land was to be possessed, and for that reason presumably it was to be left unfortified but not unoccupied (Josh. 6:26, 18:21; 2 Sam. 10:5).

Israel was not to forget the nature of her entry, and the particular theological deliberation which marks these chapters of Joshua is evidence of the way in which Israel presented her history. Thus, while the supernatural features in the Jericho narrative can find other explanations (parallels for the miraculous damming of the Jordan can be provided, and the natural phenomenon of an earthquake can be advanced to explain the fall of the famed walls), we are finally left with the account of the capture of the city, which is totally reliant upon explicit divine intervention.

Early Jericho Since the fall of a major city of that time ought to have left tangible reminders, the area of Jericho has proved attractive to modern archaeology from the mid-nineteenth century. The mound of Tell-es-Sultan is commonly (though not unanimously) accepted as the site of the Old Testament town. The history of the excavation of this mound began with a visit in 1867 by Captain Charles Warren, but the first careful excavations were undertaken by an Austro-German team (of Sellin and Watzinger) in 1907-09. Their work penetrated to pre-pottery Neolithic levels and exposed the massive defensive system of late Middle Bronze Age Jericho.

Increasing precision achieved in pottery chronology encouraged the further work of Prof. John Garstang in 1930-36. Garstang's work suggested that Jericho offered the earliest evidence of humankind's move towards urbanism, and he uncovered Neolithic levels in which pottery, the accepted sign of transition to the neolithic period, was significantly absent. More importantly for the Bible student, Garstang believed that he had located the famous fallen walls of Jericho, though these proved later to be the town walls of the declining Early Bronze Age city. It was unfortunate for Garstang that he had excavated at a point in the

Tell es-Sultan (Jericho)

mound where the imposition of the later, massive Middle Bronze Age defensive system upon the earlier town walls was not evident.

Between 1952-58 Kathleen Kenyon headed a joint Anglo-American team and began further work, stimulated by Garstang's and designed to take up two main points. Her expedition aimed at tracing the origins of the site and at solving the controversy which Garstang's identification of the Jericho walls had provoked. As indicated, Garstang's fortifications proved to be the remainder of the late, Early Bronze Age city which was destroyed, perhaps by earthquake and fire *ca.* 2300 BC.

Kenyon's excavations reached bedrock in sufficient places to reveal that the height of the mound (a maximum of 82 feet, extending over 10 acres) represented successive stages in human occupation from the Mesolithic to the biblical period. The earliest slender remains were found at the north end of the mound and were dated to at least the eighth millennium BC, with indications that the earliest site was a sanctuary frequented by mesolithic hunters (the name Jericho, probably a compound formed from the name of the West Semitic moon god Yarih, suggests sanctuary connotations).

The early attractiveness of such a site, and its potential for growth, was doubtless to be explained by its very favorable location. Jericho is blessed by an abundance of spring water, making prodigious agriculture possible once irrigation has been introduced. Its climate is tropical in summer and mild in winter. It is placed strategically near one of the fordable areas of the lower Jordan and would always have provided an important communications link. Jericho, situated in the great Rift valley and some 810 feet below sea level, has the distinction of being the lowest city on the earth's surface. It is distinguished from its bleak Dead Sea environment (some eleven miles south) by the natural resources with which it is endowed.

In the ensuing Neolithic period two distinct phases of activity were documented by Kenyon. The first was a pre-pottery stage (from *ca.* seventh millennium BC onwards). During the first phase (Kenyon's pre-pottery A) a town wall associated with a massive stone tower (remarkably, twenty-nine feet in diameter and surviving to a height of twenty-six feet) provided evidence of the developing civilization. Pre-pottery B that followed brought with it a distinct culture unrelated to the previous Natufian type of culture. This non-indigenous phase was principally characterized by relics of ancestor worship in the shape of artistically plastered skulls, mainly discovered beneath the floors of the houses of the period. Like so many of the subsequent towns, this phase came to an abrupt end, the town being destroyed either by an earthquake or through torrential rain.

The following two Neolithic stages indicated that the site had been occupied by pit dwellers who were distinguished by the major advance of pottery, though both groups had differing pottery types and different flint industries. After an occupational gap extending through the major portion of the Chalcolithic period (*ca.* 4000-3100 BC) new arrivals identified by

Neolithic tower

distinct burial practices (rock tomb burials, a practice continued until the Roman period) began the turbulent Early Bronze Age phase (3100-2100 BC), in which the city walls were built and destroyed some seventeen times, a fact suggesting frequent migrations and site changes. It is clear however from the solidly built town structures which characterize this Early Bronze period that Jericho had now entered upon the phase of full urban development. The end of the Early Bronze period seems to have come suddenly, for the town walls show evidence of having been built and then destroyed by fire.

The beginning of the Middle Bronze Age seems to have been

ushered in at Jericho through an occupation by nomad pastoralist invaders, who brought with them their distinctive shaft tomb burials (as opposed to the earlier multiple burials). By their practice of secondary burials they gave evidence of their migratory character. They did not establish an urban center, and it is usually suggested that the Middle Bronze Age I (2100-1900 BC) at Jericho reflects the so-called Amorite invasion of nomadic Semitic tribes.

Middle Bronze Age II (1900-1500 BC) Jericho began with an equally abrupt break. Little survives of the town of this period because of the severe erosion through flooding, to which the site was constantly subjected. What does survive lies principally under the imposing defensive walls, which are built in three stages beginning with beaten earth and are characteristic of the latter half of this age. This sloping rampart, supported at base by a stone retaining wall and bearing a rebated town wall at its top, is normally associated with the Hyksos period (*ca.* 1750-1550 BC) in Palestine and Egypt. Most of the evidence for Jericho of the period is derived from cemeteries situated outside the town walls. Many of these tombs are very richly furnished, giving an indication of the Middle Bronze Age II character of the town. Kenyon ascribed the destruction of the site, finally by fire, and its abandonment to the Egyptian expulsion of the Hyksos (*ca.* 1550 BC) under the Pharaoh Amosis, founder of the Eighteenth dynasty. Kenyon posited no further occupancy of the site until the Late Bronze period (occupancy beginning again in the fourteenth century BC) since the characteristic pottery of the sixteenth and fifteenth centuries, the Cypriote bichrome ware, was not found in Jericho. The tomb evidence, which included scarabs from the Egyptian reigns of Hatshepsut, Thutmosis III, and Amenhoptep II (fifteenth century BC) but none from the Amarna age Pharaoh Akhenaten (fourteenth century BC), seemed to belie a period of abandonment. Kenyon suggested, however, that the scarabs were heirlooms, providing upper dating criteria only. It is generally agreed that the city was occupied again in the thirteenth century, and it is normally asserted that this very small center was the Late Bronze Age (1500-1200 BC) town that the Israelites encountered. Very little apart from pottery on the mound, in the tombs, and in building (foundation) traces remains of this celebrated Joshua 6 citadel. Kenyon had suggested the site was finally abandoned *ca.* 1300 BC.

Biblical Jericho   In summary, Jericho has been attractive for over a century as a site for excavation because of the biblical tradition that the "wall fell down flat" (Josh. 6:20). The work of Sellin and Watzinger uncovered part of the Middle Bronze Age defensive wall, and this was followed by Garstang's excavations. He apparently went to Jericho determined to find evidence supporting a fifteenth-century BC date for the exodus. In excavating at Tell es-Sultan he found the remains of Bronze Age walls, one stage of which he confidently identified with those mentioned in Joshua. Prior to that time, scholars had generally supported a thirteenth-century BC date for the exodus, but Garstang now felt that he had final proof that the event actually occurred closer to two centuries earlier. His arguments that he had actually recovered the ruined walls of Joshua's period proved very attractive in many conservative circles, and have persisted to the present. But Kathleen Kenyon's work, two decades later, showed that what he had identified as a wall from Joshua's time was not a Late Bronze Age structure, as he had thought, but was actually from the Early Bronze period instead. On the basis of certain structural and ceramic discoveries at the site he concluded that Jericho had been occupied until about 1400 BC, but faulty identification of pottery has rendered this dating inaccurate also. Jericho is now seen to have had an occupational history beginning about 8000 BC, and continuing intermittently at or near Tell es-Sultan since then. Unfortunately there is virtually no evidence at the mound pointing to the Jericho of Joshua's day.

Many archaeologists can find no evidence of fortifications at the Jericho of the conquest period that are consistent with the descriptions in Joshua 6. The problem has been reviewed recently by J. J. Bimson. Generally, his study has aimed to marshall support for an earlier dating for the exodus (mid-fifteenth century BC). This in particular involves the proposal that the Jericho of Joshua 6 was the Jericho whose destruction was normally associated with the Hyksos expulsion from Egypt. Bimson proposes that the destruction date of Jericho should be lowered and disassociated from the Hyksos. He argues that the rampart defensive system, peculiar to the Palestine of the Hyksos period (but not certainly found in Egypt where the Hyksos at this time were in occupancy) is not to be linked with the Hyksos, thus leaving the way open for the Israelite conquest date of Jericho to be placed ca. 1400 BC.

Further, the absence of Cypriote bichrome pottery ware from Jericho is irrelevant, Bimson claims, to the question of Jericho's fall, since it is probable that this pottery type, which was introduced from Cyprus, never penetrated to the Jordan valley. The arguments in this latter connection are technical and difficult to evaluate without a complete revision of pottery chronology in the Palestine of the period. Though Bimson's arguments have received varied reviews, his study does point to the looseness in some assumptions that have been applied to the Jericho problem. Certainly the transition from the Middle Bronze Age to the Late Bronze Age in Palestine is still an open question.

Bimson's attempt to correlate the Joshua 6 evidence with a Late Bronze destruction, and the mound evidence for the thirteenth century with the occupation of Eglon of Moab (Judg. 3:13), is feasible, and he could have presented a stronger case had he been prepared to associate the incoming Israelites with the prevalent Habiru of Palestine in the Amarna period. This means that the biblical account in Joshua 6 presents no features which, in terms of date and topographical knowledge, cannot be reconciled with a feasible historical hypothesis. In the absence of precise historical correlations archaeology may only generally support, but cannot categorically deny, the biblical evidence.

Jericho seems to have been a military station in David's time (2 Sam. 10:5). Hiel (1 Kings 16:34) suffered Joshua's curse when he attempted to refortify the city. The prophetic schools of Elijah and Elisha freqented the area (2 Kings 2:15, 18). Jericho was destroyed by the Babylonians in 587 BC but was resettled by post-exilic returnees (Neh. 7:36). The city was abandoned during the Hellenistic period. It received growing attention during the Hasmonaean period (134-63 BC), though it was Herod the Great who dignified this new Jericho, situated on both sides of the Wadi Qelt, a mile south of the earlier Old Testament city, as a garden city once again. From the time of its destruction by Roman troops during the Jewish war (AD 66-70), it declined in importance. Byzantine Jericho was relocated slightly to the southeast and this is its present day situation. The impressive mounds which stand to the west of modern Jericho witness to the involvement of the area in at least eight millennia of human history prior to the Christian era.

For further information on Jericho see:

Kenyon, K. M. *Digging Up Jericho* (1957).
"Jericho" in *Encyclopedia of Archeological Investigations in the Holy Land*, ed. M. Avi-Yonah, Vol. 2 (1976).
Bimson, J. J. *Redating the Exodus and Conquest* (1978).

W. J. D.

CHAPTER FOURTEEN

JERUSALEM

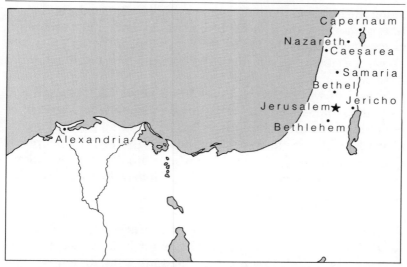

Jerusalem is certainly the city that "The Lord your God will choose to make his name to dwell there." But it is not a site that would have been a natural first choice for human beings. Admittedly the first men who settled there did so in about 4,000 BC, and this was because of the spring. Springs are rare in the area of Jerusalem, and this spring, later called Gihon, was plentiful and made the valley next to Jerusalem rich in vegetation. But it was awkwardly placed. And Jerusalem was not on any particular line of communication. It was half a mile from the main road, which runs along the hilltops from Hebron to Shechem, fifty miles to the north. But in this location it was no better than ten other cities or villages in the neighborhood.

Early Jerusalem   The awkwardness of Gihon became evident when the earliest settlement began to grow and had to be defended by a city wall. The spring was near the bottom of a valley, and the settlement was built on the spur of a hill. But for defensive purposes the city wall could not be built at the bottom of the valley and had to be higher up. Indeed the earliest wall so far to have been excavated is thirty yards up the hill, leaving Gihon outside. In peaceful times the waters from Gihon ran in canals along the hill, and there the water could be collected. But in any time of danger Gihon had to be concealed, and in fact an underground rock tunnel had to be built from inside the wall to a well above the spring, which made the drawing of water much more difficult.

Jerusalem was certainly a city from before 1750 BC, and had its present name (spelled "*Urusalim*") in some letters written in Egypt in the fourteenth century. But it was not a particular goal of the Israelites in their conquest under Joshua. "The people of Benjamin did not drive out the Jebusite who dwelt in Jerusalem: so the Jebusites have dwelt with the people of Benjamin in Jerusalem to this day" (Judg. 1:21).

Biblical   Early in the tenth century the Israelite tribes
Jerusalem   who dwelt to the north of Jerusalem came down to the kingdom of Judah, whose capital was in Hebron to the south, and they asked king David to reign over Israel as well as Judah. David therefore wished to choose a new capital, which would neither be linked to Israel nor to Judah, and this was how he came to capture Jerusalem. Interestingly enough he took the city at the very point of its weakness, and sent his men up the water tunnel.

By studying the accounts in the books of Samuel and Kings about the building works done by David and his son Solomon, the reader comes across the word *Millo*. The word refers to some kind of building, but in Hebrew it means "fullness," and that is the name of no known kind of building. The translators of the Bible have given its equivalent in English letters rather than translating it. But in the recent excavations of the earliest city Prof. Yigal Shiloh has discovered something that may be the *Millo* and was built in the tenth century. This is a lining of large stones that cover the upper parts of the hillside, a type of defense. It would make good sense as far as the Bible is concerned, for David is said to have rebuilt the buildings that are inside the Millo, that is to say on the flat top of the hill, and Solomon rebuilt the Millo itself.

David had himself built a royal palace, and then, in an apparent fit of conscience, planned to build a temple for God to replace the tent that contained the Ark of the Covenant. He revealed his plans to the prophet Nathan (2 Sam. 7:2), but Nathan came back next day with a word from the Lord. David was not to build the temple. David was to prepare the materials for building, but he was to leave the actual construction to Solomon. So under Solomon the temple was built and became the official place of worship for all the tribes of Israel. But after Solomon's death the kingdom was divided once again into Judah and Israel. The northern Israelite tribes did not regard the Jerusalem temple as holy, and this judgment is not merely that of the Israelite kings, who may have had political reasons for it, but also that of the prophets. The Jerusalem temple does not appear at all in the biographies of the prophets Elijah and Elisha, and it was evidently possible to be a good Israelite and yet have no links with the temple. On the contrary, when the kingdom of Judah was split off from Israel they continued to value the temple and to introduce into the temple area all their holiest memories. Thus for instance the temple became, in terms of prayer, Mount Moriah where Abraham went to sacrifice Isaac, according to 2 Chronicles 3:1. Chronicles is a history of the southern kingdom written in imitation of the books of Samuel and Kings, which concern all the tribes of Israel, the northern kingdom. But 2 Samuel 24 gives a very good reason why David chose the site of the temple, and has nothing to do with Abraham's sacrifice. Indeed Mount Moriah is mentioned in Genesis without any indication that it is in Jerusalem. This therefore is one of the holy places that has been added for devotional reasons, without regard for historical authenticity.

Archaeologists have not so far discovered any of the walls of Jerusalem built by David or Solomon. But in spite of this the progress of Jerusalem as a city seems clear in general terms. Before David took it Jerusalem was a walled city (or rather in modern terms a village) with fewer than three thousand inhabitants. Then Solomon extended the city northwards to include the temple. Even though the walls are missing, the location of tombs (to the west of Solomon's extension) shows the existence of a definite edge to the city, for inside a walled city tombs were not permitted.

The city of Jerusalem grew further during the remaining three and a half centuries of the monarchy, and up the western hill. The tombs were emptied and the skeletons and corpses were reburied in new tombs outside the new walls of the city. The new line of walls were all on the near side of valleys, if Professor Avigad's guess is right (*Discovering Jerusalem*, 1983). He found Israelite foundations built in the city and some houses beyond the city wall. Moreover he found one piece of a city wall, the broad bent wall on the north side of the city, and some houses that also belong to the Israelite monarchy and are outside the wall. Though Avigad did not find any more of the wall, the line he proposed certainly makes sense from the point of view of the city's defense. One result of the extension of the city was that its main street, and also its main drain, would have been between the western and the eastern hills. Another result of the expanded population of Jerusalem would certainly have been a new demand for water. This may have been satisfied by building rain-catching pools in the valleys surrounding Jerusalem and bringing the water in by channels, and it may also have been possible to draw on springs that were farther away. Water-supplying skills were good in Egypt and Mesopotamia in the time of the Israelite monarchy, and it is quite possible that during this period water already came from some of the springs at Etam eight miles to the south. The only record that has come down to us is of a defensive alteration to the water-supply. Late in the eighth century Jerusalem was threatened by the armies of Assy-

Tombs outside Jerusalem

ria, and king Hezekiah therefore cut a tunnel right through the eastern hill of the city (2 Kings 20:20) in order to conceal Gihon completely, and also to ease the task of those who drew water.

Some of the houses of the late seventh century have been excavated by archaeologists, but they were occupied for only a short time. In 597 BC Nebuchadnezzar brought the Babylonian army to besiege the city. They were successful, and they spoiled the temple, taking some of the important people away into exile. Eleven years later there was another Babylonian attack. The city was burned, and they took away more exiles. But Babylon itself was soon to fall.

In about 520 BC the Jewish exiles returned from Babylon. They were released by Cyrus, king of Persia, and encouraged, like every other Persian province, to practice their own religion and, in the case of the Jews, to rebuild their own temple. Nehemiah was in charge of Jerusalem in this early stage, and in Nehemiah 2:13-14 he gives an account of Jerusalem, which although it gives a good many place-names, none is known to us. Jerusalem was the capital of a province called *Yehud* "The Land of the Jews," and the Persian empire grew until it contained thirty provinces. But the city to which the exiles returned remained on the eastern hill, and no particular monuments of the period of Persian rule have yet been discovered.

Intertestamental Jerusalem Persian rule lasted for just under two centuries. Secular life was perhaps hard, but religious life prospered, and during this time some of the Old Testament was edited or written. But in 332 BC Alexander passed through Palestine on his way to defeat the Persian empire, and soon the Jews were becoming used to rulers who were Greek. Part of Alexander's empire was held by the Ptolemies who were rulers of Egypt, and they eventually took control of Palestine and held it until 198 BC. The Ptolemies seem to have had little effect on Jerusalem. But when their rivals, the Seleucids, took power they acted much more as missionaries of Greek culture. They were more generous than the Ptolemies in granting autonomy to cities, and accorded it to Jerusalem, whose official Seleucid name became Antioch.

Some of the Jews fell so deeply in love with the Greek way of life that they were known as "Hellenists." They took part in games in the gymnasium, were embarrassed about their circumcision, and neglected the Israelite law. Encouraged by the Hellenists, the Seleucid king, Antiochus IV Epiphanes, wanted the city to become entirely Greek. In 168 BC he took the temple treasures away, turned the temple into a holy place for Zeus or Dionysus, and forbade sacrifices to the God of Israel. But he was overly optimistic about the Hellenists. Under Mattathias the son of Asamoneus, a loyalist Jew, a revolt broke out. It was continued for twenty-seven years under his sons the Maccabees, and the end of the revolt was an independent Jewish kingdom called after their ancestor "Hasmonean." By the end of seventy years this kingdom had conquered a large area stretching from Mount Hermon, 130 miles north of Jerusalem, to Rhinocorura, 110 miles to the southwest beyond Gaza.

Model of Jerusalem Jesus knew

Jerusalem grew to almost exactly the size it had been in the late monarchy. The Hasmonean walls have been found, about half of which are traceable through their foundations. The temple area was built up with squared stones by Jonathan, working perhaps in 145 BC. The squared stones at the southeast corner of the temple enclosure may be part of his work, which is mentioned in 1 Maccabees 10:11. At this stage in its history Jerusalem might well have been taken for any other city in the Seleucid empire. Its outer trappings and its interior decoration were Greek in character. The style was Greek but not the intentions. Ever since Antiochus Epiphanes had made his error in diplomacy, most people in the city had become strict observers of Jewish Law. In the days of the early Israelite monarchy they had allowed pictures of living beings in the tabernacle and temple. They would now allow none at all, except geometric ornament and vegetation. The Sadducees, Pharisees, and Essenes, the three "Jewish philosophies" of which Josephus gives an account, are in fact none of them philosophies in the Greek sense. The Sadducees were conservative, and the Pharisees and Essenes

― 145 ―

more modern. But the main difference between them lay in the fact that they were for or against traditional teaching which added to the law revealed in the books of Moses. Large numbers of synagogues were built, and the social order was entirely set in a Jewish mold. For instance, the list of social outcasts included gamblers, usurers, herdsmen, tax collectors, and publicans, largely because they were not likely to, or could not keep, the Jewish law.

During the rise of the Hasmonean kingdom, Rome started to extend her power to north Turkey and Armenia. Later the Roman armies came south to Damascus, and in 63 BC Pompey besieged Jerusalem, and when he had conquered the city entered the temple. He split the Hasmonean kingdom, and fifteen years later there were new arrangements under Julius Caesar, which left the Hasmoneans in charge but the viceroy, Antipater, in real control. However, Julius Caesar died in Rome in 44 BC, and in 40 BC the Parthian army, now Rome's eastern rivals, marched into the Levant, and was joined as allies by the Hasmoneans. During the confusion Herod, Antipater's son, managed to escape first to Egypt and then to Rome; and in Rome, under the guidance of Mark Antony, the Senate decreed that Herod should be king of Judaea.

The Jerusalem Jesus Knew   After fighting his way back, first conquering Galilee and then, with the help of the Roman army, besieging Jerusalem for five months, Herod became king in 37 BC. His planning of Jerusalem has largely affected the layout of the walled "Old City" of Jerusalem, and enough of his work remains to show that his building activities were carried out with magnificence. One of the first buildings he rebuilt was the Hasmonean fort by the temple which he called Antonia. He finished it in 35 BC, and the lofty rock foundation is still untouched. Ninety years later it was from the steps of this castle that Paul addressed the Jews (Acts 21:40). But the main cause of rebuilding Jerusalem came ten years later, when there was a famine for two years. By the end of the famine many inhabitants of Judaea had no food and some were ruined. So Herod employed many of them on his building projects. The first building he erected was his palace, which was on the west side of the city. It had a moat around it that like many moats was dry, and inside it had a water-garden flanked by two large buildings: the Caesareum, called after Octavian (later to become Augustus), and the Agrippeum, called after Marcus Vipsanius Agrippa. To the north of these he erected what was in fact a fortress composed of three towers with solid masonry bases forty-five feet high. But when Josephus describes the towers he dwells on their decoration. One of the bases of the three towers still exists, and it most probably belonged to the tower called Hippicus, after a friend of Herod. Above the solid base it had a water-reservoir and a large decorated room. Herod laid out the city in a new way, since the road, half way between the palace and the temple, seems to run at right-angles to the eastern wall of the palace. This road was built in Herod's reign, and a house, which was occupied before the road was built, shows that Herod made a new layout of the Upper City, as the western hill was now called. Possibly the new road was part of a street grid, which was a regular feature of Greek and Roman cities of this time.

In 19 or 18 BC Herod planned to rebuild the temple, and met with considerable opposition from the priests. They knew of his favors to pagan cities, and his building of a temple to the emperor Augustus in Sebaste, and they were afraid that once he had taken down the temple in Jerusalem he would not rebuild it. They made the excuse that a miracle would be needed to rebuild the temple, since when Solomon built it "neither hammer nor axe nor any tool of iron was heard in the Temple" (1 Kings 6:7). Herod replied that all the stone should be cut in the quarry. They made the excuse that priests should build the temple and that none of them was trained in masonry. Herod then trained one thousand priests, some in masonry and some in carpentry.

Having thus got rid of the objections, the temple itself was demolished, and a new one stood in its place within eighteen months. Then it took seven years before the other buildings and courts were finished. The formal dedication took place in 10 BC, and in fact the building went on throughout Jesus' lifetime and did not end until AD 66.

The temple had an enlarged courtyard, being built out across the southern and western valleys on vaults. In fact the western extension interfered with the main drain of the city, which still cuts through the southwest corner. Inside the court there were porticoes on three sides, and on the south a covered area like a basilica in a Roman forum. The doors at the south end connected with staircases or ramps to go up to the level of the pavement, and there was a bridge across from the Upper City near the Hasmonean wall. The doors led in from ground level further to the north, and the north wall of the temple enclosure, which was also the north wall of the city, is likely to have been moated, since there seem to be the beginnings of a moat at either end. The complete area of the enclosure was known as the Court of the Gentiles, but it ended at a railing near the middle which contained notices, two copies of which have been found. The notice read as follows:

NO GENTILE TO ENTER THE FENCE AND BARRIER ROUND THE TEMPLE! ANYONE CAUGHT IS ANSWERABLE TO HIMSELF FOR THE ENSUING DEATH.

This railing therefore formed the "middle wall of partition," mentioned in Ephesians 2:14, which distinguished between Gentiles and Jews. Inside it were two courts, one of the Women, and to the west of it one containing the temple itself. When Mary came to offer two pigeons at the birth of Jesus (Luke 2:22) she went up to the golden gate which divided the courts, gave the birds to the priest, and watched him take them to the altar fifteen yards away.

The temple itself had a square facade, which was of about the same width as the width of the Islamic Dome of the Rock that now stands in its place, and one and a half times as high. Josephus was impressed by the gold inside the porch, and the golden vine which surrounded the door. A veil was hung over the door, which was like a second veil farther in, dividing the Holy from the Holiest Place. One of these veils was torn across at the moment of Christ's death (Mark 15:38).

Up to this point in our description Herod had improved Jerusalem largely by strengthening and beautifying the Hasmonean city. But he also made an extension to the north along the old main street. The position of the wall cannot be certain since none of it has so far been found, but there may be two gates. One is marked on a mosaic map made in the sixth century AD at the north end of the main street but has not been excavated. The other still crosses the road northwest of the temple enclosure, and is very like other gates made during the reign of Augustus, for instance the city gate at Nicaea in Bithynia. The gate must have been attached in some way to the Antonia fortress, and on the east it led out to the moat, across which was a drawbridge. The pattern of the streets in this new area is partly based on Prof. Mazar's excavations, and partly on the lay of the present streets.

There were a large number of reservoirs in Jerusalem. There were over ten times as many people in the city as there had been in king David's time, that is to say between 35,000 and 50,000, which would make it necessary to increase the supplies of water very considerably. The Maccabees had done so, and in about 145 BC Simon the son of Onias is credited with building a pool (Ecclus. 50:3). But several pools must have been added as well under Herod the Great, and he is known to have increased the supply that came through the channel from Etam by extending the channel another twenty-eight miles to the springs at Ain Arrub.

Two of these pools are mentioned in John's gospel. In chapter 9 the pool at Siloam is mentioned, and the smaller northern pool still exists, perhaps in a rebuilt Roman form, of which the masonry is still visible. At present the pool consists of a trench cut lengthways across the ancient pool, which in fact was square. Siloam was a spring with holy associations, and the priests from the temple were sent down to Siloam for water for two kinds of purifications (see Numb. 19:3 and Lev. 23:18).

Golden Gate of Jerusa-
lem as seen from so-
called Gethsemane

Presumably they went there because this was the water-source
that had originally been used for Solomon's temple.

The second pool, mentioned in John 5, is the one by the Sheep
gate, though whether this was a gate of the temple enclosure or
a city gate is not clear. It was called Bethesda, which was also
the name of the hill to the west. The "New City" was known in
Jesus Christ's lifetime and the streets remain in their original
grid. Indeed one of the streets goes across the middle of the pool
and has rock foundations. The copper scroll of Qumran mentions the pool of Bethesda as two pools, and the "five porticoes"
mentioned by John are explained in a third-century commentary by Origen, who had been to Jerusalem, as being four
around the edges of the pools and one across the middle. The
area of the "New City" was thus very carefully planned. The

pool was also, according to another Jerusalem writer of the fourth century AD, a place of "great infidelity among the Jews." This certainly refers to the number of sick who were in the pools, but unfortunately the text of John's gospel is not clear in the verses where we should expect him to explain the point. The moral purpose of the miracle of Jesus is perfectly clear, but any extra meaning that his visit to Bethesda may have had escapes the modern reader.

One generation after the death of Jesus' disciples there is the first mention of Christian pilgrimage to Bethlehem, and though we have no document to say so, the same must be true of Jerusalem. The holy places connected with Jesus were already visited in order to read the Bible passages concerning them and to pray. How far should reliance be placed on the holy places of early Christian faith? Are they historically authentic, or, like the identification of Mount Moriah with Jerusalem, suitable for prayer but not for history?

Each holy place should be taken on its own merits. For example the place of the Last Supper is first mentioned only in the early fifth century, and therefore is very likely to be a place of prayer rather than of history. But for Gethsemane the case is quite different. The exact garden or orchard cannot be there, since in the Roman siege of AD 70 all the trees round Jerusalem were cut to make props for earthworks, and they had to send eleven miles away to get new trees. But Gethsemane was the correct name of a place that is near the bottom of the Mount of Olives, across the Kidron valley, and is in accordance with John 18:1. So the site is still there and known by its original name, even though the particular holy places, the rock and the cave, may have been chosen by the early Christians as suitable places of prayer and nothing more.

From Gethsemane Jesus was taken to the house of Caiaphas for private questioning. Two early writers mention the ruins of this house, which was somewhere on the level patch of ground to the south of Herod's palace. It is probable that the house of a member of the high-priestly family should have been in the Upper City, since in Jesus' lifetime this was one of the newest and most fashionable parts of Jerusalem. Yet even so there is no certainty. The Christian writers on pilgrimage are the only ones to mention the ruin, and we can either believe them or not. When the private questioning by the high-priestly family was over, Jesus went to the council-chamber to be condemned by the Sanhedrin. This council-chamber in Jesus' time may have been inside the temple itself. But it is equally possible that it had been moved by them to a place in the markets, and therefore had been somewhere between the Hasmonean and the Herodian walls that come up to the west side of the temple. There was certainly a Christian holy place there, but it did not commemorate the trial by the Sanhedrin.

Jerusalem as it had grown during the time of Herod the Great, and during the next seventy years, was burned by the Romans in AD 70. Then, sixty-five years later Jerusalem, renamed as Aelia Capitolina, was rebuilt as a Roman city with temples dedicated to Roman gods. At this stage the northern part of the city was the quarter where civilians lived, and the Upper City was partly the barracks of the Tenth Legion. In other words there was an excellent reason why Christians would not have had access to the Upper City for one of their holy places, since it was a military camp.

The next thing that happened in Jesus' passion-narrative is that he went from the condemnation by the Jewish Sanhedrin to the Praetorium, the official residence of Pilate. Where was this? In fact Jerusalem offers three possibilities. The first, the fortress Antonia, is the choice of pilgrims during or just after the Crusades. This castle was certainly built thirty or more years before Jesus was born, and it is possible that Pilate lived there. Since the invention, after Crusader times, of the procession known as the Way or Stations of the Cross, it has been taken for granted that he did. But in fact Antonia was a small castle to serve as the Praetorium, and Pilate would have been less comfortable there than he would have been in the new and more spacious palace built by Herod. This question also has its psychological factor. If the Romans, who in AD 6 took over the supreme power in Judaea, had not taken over the royal palace as their Praetorium, they would not have been thought to be in full control of the country. There is therefore good reason for thinking the the Praetorium of Pilate was none other than the palace, and that somewhere in that palace Pilate erected the out-of-doors platform on which he conducted the trial of Jesus. But later, in the Roman Aelia Capitolina, the palace and part of the Upper City were under military control. Christians had to remember the trial at some other holy place.

The earliest place recorded is roughly on the site of the council–chamber of the Sanhedrin. Pilate is not known to have had anything to do with this place, but perhaps it was located there to remember "The Trial" of Jesus, and afterwards became so closely associated with the trial by Pilate that the ruins there were pointed out as Pilate's house.

Wherever the actual way of the Cross may have been, it leads to the place of the crucifixion, Golgotha. No early Christian

So-called Golgotha (Gordon's Calvary)

—— 153 ——

document is in any doubt of the site, and according to John 19:41 Golgotha was near the tomb where Christ was buried: "In the place where he was crucified there was a garden, and in the garden a new tomb where no one had ever been laid." Hebrews 13:12 says that Jesus "suffered outside the gate," and the position of Golgotha seems to be outside the gate at the time of Herod.

The first Christian reference after the New Testament to the tomb of Christ is made in a sermon, preached in AD 160 by Melito, who had just come back from a pilgrimage to Jerusalem. On the face of it his sermon contradicts the epistle to the Hebrews, since he says three times that the tomb was in the middle of the city. How can we sort out the contradiction?

To start with there is no doubt that any crucifixion would have taken place outside the city walls. The epistle to the Hebrews is therefore quite correct. But near the present tomb of Christ (which is a replica made in the eleventh century) there are other Jewish tombs which may well have been made in Christ's lifetime. At any rate they were made before about 44 AD, when they were emptied of their corpses, because it was in about that year that Herod Agrippa intended to make a new north wall to the city. The new wall was certainly finished before the Roman siege of AD 70, and by AD 160, when Melito preached his sermon, this was one of the areas next to the new forum of Aelia Capitolina, which is certainly within the city. Thus the contradiction is resolved, and in such a way that it is a help toward the identification of the site. In the fourth century the tomb was once again discovered, and this rock tomb, where the replica stands today, is very likely to be where Christ was buried and raised up. If this is not the site then no one has any idea where it might be. But of Golgotha there is more uncertainty. The situation of Golgotha depends on the finding of the tomb, so if the tomb is in the wrong place Golgotha is as well. Further, Golgotha is a rock whose outline is strange. This may have been because, when the whole area was quarried at the building of Aelia Capitolina, the rock later called Golgotha was the highest point in the whole area. In fact the biblical Golgotha may well have been quarried away, and there is certainly no room on the present rock for three crosses.

There are two other holy places to be examined. One is the holy place that commemorates Jesus' ascension, and is a rock on the summit of the Mount of Olives. Since the end of the fourth century there has been a church there. But the earliest place where the ascension was remembered was in a cave not far from the rock, and this was not the place mentioned in the Bible, even though it may have been near it. The other holy place is the one which commemorates Pentecost on Mount Zion. Mount Zion seems in the Bible to have been an alternative name for Jerusalem. For example, when Psalm 51:18 says "Do good to Zion in thy good pleasure/ Rebuild the walls of Jerusalem," it seems to be speaking of one place under two different but alternative names. The only thing that we know about this site, which would be to the south of the palace of Herod, like Caiaphas' house, was that it was the site of the earliest house church in Jerusalem. It is hard to say whether or not the disciples of Jesus, who were visiting fishermen from Galilee, would have occupied quite so exclusive a part of Jerusalem during the time of Christ. Therefore whether Pentecost took place there, with its miracle of the Holy Spirit coming down on the disciples, is uncertain. But at least this is the site of the earliest known Christian church building. To use the words of one of the earliest church services written in Jerusalem, this was "The holy and glorious Zion, the mother of all the churches."

For further information on Jerusalem see:

Avigad, N. *Discovering Jerusalem* (1983).
Benoit, P. *Jesus and the Gospel* (1973).
Finegan, J. *The Archaeology of the New Testament* (1969).
Jeremias, J. *Jerusalem in the Time of Jesus* (1962).
Kenyon, K. M. *Digging up Jerusalem* (1974).
Wilkinson, J. *The Jerusalem Jesus Knew* (1983).

J. W.

CHAPTER FIFTEEN

MARI

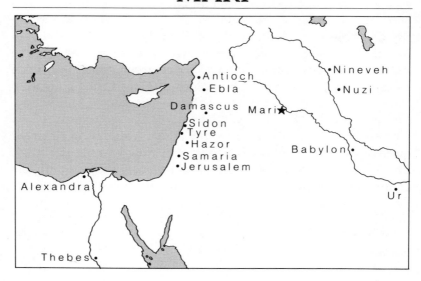

Discovery Fifty years ago in August 1933, a small delegation of Arab clansmen arrived at the of-
fice of Lt. Cabane, Deputy-Inspector of the
French military in the district of Abū-Ke-
māl, on the eastern edge of the Syrian Arab Republic. Engaged
in burying one of their deceased brethren and searching for an
adequate tombstone to place atop his grave, they had uncovered
a large stone statue bearing an inscription; they were asking the
lieutenant what should be done with it. His curiosity aroused,
he journeyed immediately to the mound, *Tell Ḥarīrī*, recovered
the statue, and shipped it to the Aleppo Museum, where it came

MARI

to the attention of F. Thureau-Dangin, who published a photograph, transliteration, and provisional translation of it the following year. The "Cabane statue," as it came to be known, is actually a decapitated limestone statue of the son-god Shamash, weighing several hundred pounds, and it bears a votive inscription from Yasmah-Addu, known today as the son and vice-regent of the powerful Assyrian monarch Shamshi-Addu I.

Within two months, news of this treasure-trove had come via the Director of the Syrian Department of Antiquities to René Dussaud, then Curator of Oriental Antiquities at the Louvre. Dussaud requested and was granted speedy permission by the "Conseil des Musées Nationaux" to send out an archaeological expedition under the capable direction of André Parrot. Parrot had studied in Jerusalem in 1926 at "l'Ecole biblique," and his mentor, Dussaud, awakened within him a passion for oriental archaeology. The young Frenchman had gone on to distinguish himself in the excavations of Tello (= Girsu), where eventually he had become the successor to Henri de Genouillac. So it was that, at age 32, Parrot was selected to lead this new undertaking.

Work on Tell Harīrī began on December 14, 1933, with almost instantaneous and somewhat dramatic results: a section was opened along the northwestern perimeter at a spot where the excavator expected to find a city gate. He did. But in addition and in a manner reminiscent of Andrae's spectacular temple discovery at Asshur, Parrot's team had also begun to uncover what later would prove to be a pre-Sargonic temple of Ishtar. With practically the first plunge of the picks, workers began to unearth numerous small statuettes, and on January 23, a number of inscribed statuettes was exhumed. On the back of the right shoulder of one of these was found the following declaration: "Lamgi-Mari, the king of Mari, the great ruler [ensi] of (the god) Enlil, dedicated this statue to Ishtar." So it was that two days later, on January 25, 1934, Dussaud jubilantly announced to "l'Academie des Inscriptions" in Paris that Parrot had discovered the ancient city of Mari!

Encompassing some 280 acres (after erosion along the northeast quadrant), the ruins of Mari are located about six and

—— 157 ——

Tell Hariri (Mari) and Euphrates River

three-quarters miles north-northwest of Abū-Kemāl, and approximately fifteen and a half miles north of the Syrian-Iraqi border. The relatively low-lying mound, not more than forty-three feet above the surrounding terrain, is situated in the mid-Euphrates basin and at the base of the river's catchment area, about one and a half miles west of the present course of the river and some three and three quarter miles east of the major highway that connects Aleppo and Baghdad.

History   Archaeological evidence indicates that Mari experienced five periods of major occupation. (1) *Jemdet Nasr: Mari's formative age (ca.* 3100-2900 BC). The site apparently was founded during this epoch as there are stone structures located under pre-Sargonic palaces, but very little of this period is attested so far. Current excavations are exploring the Jemdet Nasr remains further. (2) *Pre-Sargonic: Mari's noble age* (*ca.* 2900-2340 BC). Dating to this period are seals, statues of deities and three kings, various votive objects, six temples, an archaic ziggurat, and two (perhaps three) palaces. Though few in number, pre-Sargonic epigraphic remains are consequential, in that they refer to both Ansud and Mesanepada, known from the Sumerian King-List to have been founders of dynasties in Mari and Ur respectively. Accordingly it follows that these were historical characters (not mythological) and that their reigns were roughly contemporaneous (compare contemporaneity of the biblical Judges). The palaces give evidence of at least two destructions, variously attributed to Eannatum (Lagash), Lugalzagizi (Umma), Sargon or Narām-Sin (Akkad), or Enna-Dagan (Ebla). Artistic (bearded figures), religious, and onomastic factors combined to suggest what in 1940 must have been a startling notion: a nascent Semitic civilization appeared to have existed as many as two hundred years prior to the existence of Sargon's Akkad, then thought to have been the oldest Semitic civilization known! Subsequent discovery, however, observed most especially in texts from Fara, Abu Salabikh, and Ebla, have demonstrated convincingly the reality and ubiquity of such a proposition. (3) *Sargonic: Mari's dependent age* (*ca.* 2340-2110 BC). The relative splendor of pre-Sargonic Mari was eclipsed by Sargon's conquest (see above). Included among the Sargonic materials are a few temple and bronze inscriptions, and many cylinder seals. Parrot also found a text mentioning a rebellion against Narām-Sin, and two bowls inscribed with the names of two of Narām-Sin's daughters. (4) *Ur III: Mari's twilight age* (*ca.* 2110-1828 BC). It has been customary to affirm, following the initial evaluation of G. Dossin (former chief epigraphist of Mari), that the city experienced a vassal relationship to Ur during the Ur III period. Admittedly, a ruler of Mari had one of his daughters taken by marriage into the family of Ur-Nammu. While this marriage may have cemented friendly diplomatic relations, the city-state of Mari was undoubtedly exerting an ever-increasing independence throughout most of the Ur III epoch. Excavations have furnished an array of inscribed statues of at least a dozen individuals who bear the title "governor" [shakkanakku], but these texts never refer to an overlord. The 475 or so Ur III administrative and economic texts that have been published thus far bear date-formulae of Mari, not Ur; their contents—dealing with the receipt, distribution, or consignment of grain, wine, animals, metals; and the remittance of clothing, furniture, and utensils— confer upon Mari nobility a certain stature and independence. Also bespeaking independence is the so-called "Mari Pantheon," which was exhumed from the Dagan temple of the Ur III period. (5) *Old Babylonian: Mari's golden age* (1828-1758 BC). Though the city's Old Babylonian existence spanned not more than seventy years, Mari was truly a marvel of Middle Bronze Age Mesopotamia (2100-1525 BC), an era compared by one noted historian to the age of Pericles in Greek history or to Caesar Augustus in Rome. For Mari it became a period of unsurpassed greatness in material prosperity, and its cultural remains have been matched by few other sites in the neighboring areas of the ancient Near East.

Monuments and Archives The opulent prosperity in which Mari indulged is unmistakably etched into the remains of the magnificent palace of king Zimri-Lim. Much of it constructed of brick stamped with the name of the monarch himself, this royal residence covered a nine-acre rectangular plot and contained more than three hundred rooms, including private royal chambers for both the king and queen, as well as private bathrooms (complete with covered lavatories, terracotta bathtubs, and plumbing), royal chapel, throne room, reception center, quarters for visiting dignitaries, administrative offices, schoolrooms (shells [for counting?]), benches, pottery, numerous workshops (kitchen, bakery), storage areas (wine cellar), service rooms (quarters for security guards, a funerary unit), scriptoria and archive repositories, as well as many courts and corridors.

The palace is one of the largest and best preserved buildings in all of second millennium Mesopotamia. Parrot uncovered some interior walls as thick as thirteen feet and standing as much as sixteen feet high; and the lintels in some doorways were still intact. The two-story edifice was contructed with great architectural skill and aesthetic sensitivity. Surrounding each of the many large open courts was a constellation of rooms interconnected by high doorways, thereby permitting ventilation and light to penetrate throughout a ground floor in which there were no windows. Floors were made sometimes of beaten earth, often plastered or covered with flagstone or tile. Walls were plastered and not infrequently adorned with ornate sculpture or painting, the most famous of which is a multi-colored fresco depicting the "Investiture of Zimri-Lim." Wood was employed for ceiling beams, and occasionally it was crafted decoratively to add aesthetic luster.

One should not necessarily interpret the fabulous wealth and extensive correspondence of Zimri-Lim as indicative of vast political hegemony or invincible military might; such would be a myopic and distorted historical picture. Actually, Zimri-Lim's reign was extremely circumscribed in both time and space; the monarch's rule encompassed not more than eighteen years, and his kingdom was always flanked by the forbidding desolation of the Arabian desert and the proximity of more powerful neighbors. A proper assessment of the extent of Zimri-Lim's kingdom would be as follows: by recapturing the city of Mari, wrested from his father some twenty years earlier by means of a palace *coup* in which Shamshi-Addu appears to have been implicated, Zimri-Lim succeeded in carving out a niche in Assyria's vast empire, later inherited by Ishme-Dagan. Sensing that the Assyrian was kept occupied on other frontiers, Zimri-Lim opportunistically seized the city-states of Terqa, Sagaratum, and Tuttul, thus bringing under his control the middle-Euphrates valley. But his efforts to enlarge this niche northward into the Habur regions and eastward towards the Tigris brought him inevitably into military conflict with Ishme-Dagan. Though successful in the battle (at Razamā), the glory was ephemeral; Zimri-Lim was never able to breach the barrier of the Tigris and his own city was destroyed some five to seven years later. Such, in brief, is the story told by his own date-formulae and correspondence. In the end, beleaguered by a disturbing proximity of nomads who were emboldened periodically to disavow loyalty to this throne, without natural defenses and hinterland, forced to wage war simultaneously on more than one front, and lacking substantial resistance when faced with an overwhelming military power, Zimri-Lim and his burgeoning kingdom were eliminated by Hammurabi's forces, apparently with relative ease.

How then did Zimri-Lim acquire all this wealth? The answer seems to be a combination of geographical position, physical topography, and political and commercial ingenuity. From most ancient times, Near Eastern economy has revolved around the axes of open canals and open trade. While some sites became important because they were situated strategically along established arteries of trade (Ur, Ugarit, Carchemish) and others assumed prominence because of their capacity in local commercial enterprise (Jericho, Kanish), both factors were significantly operational at Mari; the city sat astride four separate trading arteries and was itself an important agricultural producer and exporter.

Poised at one of the pivotal crossroads in international trade, Mari's geographical and commercial horizons were virtually coterminous with the limits of the Old Babylonian world. They ranged from Shemshāra, Anshan, and Tilmun in the east, to the Mediterranean and Aegean in the west (including cities in modern Turkey, Lebanon, Syria, and Israel, as well as Tema in the Arabian desert). From this enviable position, the kingdom of Mari played a crucial role in the trade of timber, stone, wool, iron, resin, garments, furniture, royal horses, wine, olive and sesame oils, and myrtle, thereby linking the Babylonian and Levantine worlds. Garments, bolts of cloth, and vases of gold were sent to Zimri-Lim as gifts from the king of Byblos. The city functioned, moreover, as a tin emporium in traffic that ultimately linked Anshan and eastern Iran with Ugarit, Crete, and points south, including Aleppo, Layish (for example, Sign-Dan), and Hazor (see below). Copper was imported from the islands of Cyprus (Mediterranean) and Tilmun (Persian Gulf); gold, precious woods, cloth, and a certain kind of metal containers were imported from Crete, while lapis-lazuli, quarried in Afghanistan, found its way to Mari. Often these metals or precious stones were employed in the manufacture of statues or works of art dedicated to temples. Beyond this, one must bear in mind that certain texts refer to tolls that Zimri-Lim imposed on both caravan and riverine trade. In short, Mari had become both an entrepôt and a tax collector.

But the sovereign from Mari opened canals as well as trade, thus adding to his lucrative proft. The flood-plain along the mid-Euphrates between Meskéné and 'Āna, which is in places as deep as 330 feet and up to seven and a half miles wide, has always offered ideal possibilities for agricultural use. In particular, below Deir e-Zōr the humus soil deposited by the Euphrates and Habur rivers is especially conducive to this usage; in this area, consequently, a whole series of Old Babylonian settlements is known from Mari literature and attested through modern archaeological survey. On the other hand, since this narrow strip of land suitable for cultivation lay outside the zone of adequate precipitation (twelve inches annually), irrigation agriculture was required. According to his correspondence, Zimri-Lim accomplished this task by excavating an entire network of primary canals, smaller feeder canals, and reservoirs, thus allowing for adequate and continuous soaking of the crops during their growth cycle, while on the other hand minimizing or preventing flooding of crops before harvest time. This excavation, maintenance, and control of the irrigation system was ultimately the responsibility of the central admininstration and one that was assigned a high priority. Nevertheless the vast areas to be cultivated sometimes necessitated cooperation between towns or even districts. The Ishĭm-Yahdun-Lim canal, for instance, coursed some seventy-five miles through three separate districts, fed many secondary canals, and had at least five towns situated close to its banks. With Zimri-Lim's consummate oversight, this rich soil received constant and adequate irrigation, culminating in extreme fertility and lush productivity. One need only reflect upon the vast riches which accrued to David or Solomon through their export of grain (1 Kings 5:11; 2 Chron. 2:15) to discover the high price such a commodity must have commanded in a market where import was required. Zimri-Lim's palace fields produced vast supplies of wheat, barley, sesame, flax, beans, vetch, and date palms; some of this was certainly exported by the entrepreneur, thereby generating still greater wealth for his kingdom.

Out of Zimri-Lim's palatial estate was dug Mari's greatest legacy of all: the royal archives. Embodying more than twenty-five thousand tablets, the Mari correspondence addresses almost every aspect within a culture: internal politics of a sub-kingdom or indigenous state, international affairs, diplomacy and treaties, domestic policy, commerce and trade, agriculture, irrigation, law and jurisprudence, transportation of caravans, ambassadors, professional artisans and courtiers, political intrigue, and religion. In point of fact, this archive contributes in a seminal manner to affirm understanding of Middle Bronze Age Mesopotamian and Syro-Palestinian culture. For example, before the discovery of Mari, Hammurabi was said to have been an unequaled sovereign, a monarch who "stood out in striking isolation." But it appears from a much-quoted but not yet published Mari document that Zimri-Lim, bidding for the allegiance of local sheikhs in the Habur region, issued them an invitation to attend a regalia he was to sponsor. When they convened, Zimri-Lim's governor of Nahur sought to curry their favor by stating: "No king is alone powerful, some 10-15 kings follow Hammurabi, king of Babylon; there are as many who follow Rīm-Sin, king of Larsa, Ibal-pi-El, king of Eshnunna and Amut-pī-El, king of Qatna. Likewise 20 kings follow Yarīm-Lim, king of Yamhad." In juxtaposing these five kings and in according them an equipotent status, the text rightfully portrays Hammurabi merely as a man among other men.

The archive contributes as well to ancient chronological discussions. Modern formulations of second millennium chronological systems use as a linchpin the Hammurabi—Shamshi-Addu synchronism established in a Mari text; this datum, taken together with the Babylonian's year-names, establishes a minimal synchronism of eleven years, while other factors require a maximal synchronism of fourteen years. In addressing this issue, Albright averred: "There can be no doubt that the Mari documents and the Khorsabad List made a really organic picture of the historical evolution of the ancient Near East possible for the first time. Henceforth, ancient Near Eastern history becomes *history*, not merely a congeries of more of less refractory data." Now while it is true that the Khorsabad king-list adds significantly to the second millennium chronological reservoir, because of certain linguistic and historical complications, as well as two lacunae at critical places in this text, it has not proven to be of exacting assistance for dating before the fifteenth century BC. Moreover, those studies which gave rise to chronological systems (low, middle, high) all appeared before the year in which Poebel published the Assyrian list. Therefore, to suggest that Old Babylonian chronological systems largely owe their genesis to Mari literature does not appear to be an exaggeration.

This is not the place for a lengthy discussion of chronology, but we might summarize diagrammatically what the Mari chronological notices permit to assert, when studied together with other pertinent data (according to a middle chronology):

Shamshi-Addu I	1813—1781
Yahdun-Lim	*ca.* 1801
Yasmah-Addu	1796—*ca.* 1776
Hammurabi	1795/2—1753/0
Dādusha	1796—1785
Ibal-pī-El II	1785—*ca.* 1758/5
Ishme-Dagan	1781—(attributed 40 years)
Zimri-Lim	not before 1776—1761/58

Thus both historically and chronologically, one is now able to ascertain from Mari documentation that Hammurabi's proclivity to treaty-making was necessary for survival amidst a veritable chess board of political exigency.

But if the Babylonian no longer stands in striking isolation, the whole of Northern Mesopotamia and North Syria no longer stands in haunting silence! The highlands of the Habur triangle, the valleys of the Balīh and Habur rivers, the "island" of land betwen the Euphrates and Tigris, once only a blank spot on the map of western Asia, today throb with historical, geographical, and social dimension. Attested at Mari are the names of virtually all the great Mesopotamian centers and city-states, as well as many scores of lesser known but now reasonably well-located sites. Armed with this new knowledge, scholars from Europe, North America, and Japan, in conjunction with national representatives, have undertaken a great number of archaeological explorations. Their efforts in these regions have been rewarded handsomely by the discoveries of Dur-Katlimmu, Kahat, Tuttul, Harrān, Karanā, Imār, Ebla, and perhaps Shubat-Enlil. In landscape dotted with a concentration of tells, additional significant discovery is imminent.

Culturally speaking, Mari's contributions again have been seminal, although space permits the brief mention here of only a few items. This archive has supplied both the oldest evidence of Amorite political centers outside the land of Amurru and the oldest religious documents written in the Hurrian language. Mari documentation also provides vivid illustration of the procedure employed in the river trial-by-ordeal (compare Numb. 5:11-22). These texts settled what had been a debate that raged up to the time of their publication, demonstrating incontestably that the participant was uncondemned if he did *not* die in the water when dunked. Attested also at Mari is the earliest and most extensive information on tribalism and tribal life, so much so that Gelb has stated that the study of nomadism was well nigh impossible before the discovery of Mari. The most ancient examples of hepatoscopy (observations of a liver of a slaughtered animal) and extispicy (observations of the entrails of an animal) are exhibited in the Mari texts. And feminine correspondence, part of this archive, is a virtual anomaly in other ancient Near Eastern literature.

**Mari and
the Bible**

Mari's contributions to biblical studies have been no less significant. But this should come as no surprise inasmuch as one can observe an international cognition both in the Bible (migrations of Abraham, Eliezer, Jacob; Assyrian and Babylonian deportation) and from the archaeology of Israel (cuneiform tablets [both alphabetic and syllabic], cylinder seals, and scarabs). Documentation from Mari has helped in understanding the region of Upper (nothern) Mesopotamia, which included the homeland of the biblical patriarchs. The whole notion of tribal or ethnic movement of peoples, the categorization of clan leadership, and the relocation and resettlement of such peoples is amply attested in Mari literature. The question of meaning of the world "Hebrew" and its possible relationship to "Habiru" can now be addressed more intelligently, owing in part to the existence of a verb *habuāru* which occurs in Mari texts and means "to emigrate, seek refuge," Studies of social structure at Mari, defined by Rowton as "dimorphic society" (a social structure based on the essential interplay of tribal and urban elements), have led to a repudiation of that socio-economic model which impelled Noth to formulate his "amphictyonic hypothesis." The same studies have demolished the ethnological theory that all Semites migrated out of the desert, and that an agrarian way of life was *necessarily preceded* by a nonsedentary life. Tribal traditions, which include the manner of warfare, a solemn ban on certain cities, and the making and ratifying of covenants, are illustrated elaborately in the royal archives. Furthermore, Mari's regard for genealogy and ritualistic religion contribute to the reshaping of Wellhausen's axiom in the history of religion that freedom and spontaneity were wholesome and primitive, whereas organization and ritual were stifling and late.

In the cultural sphere, the present writer has argued elsewhere that king Zimri-Lim was responsible for opening the Palestinian market to tin, an essential component in the manufacture of bronze, and that this move paved the way for the inauguration of the Bronze Age in an industrial and technological sense. Some features of Israel's religion (for example, "god of the fathers" concept, *aštōret*, *ašerîm*, *maṣṣēbôt*) find helpful parallels in Mari tablets, as do certain types of biblical literature (prophecy and wisdom literature). While the question of the right of the firstborn in a patriarchal society has been related to a number of archaeological archives, including Mari, the amount actually inherited by the firstborn is elucidated through Mari literature. It seems that at Mari, the inheritor received "two-thirds" of his father's estate, not merely a "double portion." In a forthcoming study on the amount of the firstborn's inheritance in the Bible (Deut. 21:17), the present writer will argue that the expression normally rendered "double portion" (literally "mouth of two") should be understood to connote a bona fide successor, that is, a majority stockholder as it were, and that as such it should be rendered "two-thirds." Such an interpretation makes sense in a culture where the purpose of primogeniture was to guarantee estate succession.

Beyond these historical and cultural contributions, the Mari archives also provides linguistic elucidation. These include geographical entities, military terms, settlement patterns, tribal terms and leadership, compass points, flora and fauna, and census taking, to name but a few. Certain name-types similar to those of biblical characters occur at Mari, including Abri-ram (Abram), Laban, and Yahqub-El (Jacob). Alternatively, the name-types of David and Benjamin do not occur in published Mari documentation, despite what numerous authors say to the contrary.

It must be stated, however, that it is precarious methodologically, if not erroneous, to presuppose tacitly that similarity and identity are one. The historical, cultural, and linguistic parallels adduced in the last portion of this essay should lead the reader to conceptual but not necessarily chronological conclusions. One must bear in mind that the ancient Near East sometimes exhibits aspects of tradition that persist over many centuries and in numerous places.

MARI

For further information on Mari see:

Mission archéologique de Mari (= MAM). Mari's archaeological and architectural remains have been published in this series. Most of the published epigraphic remains appear in the series *Archives royales de Mari* (= ARM). Both of these series are published in Paris by the Librairie Orientaliste Paul Geuthner (1950—). Besides these official publications, some 320 texts and a countless number of excerpts have been published in extraneous sources, on which see now J.-G. Geintz, *Index documentaire des testes de Mari* (ARMT 17). Paris, Geuthner, 1975. A new journal *Mari: Annales de Recherches Interdisciplinaires* (= MARI) was recently begun in part to report the results of current excavations at Tell Hariri. This series is published in Paris by the "Editions Recherche sur les civilisations" (1982—).

Gelb, I. J. "The Early History of the West Semitic Peoples." *Journal of Cuneiform Literature* 15 (1961), 27-47.

Heintz, J.-G. "Prophetie in Mari in Israel." *Biblica* 52 (1971), 543-55 (bibliography on prophecy at Mari).

Kupper, J. -R. *Les nomades en Mesopotamie au temps des rois de Mari* (1957).

Parrot, A. "Mari." *Archaeology and Old Testament Study.* ed. D. Winton Thomas (1967), 136-44.

———. *Mari, Capitale fabuleuse* (1974).

Young, G. D., ed. *Mari at Fifty* (1984).

B. J. B.

CHAPTER SIXTEEN

NAZARETH

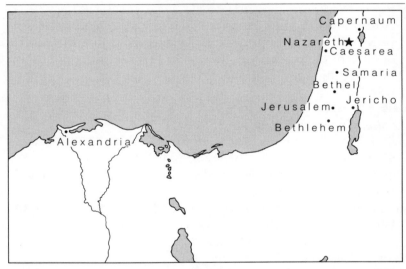

Located strategically in a high Galilean valley at the southern extremity of the Lebanon mountains, Nazareth has always attempted to exert an influence that was out of all proportion to its physical size. It was situated to the north of the plain of Esdraelon, about 1250 feet above sea level, and the basin which gave the settlement shelter opened only to the south, where there was a sharp descent to the plain below. On all other sides the community was protected by imposing hills which served to shelter it from extremes of climate and ensured it an adequate amount of rain. This was an important consideration in view of the scarcity of wells and springs in the area. Fifteen miles to the northeast lay the Sea of Galilee, while some thirty miles due west was the Mediterranean.

Name There is some debate as to how the name Nazareth originated, and what its precise meaning is. Some scholars have suggested that it is related to the word *nazir*, meaning "separated." If this were truly a reminiscence of the Nazirites (Numbers 6), it would not be unreasonable to expect some connection between the vigorous Nazirite tradition and the site itself. But if there was such a link it has disappeared with the passing of time. Other scholars have associated the name with the Hebrew word *neser*, "sprout, shoot, branch," and have seen an allusion to the messianic prophecy of the "branch" in Isaiah 11:1. This may perhaps have been what Matthew (2:23) had in mind when he could speak of Jesus being designated a Nazarene by "the prophets." Yet another suggestion reflects the topography of the city as a possible "watchtower" (Aramaic *naserat*) over the plain of Esdraelon. At best, however, this is uncertain, as are all the other attempts to explain the origin of the settlement's name.

What seems to be the earliest Jewish reference to Nazareth as a settled community of the first century AD occurred in a fragmentary Hebrew inscription unearthed at Caesarea in 1962 by archaeologists from the Hebrew University of Jerusalem. This source mentioned Nazareth as one of the towns where members of the twenty-four priestly courses (compare 1 Chron. 24:7-19; Luke 1:5) went *ca.* AD 135. All New Testament references to Nazareth obviously predate this event.

Location In ancient times the village settlement was apparently restricted to the side of a hill that faced southeast, enabling the inhabitants to survey the plain of Esdraelon below. An important caravan route from Egypt to Damascus came to within six miles of Nazareth. A well-traveled road from Sepphoris, three miles to the north, ran through Nazareth on its way south to Sychar and Jerusalem, while Gileadite caravans forded the Jordan and passed south of Nazareth to join the Egypt-Damascus road. Yet another road led from Nazareth through En-dor, about seven miles to the southeast, then down to Jericho and southwest to Jerusalem. In Roman times the legions marched along the highway from Ptolemais south and east to the Decapolis, a group of ten Hellenistic cities located in Transjordan south and east of the Sea of Galilee.

From the foregoing it will be apparent that Nazareth possessed admirable natural advantages. Its mild climate and sheltered location made it a most desirable place in which to live, while its position as a border town of Zebulun, perched up in the hills, gave it a certain measure of isolation. If contact with the outside world was necessary, there were several trading routes and major roads within easy reach. But with all this the one major disadvantage that Nazareth possessed was that the water supply for the settlement was restricted to one main spring, now known as Mary's Well or Ain Maryam, and this was at the foot of the hill which sheltered the town. A much smaller well was located in a cleft of the same elevation, but at some distance from Ain Maryam. Perhaps it was this natural disability that prevented Nazareth from becoming as prosperous as its neighbor Sepphoris, which in the Maccabean period was the largest city in Galilee.

Excavations   Nazareth is unmentioned by name in both the Old Testament and the Apocrypha, as well as in the works of Josephus, but this deficit should not be taken to imply that it only came into existence during the Graeco-Roman period. The very fact that there was a large perennial spring of sweet water in the area would be sufficient to guarantee a lengthy occupational history for such a site in a land where fresh clean water has always been at a high premium. One of the great difficulties connected with attempts to establish the history of the settlement is that the valley is still completely occupied by buildings. Modern Nazareth, or En-Nasira as it is called, has more than

En-Nasira (Nazareth)

twenty-seven thousand inhabitants and accommodates the largest Arab and Christian population segments in the State of Israel. Consequently it is impossible to undertake archaeological excavations as such, and whatever is attempted can only occur when old buildings are demolished to make way for new ones, or when extensions to already existing properites are being undertaken.

Because of this, the excavations commenced by the Franciscans near the Church of the Annunciation hold special interest for the history of Nazareth. The site is south of St. Joseph's Church, which itself was important for establishing the antiquity of the location because of the discovery beneath a Crusader church of a large water reservoir hewn out of the rock. At an even lower level the archaeologists uncovered a pit and a granary. Fragments of pottery from the period of Israelite occupation to the Middle Ages were recovered from the site, all of which attested to the long history of settlement there. A skull recovered from the valley at the base of the western hill is unfortunately of uncertain antiquity.

This picture was enhanced when constructional work was undertaken at the Church of the Annunciation, which is reputedly the largest Christian church in the Near East. It contains a grotto or cave where, according to legend, the angel Gabriel appeared to Mary with tidings about her coming conception and the birth of Jesus (Luke 1:26-31). A portion of a mosaic floor was discovered in the church, but it was Byzantine in character and probably no earlier than the fifth century AD. Apparently from an earlier period came a pool and stones bearing graffiti which included *IH*, a shortened form of the name Jesus. Underneath the floor of a small monastery were the remains of an older building, perhaps a third-century church, where other graffiti including charcoal crosses on a white plaster surface, a boat, and a man bearing a cruciform staff were found. Some small coins from the third and fourth centuries AD were unearthed, along with Byzantine potsherds. Excavations at the church in 1955 uncovered subterranean storage vaults for wine and oil, small wells and pits for grain, as well as traces of foundation walls and surface oil presses. Fragments of pottery from the Israelite period were also found, including pieces of two-handled jars that had blunt spouts. When digging took place in order to accommodate the foundations for the pillars of the new church, some subterranean caves came to light which contained metal objects, pottery, and a scarab, all of them dated in the Hyksos period (*ca.* 1700-1550 BC). Another recess was similar in nature to the Bronze Age graves uncovered at Megiddo, and this discovery established beyond question the fact that Nazareth was a settled community at least as early as the Middle Bronze Age (*ca.* 2000-1500 BC).

An additional discovery of a rather accidental nature occurred while construction work was in progress near the Church of the Annunciation. A necropolis of twenty-five graves from the late Roman period was uncovered on a hillside west of the church, and this burial site was associated with a number of other graves on the slope of a hill to the east, across a small valley. Most of the graves were simple horizontal recesses, known as *loculi*, in which the body was placed. One grave that had a

Church of the Annunciation

rolling stone as a cover for the aperture contained *loculi* in the interior burial chamber as distinct from the more elaborate *arcosolium* type of grave, where a horizontal recess in the wall, containing the body, was covered by a stone slab. Some small artifacts recovered from the site included coins from the first four centuries AD.

Despite the lengthy period of human occupation at Nazareth, the town never claimed any great regard. In fact, in the time of Christ it was the fashion to speak scornfully of it (compare John 1:45-46). As a boy, Jesus lived there with his parents (Luke 2:39, 51), hence his designation as "the Nazarene" or "of Nazareth" (compare Mark 1:24; 10:74; John 18:5; Acts 2:22, etc.). The site of his residence is, of course, unknown, and the "Carpenter's Workshop" associated with St. Joseph's Church is a tourist attraction that has no demonstrated connection with either Joseph or Jesus. Even the location of the ancient synagogue in which Christ read from the book of Isaiah (Luke 4:16-29) cannot be identified with certainty, although several possible sites have been suggested.

Of other areas with supposed New Testament connections, the Mensa Christi or "Table of Christ" marks the location where Christ is alleged to have eaten with his disciples after the resurrection (compare John 21:9-12), but this is without any historical foundation. The same is regrettably true of the Basilica of Jesus the Adolescent, and also the Maronite Church of the Precipice, which confuses the location of Jebel Qafsa with the hill on which the city was built (Luke 4:29). There is a steep cliff closer to the town in proximity to an ancient synagogue which would appear to be a more probable claimant to the dubious honor of being witness to Christ's attempted murder. According to Matthew (4:13-16), Jesus left Nazareth for Capernaum in order to fulfill the prophecy of Isaiah (9:1-7), but an equally valid reason would have been the repudiation of his ministry by the citizens of his home town on another occasion (Matt. 13:54-58; Mark 6:1-6).

| **Nazareth** | An artifact of great historical interest for |
| **Decree** | the study of early Christianity consisted of |

An artifact of great historical interest for the study of early Christianity consisted of a marble slab which was discovered in the collection of a German antiquarian named Froehner by the historian Rostovtzeff in 1930. Apparently it had been recovered from Nazareth about 1878, and consisted of an inscription in Greek uncial lettering amounting to twenty-two lines of text. It is usually described as the "Nazareth Decree" or the "Nazareth Inscription," and the fact that the Greek seems to be a rather poor rendering of an original Latin document has led most scholars to assign it to a date about AD 50, and to regard it as a decree issued by the emperor Claudius.

Apparently there had been some disturbance in Palestine that had religious origins, which was not an uncommon feature of the period, except that this particular one appeared to be different in that it involved the disturbing of graves. As Rostovtzeff translated it, the inscription is as follows:

Nazareth Decree

"Ordinance of Caesar. It is my pleasure that graves and tombs remain undisturbed in perpetuity for those who have made them for the cult of their ancestors, or children, or members of their house. If however, any man lay information that another has either demolished them, or has in any way extracted the buried, or has maliciously transferred them to other places in order to wrong them, or has displaced the sealing or other stones, against such a one I order that a trial be instituted, as in respect of the gods, so in regard to the cult of mortals. For it shall be much more obligatory to honor the buried. Let it be absolutely forbidden for anyone to disturb them. In the case of contravention I desire that the offender be sentenced to capital punishment on charge of violation of sepulture."

—— 177 ——

Historians and New Testament scholars alike have seen this inscription as additional evidence of the difficulties that Claudius encountered with Jews in different parts of his vast empire. Although an individual of rather bizarre behavior, which may actually have been the result of some neurological deficit, Claudius was an intelligent person who was anxious to continue the policy of religious reformation that Augustus had instituted. He must obviously have been either profoundly interested in the perculiarities of the Jewish religion, or else he had an adviser in Rome who was knowledgeable in such matters, because his communications to his Jewish subjects were both informed and pointed.

A few years before Claudius actually expelled from Rome all the Jews who were living there (Acts 18:2), he had had occasion to communicate with the Jewish population in Alexandria. In a letter written in AD 41 he specifically prohibited the Jews of that city from bringing or inviting "other Jews to come by sea from Syria." He continued tersely: "If they do not abstain from this conduct I shall proceed against them for fomenting a malady common to the world." This document contains what had been regarded as the first secular reference to Christian missionary activity, and it is difficult to deny that the style and intent have much in common with the Nazareth Inscription.

According to the Roman historian Suetonius, the expulsion of the Jews from Rome in AD 49 had been the result of public disturbances relating to "a certain Chrestos." Quite probably the Jewish authorities had tried to restrain the early Christian missionaries in Rome from preaching the resurrection of Jesus, and may have adduced as an explanation of the empty tomb the fabrication of the chief priests and elders recorded in Matthew 28:13. If this was actually the case, and was sustained on further enquiry of the emperor, the local governor in Palestine would have set up the decree at the town named in connection with the alleged offense. Certainly the correspondence between the historical background of the Nazareth Decree and the accounts of the empty tomb in the Gospels is too striking to be entirely coincidental.

For further information on Nazareth see:

Kopp, C. *Journal of the Palestine Oriental Society* 18 (1938), 187-228.
Prawer, J. *Israel Exploration Journal* 24 (1974), 241-51.
Bagatti, B. *Encyclopedia of Archaeological Excavations in the Holy Land*, Vol. 3 (1977), 919-22.
Mare, W. H. *New International Dictionary of Biblical Archaeology* (1983), 329-30.

R. K. H.

CHAPTER SEVENTEEN

NINEVEH

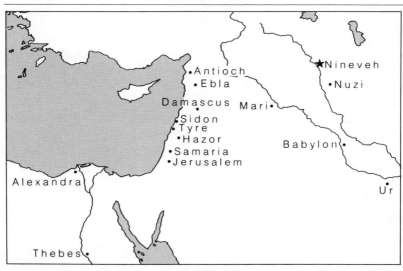

Nineveh is one of the oldest and most important cities of Mesopotamia. Excavations at Nineveh have provided more light on ancient Assyrian history, literature, and culture than any other site. The description of this ancient capital as "an exceedingly great city" (Jonah 3:3) is hardly hyperbolic. From Nineveh's walls, temples, palaces, inscriptions, and reliefs, mute yet elaborate witness is given to a city that flourished up to its destruction in 612 BC. Accordingly, the magnificent buildings, artistic designs, and water-supply projects of Nineveh have resulted in its being likened to ancient Versailles.

—— 180 ——

Exploration of Nineveh

The ruins of Nineveh are located about one mile east of the Tigris River, opposite modern Mosul in northern Iraq. The River Khosr divides ancient Nineveh into two large tells. The mount Kuyunjik ("many sheep") is to the northwest and Nebi-Yunus ("the prophet Jonah") to the southeast. Both mounds are surrounded by a brick-rampart enclosure nearly eight miles long, the height of which varies from ten to twenty feet. Kuyunjik, the larger of the two citadel mounds, is the site where the royal Assyrian palaces and temples have been excavated. About a mile long and a half mile wide, Kuyunjik rises in sharp relief to a height of ninety feet above the Tigris valley. The smaller mound of Nebi-Yunus, according to Islamic tradition, is the site where the prophet Jonah lies buried. Today, a mosque is built over the burial place. A Moslem village and cemetery surround the mosque, covering a large portion of the tell. Hence, the prospects for excavating Nebi-Yunus remain slight.

The name *Nineveh* may be traced to a Cappadocian cuneiform tablet from the twenty-first century BC and found in Asia

Keyunjik (Nineveh)

Minor at modern Kultepe. The name *Ninē* is found on this tablet as an ideogram with the picture of a fish within an enclosure. The name is linked to the Ninevite goddess Ishtar, whose symbol was the fish. Hammurabi (eighteenth century BC), in the prologue of his law code, describes himself as "the king who in Nineveh glorified the name of the goddess Ishtar." From about this same period of time comes an inscription of Shamshi-Adad, king of Ashur, a city on the Tigris about sixty miles south of Nineveh. He also links the name of Ishtar with Nineveh. The temple of Ishtar, goddess of love and war, was uncovered at Kuyunjik along with another temple dedicated to Nabu, god of writing, the arts, and science. Statues of Ishtar of Nineveh were sent to Egyptian rulers as treasured gifts by the kings of Mitanni. Despite the statements in certain secondary dictionary sources, there is no conclusive evidence that links the Hebrew word *nūn* "fish" to the name Nineveh.

At Kuyunjik, excavations down to virgin soil reveal that the site was first occupied in prehistoric times at about 4500 BC. The earliest stratum of the tell has pottery similar to that of Hassuna, a site just south of modern Mosul. Here at Hassuna the cultural remains and artifacts date to about 5000 BC.

The city of Nineveh was first explored by C. J. Rich in 1820. He sketched a plan of the ruins and collected some tablets and inscriptions which, at that time, no one was able to decipher. In 1842, Paul Emile Botta, a French consul at Mosul, was the first to excavate briefly at Nineveh. After several months of work, Botta left Nineveh to dig at nearby Khorsabad, there discovering Sargon II's palace. In 1845, an Englishman, A. H. Layard, came to Mosul. In 1849 he resumed digging at Kuyunjik at the location Botta had earlier abandoned. His discovery of bas-reliefs from the palace of Sennacherib, and the Taylor Prism that contains the annals of Sennacherib including his attack on Hezekiah in Jerusalem, aroused considerable interest in Layard's homeland. The British Museum now became involved. During the last half of the nineteenth century, British expeditions led by H. Rassam (1852-54, 1878-82), George Smith (1872-76), and E. W. Budge (1888-91) continued the excavation. Of particular sig-

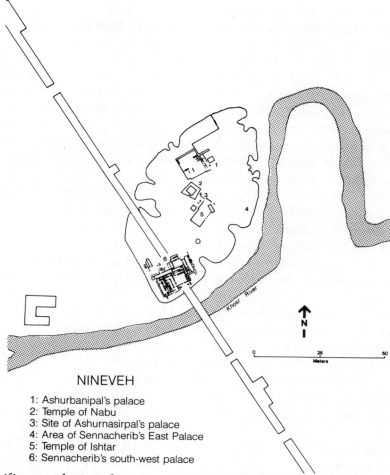

NINEVEH

1: Ashurbanipal's palace
2: Temple of Nabu
3: Site of Ashurnasirpal's palace
4: Area of Sennacherib's East Palace
5: Temple of Ishtar
6: Sennacherib's south-west palace

nificance during this time is George Smith's discovery of the Babylonian Flood story (Gilgamesh Epic) and his pioneering efforts as an epigraphist.

Further significant excavation was carried on by R. Campbell Thompson and others, especially from 1927-32. The clearing of the Temple of Ishtar and the stratification of the mound down to prehistoric levels and virgin soil are among the most noteworthy developments. In recent years, the government of Iraq has continued work around the tell.

The first biblical mention of Nineveh is Genesis 10:10-12 in the Table of Nations. It is one of a group of Mesopotamian cities founded by Nimrod. Genesis 10:12 speaks of "Resen between Nineveh and Calah; that is the great city." Three times in the book of Jonah (1:2; 3:3; 4:11) the expression "great city" is used for Nineveh. It is questionable, however, whether the "great city" of Genesis 10:12 is referring specifically to Nineveh. Some scholars take Jonah's "great city" to apply to a group of Assyrian cities in an administrative district of which Nineveh was a part. The first to suggest this idea was Diodorus Siculus, an ancient geographer. He projected that "greater Nineveh" was a parallelogram shaped area of some sixty miles in circumference. In modern times, André Parrot has argued that "greater Nineveh" was a metropolitan district comprising a so-called "Assyrian triangle" of Nineveh proper, Khorsabad, and Nimrud.

Further indication of the size of Nineveh is found in the biblical mention of "more than a hundred and twenty thousand persons who do not know their right hand from their left" (Jon. 4:11). The phrase has traditionally been understood to refer to children, thus making a projected total population of about 600,000 for "greater Nineveh." Evidence, however, is lacking to demonstrate that such a phrase refers to infants. Besides, the survey of Nineveh by Felix Jones in 1834 revealed that no more than 175,000 could live within the approximately eight miles of city walls encompassing the areas of Kuyunjik and Nebi-Yunus.

Jonah and Nineveh   Another expression related to the size of the city is "three days' journey in breadth" (Jon. 3:3). If one accepts the hypothesis that "great city" means "greater Nineveh," then the expression would mean that the prophet probably traveled through a circuit of cities within the district, moving at the normal pace of fifteen to twenty miles a day. On the other hand, one may understand "three days' journey" in reference to Nineveh proper. If one posits that the city had a maximum axis of considerably less than three miles, then the prophet may have taken "three days to go all through it" (Jon. 3:3 NIV). This assumes that he walked slowly from street corner to street corner. D. J. Wiseman, however, suggests an alternative explanation in accord with the ancient oriental practice of hospitality. Thus, the first day is for travel in from the suburbs and arrival in the city. The second is for visiting, business, and rest. The third day is for return. This interpretation also fits in with the time-scale associated with the "three days and three nights" in the deep (Jon. 1:17) and parallel experience of Jesus in the grave (Matt. 12:38-40).

Long before the time of Jonah, which was the first half of the eighth century BC, Assyrian kings had a reputation for being ruthless and cruel. For example, King Ashurnasirpal II (883-859 BC) boasted of the cruelty brought upon his enemies: "I stormed the mountain peaks and took them. In the midst of the mighty mountain I slaughtered them, with their blood I dyed the mountain red like wool. With the rest of them I darkened the gullies and precipices of the mountains. I carried off their possessions. The heads of their warriors I cut off, and I formed them into a pillar over against their city, their young men and their maidens I burned in the fire."

With savage ancient Near Eastern rulers like Ashurnasirpal II, the Israelites acquired an intense nationalism. Such is displayed in the book of Jonah toward Nineveh. Jonah directs his flaming, patriotic zeal against Israel's powerful and cruel enemy. The prophet wanted the Ninevites destroyed not saved. So Jonah resisted God's first command to preach repentance to the "wicked" city (Jon. 1:1-3). He knew God was gracious and merciful and that he would relent of judgment (Jon. 4:2). This is the human side of Jonah. He could not stand to see Nineveh, this despised enemy of God's elect, spared from sure destruction.

The people of Nineveh, however, did repent and were spared (Jon. 3:10). The suddenness of the Ninevites' repentence has proven difficult for certain scholars to accept. The miraculous power of God, however, which must have accompanied Jonah's preaching, should not be minimized. In addition, the Ninevites may have been somewhat preconditioned and open to Jonah's message due to the religious reforms of king Adad-nirari III

(810-783 BC). This Assyrian king had established a trend toward monotheism by focusing the cult-worship upon the god Nebo. Typical of ancient historiography, Assyrian records are silent about the conversion of Nineveh. It is impossible, therefore, to measure how deep and lasting were the results of Jonah's mission. But its historic importance, as an event to be remembered and as a "sign" to the Jews of Jesus' day, is clearly affirmed by the New Testament writers (Matt. 12:38-42; Luke 11:29-32).

The Assyrian Capital Though Nineveh did not become the permanent capital of Assyria until Sennacherib ruled (705-682 BC), Assyrian kings had their seats in Nineveh as early as the thirteenth century BC. As a royal residence, Nineveh alternated with Ashur and Calah (Nimrud) throughout the Early, Middle, and Late Assyrian periods. Among the more significant monarchs who built their palaces in Nineveh were Tiglath-pileser I (*ca.* 1115-1077 BC), Ashurnasirpal II (883-859 BC), Sargon II (722-705 BC), and Sennacherib (705-681 BC). It was under Sennacherib, however, that Nineveh reached its highest peak of development. Nineveh's rivals were few in the ancient world.

Sennacherib's father, Sargon II (722-705 BC), claimed credit for the downfall of Samaria and the northern kingdom (722-21 BC). In his extravagant palace at Khorsabad, twelve miles northeast of Nineveh, he wrote an inscription that states, "I besieged and conquered Samaria, led away as booty 27,290 inhabitants of it." Some of these Israelite deportees must have made their way not only to Khorsabad but also to nearby Nineveh. When Sargon II died in battle he was succeeded by his son Sennacherib, who moved the royal capital to Nineveh.

The excavation of Sennacherib's magnificent palace at Kuyunjik by Layard (1849-1851) heightened interest in the rapidly growing field of Assyriology. Sennacherib referred to his new palace as "the palace which has no equal." Such could only fit his boast to be "king of the universe, king of Assyria." Layard unearthed a palace of seventy-one rooms which included two large halls forty feet wide and 180 feet long. A total of 9,880 feet of sculptured walls decorate the structure. These depicted such biblical events as Sennacherib's victory over Lachish and his receipt of tribute from king Hezekiah of Judah (2 Kings 18:13-18). On four sides, marble stairs led up to the palace, its entrances adorned with such figures as winged sphinxes and human-headed bulls. Inside the palace, numerous huge winged bulls and lion-sphinxes were scattered throughout.

Sennacherib also strenghtened and beautified the city. He rebuilt the city walls, including fifteen impressive gateways guarded by stone bulls. He laid out a botanical garden with vines and fruit-bearing trees from around his empire. He also built parks and a zoo. In addition, he channeled water into Nineveh by building a thirty-mile aqueduct.

The Taylor Prism of the British Museum records Sennacherib's campaign against Hezekiah and Jerusalem (compare 2 Kings 18:13—19:37; Isa. 36:1—37:38). The king of Nineveh states on his inscription, "As to Hezekiah, the Jew, he did not submit to my yoke. I laid seige to 46 of his strong cities, walled forts and to the countless small villages in their vicinity, and conquered them...[Hezekiah] I made a prisoner in Jerusalem, his royal residence, like a bird in a cage." Sennacherib suffered a crushing defeat outside the walls of Jerusalem due to divine intervention (2 Kings 19:35). Herodotus suggests a plague spread by mice was the agent. At any rate, Sennacherib then returned to Nineveh. There, some time later, he was murdered in the temple of Nisroch by his two sons (Isa. 37:38).

Esarhaddon (681-669 BC), Sennacherib's favorite son, succeeded him. He built his own palace in Nineveh at Nebi-Yunus. His administration was marked by the rebuilding of the city of Babylon. He also led Assyrian forces in the conquest of Egypt.

Ashurbanipal, last of the great Assyrian monarchs, came to the throne in Nineveh in 669 BC. He is the Osnapper of Ezra 4:10. The palace of Ashurbanipal was discovered in 1853 by Rassam who had resumed Layard's dig at Kuyunjik. Largely due to rebellions in the Assyrian empire, Ashurbanipal subdued Babylon, Elam, Tyre, and Egypt. Nahum 3:8-10 recalls Ashurbanipal's sack of Thebes, one of the great cities of the ancient world. In warning of the impending fall of the "bloody city" (3:1), the prophet employs a lesson from history by stating, "Are you better than Thebes, that sat by the Nile" (Nah. 3:8)?

Ashurbanipal, however, is best known for his literary pursuits. Rassam's discovery of Ashurbanipal's massive royal library brought tens of thousands of clay tablets to light. The library included an older collection of texts originally assembled by Tiglath-pileser I (*ca.* 1115-1077 BC). But it also included many new texts which had been copied by Ashurbanipal's scribes from libraries scattered throughout Mesopotamia. The royal library of Ashurbanipal at Nineveh contained copies of the Babylonian Creation and Flood epics. Because of Ashurbanipal's interest in culture and sports—beautiful bas-reliefs of his lion hunts now hang in the British Museum—his empire gradually began to crumble. As revolt followed revolt, Ashurbanipal's sons could not keep the once powerful empire of their father from collapsing. What is more, Nabopolassar (625-605 BC), a new and powerful ruler in Babylon, was now securely enthroned.

Ashurbanipal anointed

In August of 612 BC, Nineveh fell. It was a combined attack. The armies of the Babylonians, the Medes, and Scythians laid siege to the Assyrian capital. Nabopolassar was greatly aided by his brilliant son Nebuchadnezzar and by the flooding of the rivers about the city (Nah. 2:6-8). The prophets Nahum and Zephaniah had predicted this onslaught in the most graphic of terms: "An attacker advances against you, Nineveh. Guard the fortress, watch the road, brace yourselves, marshal all your strength (Nah. 2:1, NIV; compare Zeph. 2:13-15)!" The "lions' den" would be no more (Nah. 2:11-12).

For further information on Nineveh see:

Brackman, A. *The Luck of Nineveh* (1978).
Finegan, J. *Light From the Ancient Past* (1959).
Luckenbill, D. D. *The Annals of Sennacherib* (1924).
Kubie, N. *Road to Nineveh* (1965).
Parrot, A. *Nineveh and the Old Testament*, trans. by B. E. Hooke (1955).
Thompson, R. C. and R. W. Hutchinson. *A Century of Exploration at Nineveh* (1929).
Wiseman, D. J. "Jonah's Nineveh." *Tyndale Bulletin* 30 (1979), 29-51.

M. R. W.

CHAPTER EIGHTEEN

NUZI

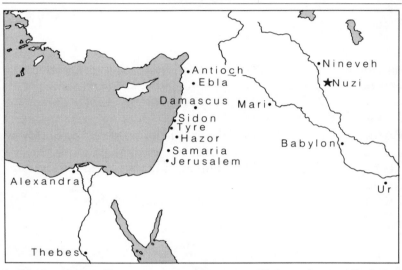

About thirty-five centuries ago a small kingdom called Arraphe flourished two hundred miles north of Babylon. In this
area the arid Mesopotamian plain, where gradual salinization of
the soil brought an end to the world's first great civilization,
gives way to the more fertile hills of Kurdistan. The ancient
kingdom's principal settlement, today a city known as Kirkuk,
has, like Jerusalem and Alepo, occupied the same site for more
than four millennia. It overlooks a vast oil field, now at stake in
the most recent of innumerable wars found between the lowland
and the mountain peoples since the dawn of recorded history.

The kingdom of Arraphe was inconsequential in the power

politics of the ancient Near East. But it is of great interest to modern biblical scholars, for about twelve miles to the southwest of Kirkuk the deserted mound of Yorghan Tepe, site of the very old town of Nuzi, has yielded abundant written records. Most importantly, these records illuminate many passages from the patriarchal narratives of Genesis. They also point up the uniqueness, in a later period, of Elijah's dramatic confrontation with king Ahab, as well as indictments by Amos and Hosea of injustices inflicted on the poor.

Such abuses were ubiquitous throughout the ancient Near East. Ahab's kingdom of Samaria, like Nuzi about six hundred years earlier, suffered a terrible fate—destruction by the armies of imperial Assyria—but it was only in Judah that another prophet saw Assyria as the agent of a just God: "Woe to the Assyrian, the rod of my anger, in whose hand is the club of my wrath!" (Isa. 10:5).

Discovery The attention of scholars was drawn to Arraphe in an unusual way. Unlike Nineveh, Ebla, and Nippur (holy city of the ancient Sumerians), the town of Nuzi does not lie beneath a very large mound of obvious importance. Nor was it, like Mari and the Syrian port city of Ugarit, discovered by chance when artifacts were found by local peasants. At these other sites the exciting discovery of archives came only after excavations had begun, but not so at Nuzi.

Around the turn of the century a distinctive kind of clay tablets—recording land deeds, contracts, and court cases—began to appear on the antiquities market. The language was Akkadian, an older cognate of Hebrew and Arabic, but the dialect was bizarre, showing strong influence from an unknown language that was not Semitic. Though most of these tablets were acquired by museums and published in London, Paris, Berlin, Leiden, and elsewhere, some are still available from dealers. Recently the present writer held one in his hand. It was about the size and shape of a shredded wheat biscuit but heavier. The rather coarse clay was almost black in color and finely incised with cuneiform "wedge" writing by the stylus of a professional scribe about thirty-five hundred years ago.

In 1925, sudden proliferation of these tablets in Iraqi bazaars prompted the distinguished British civil servant, Miss Gertrude Bell, first director of antiquities under the post World War I mandate, to invite Edward Chiera, then annual professor at the American School of Oriental Research in Baghdad, to investigate their provenance. With assistance from an English surgeon, who had intimate knowledge of the area, the main source was found on the ancient mound of Kirkuk. Since the foundations of modern buildings could not be undermined by digging, excavations were begun at the alleged location of a cache of similar tablets about twenty-five years earlier, the mound of Yorghan Tepe, Nuzi.

Success was immediate. A splendid villa was uncovered. It was the residence of one Tehiptilla and his wealthy descendants for four or five generations. Until the town was violently destroyed by the Assyrians, the family's achives had been kept in perfect order. They comprised more than a thousand clay tablets recording trade and real estate transactions, neatly stored in rectangular baskets. In subsequent seasons about three thousand more tablets were recovered from other houses and the local temple, providing a remarkably complete picture of daily life in Nuzi during the fifteenth and fourteenth centuries BC.

Patriarchal Customs   As soon as these texts began to be published, the attention of W. F. Albright and other biblical scholars was arrested by striking parallels with the social customs of the Hebrew patriarchs attested in the book of Genesis. Details of adoption, concubinage, and disposition of property were stressed in a spate of early articles. In addition to material relevant to Genesis, the Nuzi records illustrate the means by which large estates were acquired by a handful of rich landowners: a practice almost universal in the ancient world and persisting in many countries until the enactment of modern land reforms. It was only in ancient Israel that such concentration of holdings

Nuzi land deed from *ca.* 1500 BC

was forbidden in order to protect the rightful owners of the land. If obeyed, the law set forth in Leviticus 25 would have prevented alienation of a family's property. Land sold, or rather leased, must be returned during the Jubilee that was celebrated every fifty years. Certain Mesopotamian laws, known from the Nuzi tablets and the older code of Hammurabi, did indeed forbid farmers to sell their holdings but for a very different reason: each landowner was required to render annual service to the state.

One method of circumventing this law at Nuzi was to foreclose an impoverished peasant's mortgage. Another was to take a good field in exchange for a worthless one and a small sum in silver. But the device of primary interest was the contract of adoption. By making the purchaser their legal heir, the seller and his descendants gave up forever any claim to their property. Thus Tehiptilla and other rich men were "adopted" by hundreds of peasants. A childless couple might also adopt a young man who agreed to care for them as long as they lived. Such adoption for economic consideration or to secure a debt is probably remembered in an obscure reference by Abraham to Eliezer of Damascus (Gen. 15:2b) and in his further complaint that "a member of my household shall be my heir."

The ancestral home of Abraham's clan was Haran near the present border between Turkey and north central Syria, the heartland of an ancient empire called Mitanni that flourished in the middle centuries of the second millennium BC. It is now known that most of the settled population were Hurrians, a people who must have come from the mountainous regions northeast of Mesopotamia, speaking the non-Semitic language that influenced the Nuzi texts. Unless their great capital of Washukani, well known from various ancient sources, is found by archaeologists, our best evidence for the social and economic customs of the Hurrians, among whom the patriarchs lived, must be sought near the eastern border of Mitanni, in the thousands of clay tablets from Nuzi.

So abundant and varied is the material that work on it continues today. The excavations, completed in 1931, revealed that the mound had been built up layer upon layer since the Chalcolithic period, *ca.* 2250 BC, when the site, then called Gasur, was part of the first great Semitic empire of Sargon of Akkad. The biblical name Ishmael, known also from Ebla, is here attested. And among the quotidian business records was the most ancient map yet found; difficult to interpret but perhaps showing the city of Ebla. A few precious texts from intervening centuries bear witness to continuing commercial activity at the site until the arrival, perhaps about 1700 BC, of the Hurrians who renamed the town Nuzi.

The exacting task of publishing thousands of tablets, often broken and hard to read, was carried forward in forty years of dedicated labor by Prof. Ernest R. Lacheman of Wellesley College and Brandeis University. His accurate handwritten copies of the cuneiform writing, traced from bleached-out photographs of the tablets, have been much admired by Assyriologists. Professor Lacheman has been honored by a handsome jubilee volume of *Studies on the Civilization and Culture of Nuzi and the Hurrians* by his own students and other scholars writing in French, German, and Italian.

**Nuzi and
The Bible**

With most of the Nuzi texts now pubished, it is useful to reassess, in the perspective of half a century, their relationship to the patriarchal narratives of Genesis. A number of parallels, initially drawn on the basis of incomplete data, are now subject to correction in matters of detail. Nevertheless, the overall significance of the Nuzi records has been strongly enhanced by new knowledge, including a wealth of complementary material from Mari, Ugarit, Alalakh (near classical Antioch), and many other sites. Some customs, once considered peculiar to the Hurrians—among whom the Semitic clan of Abraham sojourned—are now known to have been widespread in Mesopotamia and adjacent areas. But one salient fact remains: many of these practices were unknown in Israel centuries later, when the patriarchal narratives are believed to have been committed to writing, or are at least unattested in the biblical books of Judges, Samuel, and Kings.

In addition to the adoption contracts, second millennium sources from Nuzi and elsewhere indicate that primogeniture was not the sole criterion for inheritance. At Nuzi a father on his deathbed could designate orally his principal heir, as Jacob did when he deprived Reuben of his rights as firstborn (Gen. 49:3, 4; 1 Chron. 5:1) and placed his right hand on the head of Ephraim instead of his elder brother Manasseh. Likewise, before his death Isaac blessed Jacob, the supplanter, instead of Esau. Interestingly, a Nuzi tablet records that, like Esau in Genesis 25:29-24, a man made over his inheritance rights to his brother in exchange for three sheep.

Contracts between herdsmen and livestock owners, and court cases settling their disputes, often accord in detail with the biblical account of Jacob and Laban. For example, the legal obligation of a herdsman to make good a shortage of livestock, unless caused by predatory beasts or "the touch of a god," illuminates Jacob's contention: "Your sheep and goats have not miscarried, nor have I eaten the rams from your flocks. I did not bring you animals torn by wild beasts; I bore the loss myself. And you demanded payment from me payment for whatever was stolen by day or night" (Gen. 31:38-39).

Nuzi marriage contracts stipulated that a wife, if childless, should provide her husband with a concubine, a requirement applying in the code of Hammurabi only to a class of priestesses to whom childbearing was prohibited. Further stipulations as to the wife's authority over the concubine are analagous to the biblical account of Sarah and Hagar.

Frequent in the Nuzi texts is the adoption not only of a son but also of a woman as a sister, and the woman was occasionally married to her adoptive brother. Initial indications of a high social status accorded to the sister-wife have not been borne out by additional texts, which indicate that such a woman was often a former slave, but an authentic and specifically Hurrian tradition is still reflected in the statements made by Abraham and Isaac, when they wished to conceal the identity of their wives: "She is my sister."

Early evidence that inheritance of a family's household idols may have signified an entitlement to other property has not been confirmed, but it is nonetheless significant that the disposition of household gods was carefully provided for in many testamentary tablets. This affords striking evidence that these sacred images were highly valued and might well have been taken surreptitiously by Rachel when Jacob left the household of Laban.

Still other parallels between the Bible and the Nuzi texts might be cited, such as the complaint of Laban's daughters that a portion of their bride-price had not been returned to them as dowry. But the general significance of the Nuzi material far outweighs any parallel to a bibical passage that might be cited to prove its Hurrian background or a particular date for the patriarchal narratives. The world of the second millennium is well known from many sources that complement the evidence from Nuzi. Led by W. F. Albright and R. de Vaux, many scholars have placed the patriarchal narratives firmly in the early part or middle part of the second millennium. While specific parallels may be called into question, the tablets from Nuzi still add many convincing details to the general picture of Semitic pastoral nomads moving about the fertile crescent from Haran to Ur in the south, and westward to the Mediterranean coast. The probability that among them were sheiks of the desert named Abraham, Isaac, and Jacob cannot easily be set aside.

For more information on Nuzi see:

Chiera, E. *They Wrote on Clay* (1938).

Frymer-Kensky, T. "Patriarchal Family Relationships and Near Eastern Law." *Biblical Archaeologist* 44 (1981), 209-213.

Morrison, M. A. "The Jacob and Laban Narrative in Light of Near Eastern Sources." *Bibical Archaeologist* 46 (1982), 155-164.

Morrison, M. A. and D. I. Owen, eds. *Studies on the Civilization and Culture of Nuzi and the Hurrians* (1981).

Thompson, T. L. *The Historicity of the Patriarchal Narratives* (1974).

P. W. G.

PHILIPPI

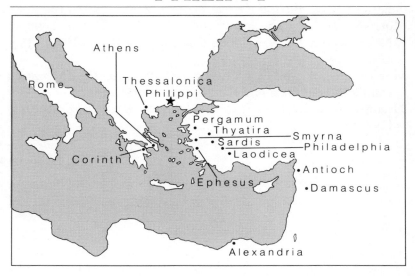

Early History   The site of Philippi was first settled by colonists from the island of Thasos, when the
area still belonged to Thrace, and they
named their settlement Krenides (springs).
Four years later in 356 BC, Philip II, who was the first to unite
Macedonia and Greece, incorporated Thrace into his kingdom
and founded the city of Philippi. It was made the chief mining
center of the Pangaeus gold fields, a source of much of the area's
wealth in the early period, and later a resource for the expeditions of Philip and his famous son Alexander the Great.

The city is situated on the western end of the Philippian plain, a fertile area surrounded by Mounts Orbelos, Symbolon, and Pangaion. Some twenty-two miles to the West is the Nestos river, and about twenty-five miles to the southwest lies the river Strymon, in antiquity called the Gangites. To the south, below the city of Philippi, there is a sizeable marshland (which is bypassed by the road from Neapolis), as there is in the west also.

Trouble with Rome began to develop in the late third century BC when Demetrius, the former ruler of Illyrium, fled to Macedonia to escape the reach of the Senate and the Roman army. Demetrius had been set up as ruler by Rome, but had rebelled against his masters and spread anti-Roman sentiment in the east. Then during the Second Punic War (218-01 BC), Philip V supported Hannibal the arch-rival of Rome.

Aetolia and her Greek allies enlisted the aid of Roman legions to check the expansion of Macedonia under Philip V, and the peace treaty was signed in 215 BC. But convinced that the kingdom was a continuing threat to her power and her allies' security in Greece, Rome invaded again in 200 BC and four years later proclaimed victory and freedom from Macedonia for all Greek cities.

Roman Dominance   Although Macedonia was briefly a free ally of Rome, increasing political tensions on the Grecian peninsula and pretensions of Philip V's son, Perseus (who had allied himself with the Achaean league against Rome), brought the Roman legions once again into the kingdom in 171 BC. The battle of Pydna ended the last fight for Macedonian independence in 168 BC, and Macedonia was divided into four regions or republics to enhance Roman government and to discourage uprisings. The first district included the territory between the Nestos and Strymon rivers and had Amphipolis as its capital. The second, extended from the Strymon to the Axios River with Thessalonica as the capital. The third stretched from the Axios to the Peneios with Pella as the capital, while the fourth reached from Peneios to the borders of Illyria and Epirus, with Pelagonia as the capital. The Roman Senate immediately moved to forbid the exploitation of all the old royal properties and monopolies, including mines, forests, and even the salt trade. Later on these restrictions were amended to allow for necessary salt and industrial metals, and also the minting of coins.

The city of Philippi was a part of the first region, the richest of all, especially in mining. When the senatorial restrictions were relaxed in 158 BC, the first district showed its pride by issuing a great number of silver tetradrachmas, on the obverse of which was Artemis on a Macedonian shield. Artemis was the most honored goddess of Philippi, perhaps the patron of the city. In 148 BC Macedonia was established as a permanent Roman province, governed by a proconsul resident in Thessalonica.

From 148 to 55 BC Philippi, along with all of Macedonia, suffered from several uprisings, from raids by neighboring states, and from the heavy toll of supporting Roman troops. The wealth of the first district was dwindling away, but two major conflicts served to reduce the region to real poverty just prior to the Christian era.

The first conflict was between Julius Caesar and Pompey, who fought out their rivalry in the east and conscripted men, money, and arms as they went. The second conflict, by far the worse of the two, was between the old Republican forces of Brutus and Cassius and those who supported the Principate, led by Antony and Octavian (later Augustus). Following the assassination of Julius Caesar, Brutus and Cassius arrived in the East in 43 BC. In their haste to obtain men, ships, money, and military equipment they did not hesitate to resort to violent measures. Two legions were formed of Macedonians, and the land was forced to quarter their forces. Philippi alone is said to have lodged one hundred thousand men and their fleet. The last and decisive battle with Antony and Octavian was fought on the nearby Philippian plain (42 BC).

There was no rest, however, for the conquered region! Mark Antony demanded of the already plundered city a contribution equal to that given to the armies of Brutus and Cassius, as a fine for their part in the civil war, and so that he might have money to dismiss his own armies peaceably. One citizen wryly asked if Antony might be so kind as to send them two harvests in the same year, since they had twice been asked for almost more than they could bear.

Following the historic battle of Philippi, the city was constituted a colony and veteran soldiers settled there. After the defeat of Antony's forces at Actium, Octavian (Augustus) named the colony Colonia Iulia Philippensis, in honor of Juilius Caesar. But three years later the Emperor renamed it in honor of himself: Colonia Iulia Augusta Philippensis. According to Rostovtzeff, Roman rule and military protection were less efficient than that of her Hellenistic predecessors but opened up great areas of trade in the West for the impoverished Eastern provinces, and this eventually led to great prosperity.

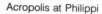

Acropolis at Philippi

Paul's Journeys   The city of Philippi in Paul's day was proud of its status as a Roman colony. As such, all its citizens held Roman citizenship as well, a privilege that had not yet been devalued by becoming the common property of the masses, as it did in the later empire. Undoubtedly there were still many ex-soldiers and their descendants living at Philippi, which would contribute substantially to the pro-Roman sentiment of the town. Unlike many cities Paul visited, Philippi had no synagogue, and hence must have had a very tiny Jewish population. Only ten or twelve men might form a synagogue, but all that Paul found was a prayer meeting dominated by women when he arrived (Acts 16:13). The remains of an archway at the west gate (or Krenides gate) have been uncovered by archaeologists, and it is thought to date to the time of Paul. A road led from here down to the river Gangites, where the prayer meeting probably occurred.

There were three elements common to the Roman provincial government of the time: permanent military occupation, regular taxes, and Roman supervision of public order, including the municipal government. As a colony, we might expect that civil order and legislation in Philippi closely paralleled that in Italian towns. There were two officials over Philippi, known as *duoviri*. Luke uses the Greek term, *strategoi*, which some think points to a preference for the older term of *praetores*, but Sherwin-White finds it a general Greek term for an untranslatable Latin title. We must keep in mind that at this time the magistrates had power unlike that given to modern ones. They were often judge, jury, police, and law-maker all at once. The moral codes developed under Augustus applied primarily to the aristocracy, and in Italy the crimes of the common man were left to the summary jurisdiction at Rome of the annual magistrate. In the provinces, especially here in a colony, jurisdiction fell to the discretion of the local magistrate.

The city was bisected by the celebrated Ignatian Way, a major Roman military highway that ran across Macedonia from the Adriatic Sea in the west to the Bosporus in the east. A road led from the east gate to the port of Neapolis, which was regularly used by the inland city, Philippi. The city was well endowed with public works of every sort. An agora or central market-place some three hundred feet long and one hundred fifty feet wide was uncovered by the French school at Athens in 1914. Porticoes, temple facades, and public buildings bounded the agora. There is also evidence that the jail Paul and Silas were kept in was adjacent to it. A large public lavatory has been uncovered, replete with stone seats, urinals, and equipped for running water. An acropolis was situated on a nearby mountain spur, over one thousand feet above sea level. On its east slope stand the remains of a theater which once held up to fifty thousand people. On the north end of the agora have been found the four steps which would have led up to the *bema* or seat of judgment, possibly the place where the young missionaries were sentenced (Acts 16:20). On the east side what appears to be a library and reading rooms have been found.

Pagan Religion

In terms of religion, the city held a diversity of temples, and there is evidence for devotion to many major deities, as was common in cities of the Hellenistic east. There were temples dedicated to Faustia, Antonia, the Egyptian Isis, and Artemis. Inscriptions reveal cults dedicated to Jupiter, Minerva, Cybele, and above all to Artemis (Diana). Over a hundred inscriptions and reliefs have been found on the acropolis dedicated to this goddess. She is pictured as the huntress with bow and arrow, accompanied by her stag and dogs, or with the war-lance, or astride her prey with knife ready to deal the death-blow, or as the divine light-bearer. A temple dedicated to Apollo and Artemis was located to the south of the agora, which is reminiscent of the illustrious history of the city. The goddess Artemis is traditionally associated with her brother Apollo, and often appears with him in Grecian inscriptions or reliefs. Apollo is associated with the royal house of the Macedonians, for according to legend he came to Philip II's wife in the form of a serpent and fathered Alexander the Great. Thus it is possible that devotion to Apollo continued alongside the major honors paid to Artemis, as is evidenced also by the existence of the "Pythian" prophetess.

Paul and Silas entered the town some time in the mid to late AD 40s, during the reign of Claudius and probably after he had restored the province of Macedonia to senatorial control in AD 44. They soon encountered trouble with a female prophetess who had a "Pythian spirit" (*pneuma pythona*, Acts 16:16), which the NIV translates as "a spirit by which she predicted the future." F. F. Bruce thinks she was linked with the famous Delphic oracle, for the lord of this Hellenic center of prophecy was the Pythian Apollo, and the prophetesses who were thought to have contact with the god in ecstatic experiences were styled *pythona*. Others believe that the influence of this oracle had so dwindled by this late date that it is unlikely that there was any direct connection. Possibly, the name was simply a catch-word to describe any female who, like those at Delphi, claimed to have intimate contact with the gods, uttered mysterious messages in ecstatic speech, and offered predictions of the future. Either that, or her owners claimed for her a *pneuma pythona* in a clever advertising scheme to evoke images of that well-known and reputedly accurate oracle.

Paul and Silas in Court   Incensed over the loss of income that the apostles had caused by exorcising her, the woman's owners immediately hauled them before the magistrate on a trumped-up religious charge. An appeal was made to the ancient (Roman) principle of "incompatibility," which may indicate that the apostles' accusers were aware of Claudius' efforts to discourage the spread of Oriental religions, including Judaism. The charges, he avers, are not without parallel in the Julio-Claudian administration. The magistrates, even more aware of the emperor's tendencies and seeing before them only two poor, obscure men traveling through on no "real" business, quickly ordered them beaten and thrown into prison.

Contrary to some commentators, the apostles would not have

PHILIPPI

Agora at Philippi

been in immediate danger merely from preaching a new religion, for though unrecognized cults were officially forbidden they were unofficially tolerated as long as no social or political crimes were involved. Be that as it may, the apostles found themselves summarily thrust into prison without a hearing. Bruce finds no connection between the earthquake and the apostles' release, supposing that the magistrates intended no more than a night in jail to discourage their return and to satisfy the crowds. But the authorities received a rude shock when they ordered the prisoners to leave the next morning, for these "vagabonds" were really Roman citizens.

It is not known exactly how someone in ancient times might have verified his citizenship, although there are examples of portable certificates being issued to soldiers on pieces of lead. In any case, the claim of Paul and Silas was taken seriously. If the magistrates had been influenced earlier by a desire to please the emperor, they would have been horrified by that same desire now. The *lex Iulia* forbade the beating or binding of a Roman citizen *adversus provocationem* (without appeal). Furthermore,

205

Claudius was much more stern about the administration of justice in the provinces than his immediate predecessors. During his reign several governors were recalled to Rome to account for their crimes in maladministrations.

Sherwin-White argues that the laws did allow for special circumstances under which a citizen might be beaten, and thus concludes that Acts gives an exact representation of the historical situation. But this was still a very delicate matter. Above all, Roman law did not allow for autocratic power by the magistrate. By clearing up their status and rights before they left, Paul and Silas undoubtedly did the infant church at Philippi a great benefit. For they would henceforth be associated with the teaching of Roman citizens, rather than common criminals.

Christian Philippi   The evidence of Acts suggests that Luke remained at Philippi when Paul and his companions (the "we" of Acts 16:9, 10) moved southward toward Thessalonia. Bruce thinks him to be the "true yokefellow" addressed in Philippians 4:3.

It is plain to a reader of the Philippian epistle in Greek that it is keyed to this community. They are urged to act as "citizens" worthy of the gospel (*politeuesthe*, 1:27). Appropriate military terms are used at several points (indicating the presence of soldiers in the early church?): for example, *isopsuchos* 2:20, translated by the NIV as "like him", but frequently used in military contexts of a comrade-in-arms; or *sustratiotes*, NIV "fellow soldier".

It was in Philippi, and further along the *Via Egnatia* through Amphipolis, Apollonia, Thessalonica, and Beroea, that the gospel first took root in Europe. Like the leaven of Jesus' parable, it grew slowly but surely, gradually to become the dominant force in the region, as, indeed, throughout the empire. At the beginning of the fourth century AD, the Roman ruler Galerius settled in Thessalonica. In 303 he and the emperor Diocletian initiated the most famous of all the persecutions of the Christian faith throughout the empire. But it was too late. Christianity had become too much a part of the lives of the people in the provinces. In spite of the severity of the persecution, "the blood of the martyrs" was indeed "the seed of the church." Galerius was forced to issue an edict of toleration on his deathbed (AD 311).

In 313 Constantine became emperor and with his fellow ruler in the east issued the Edict of Milan, which granted Christianity the same legal standing as other religions for the very first time. In 330, Constantine moved the official capital of the empire to Byzantium (renamed Constantinople), thus transfering the center of power to the Greek territories. Within two generations Christianity had almost totally replaced the old paganism of both the west and the east.

Among the Christian architectural remains in Philippi are the following: an early fourth-century basilica a short distance outside the Neapolis Gate near a small stream (possibly the location of the first meeting of Paul with Lydia and her friends [Acts 16:13-14]); a crypt with seventh-century paintings depicting the imprisonment of Paul and Silas (possibly the jail where Paul and Silas were kept overnight); two large Christian basilicas dating from the mid-fifth century ("Basilica A") and the sixth-century basilica much more elaborate in nature; and an octagonal church dating from the time of Justinian (AD 527-65).

For further information on Philippi see:

Bruce, F. F. *Commentary on the Book of Acts* (1954).
———— . *Philippians* (1984).
Collart, P. *Philippes, ville de Macedoine* (1937).
Rostovtzeff, M. I. *The Social and Economic History of the Hellenistic World* (1941).
Sherwin-White, A. N. *Roman Society and Law in the New Testament* (1963).

W. W. G.

CHAPTER TWENTY

ROME

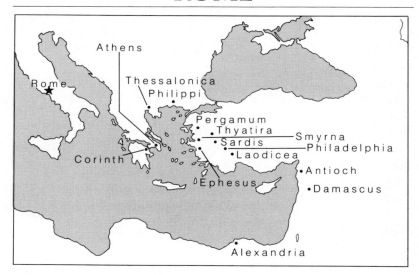

Urban Development
Rome is at the center of communications in Italy, where the north-south route below the Apennines is intersected by the east-west route in the valley of the river Tiber. Close to the river rise three hills, the Capitol (the Campidglio), the Palatine, and the Aventine. In the flat land between the Capitol and the Palatine stood the Forum. Four spurs from the table-land further inland, the Quirinal, the Viminal, the Esquiline, and the Caelian complete the Seven Hills of Rome. Outside the ancient city was another hill, the Collis Hortulorum (Hill of Gardens) or the Pincian. Facing it across the Tiber rose the Vatican hill.

The Tiber was spanned by many bridges. The Pons Fabricius, joining the island to the city, was built in the first century BC. The most northerly bridge, outside the ancient city was the Pons Milvius (Ponte Molle), parts of whose ancient piers still survive. It is here that Constantine the Great (AD 306-37) defeated his rival Maxentius (AD 306-12), as he claimed, in the sign of the Cross. The Tiber provided defense for Rome in one area; elsewhere there were earthen ramparts, which were later replaced by a stone structure, the Servian Wall, that Rome soon outgrew. Traditionally founded in 753 BC, Rome then consisted of small shepherd communities on the hills. The draining of marshy area between them and the commencement of the Forum was a major step forward. The growing city was almost destroyed in the Gallic invasion of 391 BC. During the second and first centuries BC Rome blossomed both architecturally and artistically. She reached the height of her splendor in the century from the dictatorship of Julius Caesar (d. 44 BC) to the time of Nero (AD 54-68 BC). The first Roman emperor, Augustus (31 BC—AD 14), claimed to have found Rome brick and left it marble.

Exterior of Colesseum

Emperors after Nero continued to build lavishly in Rome, and Constantine initiated Christian public architecture in the city. A brief description of some the main features of Rome in the first century AD may now be given.

The Capitol   Rome's most important temple, that of Jupiter, Juno, and Minerva stood on the summit. Parts of the foundations can be seen in the floor of the museum in the Palazzo dei Conservatori. Triumphal processions ended at it, where the celebrating general sacrificed to Jupiter. At the foot of the hill was the Carcer or Prison, now built into a church because of its Christian associations. Its lower chamber, accessible through a hole in the roof, was called the Tullianum and served as the place of execution.

The Forum   Like the agora in a Greek city, the Roman Forum was originally a market place. But as the city grew, more mundane business was displaced elsewhere. The Forum became the civic center of Rome, where much of its important commercial, political, legal, and religious business was conducted. The Curia or Senate House stood in the northeast corner. The present structure is a reconstruction by Diocletian (AD 284-305) according to the original plan of Caesar. The open space in front of it, the Comitium, was where the Roman people held some of their political assemblies. They were addressed by the politicians from the Rostra or high platform at the one end. A praetor administered civil justice from a Tribunal or raised platform near this area. Legal business was also conducted in the basilicas. Of these the two most important were the Basilica Aemilia next to the Curia and the Basilica Julia of Julius Caesar on the opposite side of the Forum. The Forum was full of temples. Eight columns of the Temple of Saturn, where the state treasury was housed, are still standing, as well as the foundations of the temple erected to Caesar after his deification. Three columns of the circular Temple of Vesta have been re-erected.

She was the goddess of the hearth (of the city). Her priestesses, the Vestal Virgins, tended the sacred fire that was kept constantly burning in the temple. They lived in a large house behind the temple under the care of the Pontifex Maximus, the floor-level of whose official residence, the Regia or Palace, can be seen behind the Temple of Caesar. The Arch of Augustus stood next to this. A road, along which triumphal processions passed, the Sacred Way, led through the Forum to the Capitol.

The Palatine Postholes of the huts of the early inhabitants of the hills have been uncovered by archaeologists in the soft tufa surface of the Palatine. The Romans themselves long preserved a reconstructed Casa Romuli (Hut of Romulus, the first king of Rome) as a reminder of their origins. The Palatine eventually became an exclusive residential area. Augustus lived on it and his successors built their houses or palaces there. Little remains of the palaces to testify to their former magnificence.

Roman forum

There were various temples on the hill, such as that built by Augustus to Apollo, a god whom he particularly favored. He also built a library whose separate Greek and Latin reading rooms have been distinguished close to the temple.

Campus Martius   The Campus Martius was outside the *pomerium* or sacred boundary of the city. The senate would meet in the Temple of Bellona (a goddess of war) there when dealing with certain military affairs or receiving foreign ambassadors, who were housed in the Villa Publica or State House, where certain types of military business were also conducted. Some Roman political assemblies were held on the Campus. Caesar built the Saepta Julia, an enormous voting-hall, to accommodate these.

Pompey the Great (*d.* 48 BC) built the first permanent theater in Rome on the Campus, with a temple to Venus above the auditorium. In front there was a large Porticus or square enclosed by

Arch of Titus

colonnades. This included a hall or exedra (an open recess with seating) called the Curia Pompei where Caesar was murdered in 44 BC.

The Amphitheatrum Tauri, built by Statilius Taurus, a supporter of Augustus, was Rome's first permanent amphitheatre. Augustus turned much of the north part into an area particularly associated with his life and career. Early in his life he erected a large circular Mausoleum, in front of which he recorded his Achievements ("Res Gestae") on two bronze pillars. The beautiful Ara Pacis Augustae (Altar of Peace), celebrating his victories in the West, has been re-assembled and re-erected not far from its original location under cover. Its brilliant sculpture can be studied in all its beauty. It shows legendary themes in Roman history as well as the procession of the day of consecration, where the features of members of Augustus' family and of the high nobility can easily be distinguished.

Circus Maximus The form of this two thousand feet long race-course can still be clearly seen between the Aventine and the Palatine. There were two parallel rows of seats on tiers and a semicircular end. At the open end there were places for twelve teams of horses to compete: they completed several laps round a central rib (*spina*) with turning posts (*metae*) at either end.

Monumental Structures Many of the buildings mentioned so far have either disappeared or survive only as ground plans. A list of some typical surviving monuments may be of interest. *Triumphal Arches* might have a single opening flanked by sculptured panels and surmounted by an attic story with an inscription serving as a platform for a triumphal chariot. Such was the (posthumous) Arch of Titus on the Sacred Way at the southeast end of the Forum. Before becoming emperor Titus (AD 79-81) had brought the Jewish War that had broken out under Nero to a successful conclusion. Elements of his triumphal procession can still be traced in the sculptured panels, including a scene

Interior of Colesseum

showing the soldiers carrying the sacred seven-branched candle-stick, the table with the shewbread, and the trumpets carried off as spoils from the Temple of Jerusalem. Some arches were triple, with subsidiary arches on either side, like the Arch of Constantine next to the Colosseum. Much of its decoration was taken from earlier monuments.

The largest *Amphitheater* is the Flavian Amphitheater (now called the Colosseum) built by Vespasian (AD 69-79) and his son Titus, who belonged to the Flavian family. Oval in form, nearly 660 feet long and 550 feet high, it could seat fifty thousand spectators in the auditorium fitted with three arcaded stories covered by awnings during shows. The arena floor has gone, making it easy to see the warren of rooms and passages where hoists and other stage devices were kept, and wild animals and gladiators awaited their turn to appear.

Basilicas were long rectangular halls, often with apses at the end, and usually divided by interior columns into a nave and aisles. They were multipurpose buildings, used especially for legal and commercial business. The largest is the Basilica Nova begun by Maxentius and completed by Constantine at the southeast end of the Forum. Part of the vaulted structure with its three exedrae can still be seen.

The commonest form of Roman *Temples* was rectangular, although there were circular examples like the Pantheon. They were usually built on a podium or high platform fronted by steps and entered through a porch of free-standing columns leading to the cella or main room at the back where a statue of the deity stood. The altar was outside. Religious ceremonies took place there and not in the temple, which was the house of the god.

Unlike Greek theaters, Roman *Theaters* were usually freestanding and built on the level ground. The semicircular auditorium, rising in tiers on colonnades, was partly roofed. The stage, completely roofed, was backed by a high wall used for the attachment of scenery. The stage itself was a high and wide stone platform.

Daily Life   Most of the population lived in small flats or apartments in multi-storied buildings. The ground story, often built round an inner courtyard, was of concrete, but the upper floors might be of wood. The risk of fire was very great, as open braziers were used for heating and cooking. The wealthier could afford single-story homes. These presented blank wall (or walls with recesses let as shops) to the street and looked inward round two courtyards: one is the atrium or the reception area; the other is the peristyle, which often had a small private garden. Since most private homes have disappeared in Rome, it is necessary to go to Ostia to see all types of housing preserved to a good height. The wealthiest would also own villas or country estates outside the city. The remarkable Villa of Hadrian can be seen at Tivoli eighteen and a half miles from Rome.

By comparison with other ancient cities Rome had remarkably hygienic and modern public facilities: granaries, carefully laid out streets and drains, sewers, and public latrines. It was her water supply that has attracted the greatest attention. An abundant supply of fresh water was delivered to the city daily by aqueducts, some as much as thirty-eight miles long, from the surrounding hills. In essence these were artificial channels with apertures for fresh air at regular intervals that ran either underground or across valleys on tiers of arches to reservoirs in the city, from which the water was delivered to its users and regulated by gauge-pipes. Isolated arches of aqueducts can be seen at various points in Rome today, but the best-preserved stretch near the city is a section of the Aqueduct of Claudius (AD 41-54) along the Rome-Naples railway line just outside the Rome station. Its conduit, together with that of another aqueduct, can be seen above the gate in the Aurelian Wall called the Porta Praenestina (now the Porta Maggiore).

Government and Society   Augustus divided Rome into fourteen "regions," each subdivided into several wards. The aediles were responsible for much municipal administration, assisted at a higher level by various "curators" who were distinguished senior senators. Augustus stationed an elite corps, the Praetorian Guard, in towns near Rome. Tiberius (AD 14-27) concentrated the Guard in a large camp, the Castra Praetoria (near to the Città Universitaria), on the outskirts of the city. The walls of the camp are still extant. The main duty of the Guard was to protect the emperor. Augustus also created two paramilitary organizations, the Vigiles, a sort of night watch and fire brigade combined, and the Urban Cohorts, a police force under the authority of the prefect of the city, a distinguished senator responsible for keeping order in the city. Augustus also regulated the corn supply, arranging the orderly distribution of the corn dole.

The pinnacle of socity was formed by the emperor and his court. The emperors of the first century AD came from two families, the Julio-Claudian and the Flavian. A rather anomalous position in society was occupied by certain imperial freedmen, ex-slaves whom the emperor employed at the head of ministries in his bureaucracy or civil service. The imperial family was regarded with some jealousy by other members of the Roman nobility, who provided most of the executive power in the Roman empire. This they did by membership of the senate and competition for its "magistracies" or annual executive offices. Thus they became consuls—chairmen of the senate, praetors—administering justice; aediles—putting on religious shows and engaged in municipal administration, quaestors—carrying out financial functions. The nobility comprised not only the senatorial "order" as it was known, but also the less-distinguished "equestrian order," consisting of large land owners and wealthy businessmen not in the senate. They were increasingly involved in the administration of the empire, especially in finance. The rest of the free Roman citizens were called the plebeians.

The Romans owned large numbers of slaves, but manumitted them readily. Accordingly a class of wealthy and competent freedmen arose, often holding important private and public positions. Rome attracted residents from all over the ancient world. Among these was a large Jewish community.

Religion   Ancient Roman religion was animistic. It regarded the universe as peopled by vaguely conceived powers, which might be beneficent or hostile (*numina*), that affected every aspect of life. There was no rigid dividing line between the religious and the secular as in modern society. Gradually, partly under the influence of Greek anthropomorphism, the major deities were given human form. Mercury was assimilated to Hermes, the Greek messenger of the gods. There were twelve chief deities. The king or father of the gods was Jupiter, originally a sky god, whose wife was Juno. There was no separate ministry trained in theology. Each father acted as priest during religious ceremonies in the home, and major political figures served as priests at state functions. Julius Caesar was *pontifex maximus* (high priest). There were several "college" priests. Especially important were the pontiffs under the *pontifex maximus*, who supervised Roman religion as a whole, and the augurs who interpreted the will of the gods. Following Caesar's example, every Roman emperor became *pontifex maximus*, a title eventually taken over by the popes.

Gradually many non-Roman religions took root in Rome, such as Mithraism from the East, which became a powerful rival to Christianity.

Since there was also no rigid distinction between the human and the divine, the Romans did not find it difficult to regard certain outstanding individuals as more than human and even accord them worship (compare the "heroes" in Greek religion). This was the basis of the imperial cult, whereby emperors were worshiped as gods (initially only after they had been deified after death). Worship of the living emperor was taken as a sign of loyalty to the state.

The Roman Empire   Early Christians would have thought of Rome less as a city than as an imperial system. Rome had early expanded to take control of Italy, then of most of the Mediterranean littoral, and much of Western and Central Europe. The empire was divided into provinces, the Alps, the Gauls (France), Lusitania and the Spains, Illyricum and Moesia (Yugoslavia and Bulgaria on the Danube), Macedonia and Achaea (Greece), Bithynia and Pontus, Asia, Cilicia, Galatia and Cappodocia (all now Turkey), Syria, Judaea (Israel), Egypt, Cyrenaica, Africa (Tunisia) and Mauretania. Certain areas were entrusted to client kings, that is, kings enjoying Roman support with full internal autonomy but following Roman foreign policy. Such were the Herods in Judaea (when the area was not a province) and in the smaller areas surrounding it, where the lesser title of ethnarch or tetrarch might be used. Long-established provinces like Asia were governed by proconsuls responsible to the senate. The newer frontier areas were called imperial provinces, where the emperors appointed governors (also of senatorial status) called imperial legates, like Sulpicius Quirinius (the Cyrenius of the KJV) in Syria at the birth of Christ. Smaller imperial provinces were assigned to prefects (later called procurators) from the equestrian order, like Pontius Pilate in Judaea.

Peter and Paul
in Rome

According to the Western text of *Acts*, when Paul arrived in Rome he was handed over to the *Stratopedarches*, or camp commandant. However the official concerned cannot be identified. He may have belonged to the Praetorian Guard or even to a body of troops responsible to the prefect of the city. Paul spent two years in Rome under a form of house arrest. Further than that Acts says nothing.

His letter to the Romans affords a brief insight into the social ambience of the early Christian community in the city. It is clear that Paul was most involved with the "immigrant" groups in Rome, Greek-speaking easterners (called "Greeks" in Rom. 1:16) and Jews especially. Socially he was concerned with small tradesmen like Aquila, a "tentmaker" like himself (Rom. 16:3; Acts 18:3). Others were freedmen and slaves for the most part, as can be reasonably deduced from the names in Romans 16. Some of the more Jewish names in the list, like Aristobulus and Herodion, may indicate freedmen members of the household of the Herods of Judaea. Narcissus, whose "household" is mentioned, could be a famous imperial freedman of Claudius: the "imperial establishment" ("Caesar's household") appears in Philippians 4:22.

The "Babylon" of 1 Peter 5:13 (as of Revelation) is almost certainly Rome, but there is no New Testament evidence explicitly connecting Peter with Rome.

There are two pagan references (one definite, the other virtually so) to Christianity in Rome. Claudius' biographer Suetonius (*ca.* AD 60-135) states that the emperor expelled the Jews from Rome because of disturbances instigated by "Chrestus," almost certainly Christ, and a reference to the disturbances usually caused by the preaching of Christianity in Jewish synagogues. The historian Tacitus (*ca.* AD 56-120) relates how Nero blamed the Christians for starting the great fire of Rome in AD 64. The emperor crucified and otherwise tortured them in his gardens and circus in the Vatican.

Specific references to the fate of Peter and Paul do not antedate the late second or third century AD. Irenaeus (*ca.* AD 130-200) is the first to connect Peter explicitly with the church in

Rome. Eusebius (*ca.* AD 260-340) says that he was crucified there. Tertullian (*ca.* 160-220) is the first author to say that Paul was beheaded in Rome.

Christian Rome
The house churches to which Paul refers in Romans 16:5 must have met in private buildings or houses as the case may have been. Churches were later identified by the name of the owner who had "title" to the property; for example "titulus Chrysogoni" or "titulus Clementis." Such names, prefaced by *Saint*, might survive for late churches on the site, as S. Crisogono (in Trastevere) or S. Clemente on Via S. Giovanni (in Laterano not far from the Colosseum). This interesting church consists of a series of buildings superimposed on each other. On the lowest level—accessible to the visitor—there was a pagan building, possibly a warehouse, and a house, later converted into a chapel of Mithras. In the fourth century a small basilica-type church was erected over these earlier buildings.

Interest attaches to the early Christian cemeteries of Rome. The ancient Romans themselves, to whom proper burial was of the greatest importance, allowed infant but not adult burials within the city. Accordingly individual graves and cemeteries lined all the roads leaving the city. Those on the Appian Way are often visited, especially the monumental tomb of Caecilia Metella. The first Christians would have been buried in pagan cemeteries. About the middle of the second century AD, Christians made the catacomb a peculiarly Christian type of burial place. The word derives from a place Ad Catacumbas, possibly meaning "At the Hollows," on the Appian Way outside the city, where it was easy to dig into the soft tufa rock of the area. The Christians eventually excavated many series of enormous underground galleries several floors deep from which access could be gained to the graves themselves. Most were *loculi*, simple coffin-like recesses dug into the wall of the gallery and sealed by tiles. There were also the more elaborate *arcosolia*, arched recesses, sometimes large enough to take a sarcophagus and often decorated, and family or group graves in little chambers called *cubicula.* Some catacombs included places where Christians could meet for funeral feasts or special services in honor of their own dead or of a local martyr. The first was built *ca.* AD 150 in a tomb that belonged to Domitilla; it is still named after her. She was the niece of the last Flavian emperor Domitian (AD 81-96). Other early catacombs were those of Priscilla on the Via Salaria and of Callistus, where many of the early bishops of Rome were buried.

According to a tradition, in a persecution in the third century the bodies of Peter and Paul were moved from their respective graves in the Vatican and on the Ostian Way and taken for safety to the catacombs on the Appian Way. There certainly was a festival in their honor there at that time. In the fourth century Constantine built a memorial church there, the Basilica Apostolorum, which later developed into the Basilica of St. Sebastian.

Constantine was the first emperor to erect Christian buildings in Rome and to start the process of imparting a Christian stamp to the public architecture of the city. His most famous church is old St. Peter's in the Vatican, the predecessor of the sixteenth century church, Basilica di S. Pietro, now on the site. Constantine chose to build his St. Peter's on the side of the Vatican hill. He excavated part of it to form a large terrace above a pagan necropolis close to the old Circus of Gaius and Nero.

The reason why Constantine involved himself in the additional expense of preparing an awkward site for the basilica was that there was an *aedicula* or small shrine of Peter in the cemetery which he had had covered over. It had been built in what was presumably a Christian plot in the cemetery at some time between AD 160 and 180. It consisted of a wall behind a small niche covered by a gable and flanked by columns, with a projecting slab for offerings. Constantine chose the site deliberately for a pilgrimage church for the veneration of the memory of Peter, like the funerary halls in the catacombs at martyrs' shrines but on a much grander scale.

It is difficult to know whether the Aedicula marks Peter's actual grave. Even if it were certain that Peter was crucified in the Neronian persecution of 64, it is not certain that Christians of the time would have gained access to the body and been able to bury it nearby. The erection of the Aedicula, however, implies that the site had strong associations at least with Peter as early as a century after his death. And Eusbius quotes Gaius, a Roman priest of *ca.* 200, to the effect that the "trophy" of Peter was on the Vatican. A "trophy" was a monument to a victory over death and could refer to an actual grave.

In a brilliant and painstaking series of excavations Vatican archaeologists have cleared the magnificent tombs of the pagan part of the necropolis and the area of the Aedicula. In one of the graves under it the bones of a large man of first century date have been found, which some regard as those of Peter himself.

For further information on Rome see:

Boethius, A. and J. B. Ward-Perkins. *Etruscan and Roman Architecture* (1970).
Cary, M. and H. H. Scullard. *History of Rome* (1979).
Gough, M. R. E. *The Early Christians* (1961).
Lanciani, R. A. *Pagan and Christian Rome* (1893).
Nash, E. *Pictorial Dictionary of Ancient Rome* (1961).
Stevenson, J. *The Catacombs*, (1978, 1985).
Toynbee, J. and J. B. Ward-Perkins. *The Shrine of St. Peter and the Vatican Excavations* (1956).

D. B. S.

SAMARIA

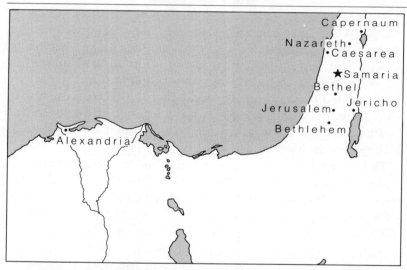

Apart from Jerusalem and Babylon, Samaria is mentioned more often in the Bible than any other major city. Samaria is unique in that it seems to be the only major city founded by the people of Israel. It was built specifically as the capital of the northern kingdom, and as such it contributed significantly to the history and culture of ancient Israel.

When Jeroboam successfully led the northern tribes in rebellion against Rehoboam, he established the first northern capital at Shechem, later moving it to Penuel (1 Kings 12:1, 25). Subsequently Baasha moved the capital to Tirzah (1 Kings 15:27-24).

Omri reigned in Tirzah for about six years, then searched for a better location. He found an ideal hill, which he purchased for two talents of silver from a man named Shemer (about 234 lb. Troy). There he built his new capital and named it Samaria after its original owner (1 Kings 21-28). It remained the capital throughout the remaining years of the northern kingdom.

Location   Located about forty-two miles north of Jerusalem and twenty-five miles east of the Mediterranean Sea, the hill of Samaria was ideal for controlling several trade routes. Standing about three hundred feet above verdant valleys of vineyards and olive orchards (Isa. 28:1) with hills on three sides, it was an easily defended observation point. The ancient hill consisted of an east-west ridge that rose to an oval summit on the west, with a steep cliff on its south side. On the east the ridge formed a long, narrow saddle that joined with the nearby hills. From his palace window on the summit of the hill, Omri had a panoramic view of the fertile valley that extended to the Mediterranean over much of the west.

The hill had not been occupied previously, except perhaps by a small primitive village in the remote past that scarcely left a trace. The city now stands in ruins, with only the small Arab village of Sebastiyeh remaining at the east end of the ridge.

There have been two periods of archaeological excavations at Samaria. The first was conducted under the authority of Harvard University from 1908-10. The excavation was done by G. A. Reisner, C. S. Fisher, and D. G. Lyon. The second (1931-35) was directed by J. W. Crowfoot with the help of G. M. Crowfoot and K. M. Kenyon. The project was conducted jointly by Harvard University, Hebrew University of Jerusalem, the Palestine Exploration Fund, the British Academy, and the British School of Archaeology in Jerusalem.

From the time that Omri built the city (about 879 BC) until the end of the northern kingdom (in 723 BC), Samaria was the northern capital. It served as the capital throughout the Omri Dynasty, the Jehu Dynasty, and the period of Israel's decline and fall.

Omri (885-874) built his palace with a skillfully constructed wall that enclosed an area about 584 by 292 feet. Inside were a series of open courts with various rooms grouped around them, with a larger court about 56 by 26 feet. The construction was of yellow limestone quarried on the site, cut with a precision characteristic of Phoenician craftsmen. There was a second wall outside the palace and a third wall lower on the hill. The construction was arranged on a number of terraces that followed the primitive contour of the hill.

During his reign, Omri conquered the Moabites and put them under tribute. He evidently made an alliance with Ethbaal, king of the Sidonians, as suggested by the marriage of his son, Ahab, to Ethbaal's daughter, Jezebel.

When Ahab (874-853 BC) became king he remodeled and expanded the palace toward the west and north. He added a large rectangular tower to the south and a strong casemate wall outside the palace wall. The northern wing contained a court surrounded by rooms. In the court was a large pool (33.4 by 16.6 feet), possibly the pool where his death chariot was washed of

Palace of Omri and Ahab

his blood. At the southern end of the new western court was a large house (37 by 104 feet), divided into three sections of six rooms each.

Archaeologists found nearly two hundred carved ivory plaques, some in fragments, on the floor of Ahab's palace. These probably are related to Ahab's "ivory house" (1 Kings 22:39) and to his "beds of ivory" (Amos 6:4). These carvings portray Egyptian gods and goddesses, revealing the strong influence of Egyptian worship on the court of Israel. Also found was a fragment of alabaster with the name of Pharaoh Osorkon II (870-847 BC).

Ahab was influenced by his wife Jezebel to bring Phoenician Baal worship into Israel. He built a temple to the Phoenician god Baal-Melqart for Jezebel. Thus Phoenician Baal worship was added to the Canaanite Baal worship already in vogue since the days of Jeroboam. During Ahab's reign a severe famine struck Samaria (1 Kings 18:2) due to the drought brought about by Elijah's prayer (1 Kings 17:1-7). This ended with the great confron-

Moabite Stone

tation between Elijah and the prophets of Baal on Mount Carmel near the Phoenician border (1 Kings 18:19-46). Baal worship suffered a great defeat at the hands of Elijah, but it managed to recover with the help of Jezebel.

Ben-Hadad I, king of Syria, besieged Ahab in Samaria, but with the advice of a wise prophet of Yahweh, Ahab defeated Ben-Hadad with a small group of young officers while the Syrian commanders were drunk. After defeating the Syrians again, Ahab made an unwise treaty with Ben-Hadad, for which Elijah reprimanded him (1 Kings 20:1-43).

Later, ca. 853 BC, Ahab and Ben-Hadad joined forces with others to resist the threat of Shalmaneser III of Assyria. They succeeded in stopping him at Qarqar on the Orontes River. That same year, Ahab and Jehoshaphat attempted to recover Ramoth Gilead from the Syrians, but Ahab was killed in the battle. He was returned to Samaria in his chariot, where he was buried. His blood was washed from the chariot at the pool of Samaria (1 Kings 22:1-38).

Ahab's son Ahaziah (853-852 BC) reigned only a short time. In his day, Mesha, king of Moab, rebelled against Ahaziah and successfully freed Moab from the tribute imposed upon them by Ahaziah's grandfather, Omri. King Mesha recorded the victory on the Moabite Stone. Ahaziah's untimely death resulted from a fall through the lattice of his upper room in Samaria (2 Kings 1:2-18).

Ahab's son, Jehoram (852-841 BC), became king and sought the help of Jehoshaphat to regain control of Moab. But King Mesha saved his people from defeat by the dramatic sacrifice of his eldest son on the city wall (2 Kings 3:1-27).

Jehu Dynasty (841-753 BC) Jehu (841-814) killed Jehoram and also Ahaziah the king of Judah, and he sent word to Samaria to defend Jehoram's royal descendants. The leaders of Samaria agreed to surrender and killed Jehoram's seventy sons (2 Kings 10:1-11). So Jehu went to Samaria, killing forty-two members of Ahaziah's family on the way. Once in Samaria, he destroyed the rest

Black Obelisk from Nimrud

of Ahab's descendants (2 Kings 10:12-17). Then he gathered all the Baal worshipers into the temple of Baal and ordered them slaughtered while the temple was destroyed (2 Kings 10:18-36).

In his day, Shalmaneser III, king of Assyria, gained dominance over Syria, Israel, and Phoenicia. Shalmaneser described his victory on his famous Black Obelisk which has a representation of Jehu or a messenger prostrated before him—the only existing representation of an ancient Hebrew king.

When Jehu's son Jehoahaz (814-798 BC) became king, Ben-Hadad II, king of Syria, gained dominion over Israel. But Yahweh delivered Israel (2 Kings 13:1-9), probably by the intervention of the Assyrian emperor Adad-Nimri III who defeated Damascus in 803 BC, bringing relief to Israel.

When Jehoash (798-782 BC), the son of Jehoahaz, became king, he recovered the cities of Israel taken by the Syrians (2 Kings 13:10-24). He also inflicted a serious defeat upon Amaziah, king of Judah, who had attacked Israel (2 Chron. 25:17-24).

The son of Jehoash, Jeroboam II (792-753 BC), reigned as cor-
egent with his father from 792-782 BC. He was one of Israel's
most successful kings, extending Israel's borders to about what
they had been under David and Solomon (2 Kings 14:23-29). He
remodeled the palace, making additions to the western and
northern wings. He added a large round tower at the southwest
corner, and rebuilt some of the walls, strengthening the city's
fortification. The western gate was made with two large towers
defending a narrow entrance approached by a ramp, hewn in
bedrock.

A group of sixty-five potsherd inscriptions was recovered
from the ruins of the royal palace by the 1908-10 expedition, being found in the great west court area of the palace in what may
have been a storeroom. Subsequent excavations made it seem
probable that these and other inscriptions could have come
from the period of Jeroboam II. While the ostraca consisted of
rough records, they were nevertheless the work of skilled writers who employed an ancient Hebrew script much like that of
the Siloam inscription (*ca.* 701 BC).

Each ostracon carried a date, apparently relating to a king's
reign, and recorded the delivery of jars containing wine or clari-
fied olive oil. Some ostraca bore place-names, the identities of
the recipients, and the names of the donors. Others named persons and places without specifying the nature of the commodity. Apart from Shechem, no other place-names are
recognizable, and the presence of the Hebrew word *kerem* "vine-
yard" preceding them might imply that the produce was from
particular areas of the royal estate surrounding Samaria. In that
event the king's tenants had evidently produced the wine and oil
for the royal palace, and had forwarded it to the steward of the
household.

The names on the ostraca are distinctively Hebrew, but some
of them differ from their Old Testament counterparts by carrying the ending *-yau* instead of *-iah*. Thus the name Shemaryau
would have read Shemariah in the Old Testament. Some
scholars have seen *-yau* as a shortened form of the divine name
YHWH, but it could just as easily be an addition to form a "pet
name" or a "nickname," as was done in Amorite and Akkadian.

Israel's
Decline
(752-723 BC)

The declining years of Israel's history were filled with moral decay, political turmoil, and many assassinations. Nearly all of our information comes from the biblical text. The assassin Shallum reigned only one month when he was killed by Menahem, who became king west of the Jordan only (2 Kings 15:13-16). Menahem's son, Pekahiah, reigned only two years when he was killed in Samaria by Pekah the son of Ramaliah (2 Kings 15:23-26).

Pekah (752-732 BC) had reigned east of the Jordan river from Samaria since the death of Shallum. With the overthrow of Pekahiah in 740 BC, he ruled the whole northern kingdom in Samaria (2 Kings 15:27). Pekah aligned with Rezin of Damascus to oppose Assyrian dominance. They tried to force Ahaz, king of Judah, to join them. Ahaz appealed to Tiglath-pileser III for help, against the advice of the prophet Isaiah (Isa. 7:1-12). Israel and Syria attacked Judah, but Tiglath-pileser gave no help. Later Tiglath-pileser made an extensive campaign into the area, putting down the resistance and killing Rezin, but not before Ahaz had suffered great losses (2 Chron. 28:5-15). Tiglath-Pileser recorded this campaign in his "Annals" inscribed on a stone slab discovered at Calah.

Hoshea (732-723 BC), a pro-Assyrian, killed Pekah and reigned in his place. He served as a vassal of Assyria for a while, but soon rebelled and sought support from Egypt. In 724 BC, Shalmaneser V, king of Assyria, invaded Israel, took Hoshea captive, and laid siege against Samaria (2 Kings 17:1-4). After a siege of three years, Samaria fell (2 Kings 17:5-6) in fulfillment of Isaiah's prophecy (Isa. 8:4). According to Thiele, this happened in 723 BC, the last year of Shalmaneser, not the first regnal year of Sargon.

Post-exilic
Samaria

Following the fall of Samaria to the Assyrians, foreigners were imported to repopulate the land under a governor appointed by the Assyrian king. Sargon II (721-705 BC) recorded in his "Annals" that he took 27,290 captives from Samaria at the beginning of his reign, settled other people there, and had Samaria rebuilt better than it was before. These new people assimilated the worship of the God of Israel into their pagan worship (2 Kings 17:24-41).

During the early years of this period a fortress was built upon the ruins of the old Israelite palace, enclosed by a massive wall. The fortress was built from the masonry of the ruined palace and walls. It is possible that the western wall and western gate were reconstructed at that time.

The city continued through the Assyrian period, the Babylonian period, and the Persian period with little archaeological evidence of the city's occupation. Historic records suggest that the city was occupied at least some of that time. For example, in the days of Artaxerxes Longimanus, Rehum, the commander at Samaria, wrote an accusation against the Jews to stop them from building Jerusalem. Artaxerxes replied with an order to make them cease, which Rehum did by force (Ezra 4:7-24). Shortly afterward, Nehemiah received permission from Artaxerxes to go to Jerusalem to rebuild the city and its walls (Neh. 2:1-10). Sanballat, the governor of Samaria, opposed Nehemiah's work, but the Jews armed themselves and continued the construction (Neh. 4:10-23) and eventually finished the wall (Neh. 6:15-19).

Archaeologists also found a letter in Egypt, written in Aramaic about 410 BC from the governors of Judah and Samaria to the Jews of Elephantine. The letter instructed them to rebuild "the house of offering of the god of Heaven" that had been "destroyed by that wretch Vidaranag in the year 14 of King Darius."

Greco-Roman Samaria In 332 BC Alexander the Great attacked and defeated Samaria when he conquered Palestine. Then Samaria was strengthened into a large fortification. Much reconstruction was done on the walls, and they were strengthened by a number of strong towers. The western gate was rebuilt with a much smaller tower. The houses were arranged in groups surrounded by narrow streets. Some houses had cisterns and some had drainage systems. Some buildings appeared to have been shops with large ovens and other evidence of craft activity. North of the palace, a temple was built for the worship of the goddess Isis.

A major change in the city's defense took place about the middle of the second century BC. A thick fort wall was constructed, probably as a defense against the Maccabees. John Hyrcanus (*ca.* 107 BC), the high priest in Jerusalem, attacked Samaria with a severe siege. He dug a ditch and built a double wall around the city. The Samarians tried to get help from allies, but all attempts failed. Hyrcanus made a large breach in the thick fort wall and took the city after a year's siege. According to Josephus, he entirely demolished the city, including the Temple of Isis, leaving no trace; and he made slaves of its inhabitants.

In 63 BC the Roman general, Pompey, captured Jerusalem and restored Samaria to the Jews, and they began to reoccupy the city. About 55 BC the governor, Gabinius, rebuilt the city walls. In gratitude the citizens changed the name of the city, naming it after him.

In 38 BC Herod the Great moved his family to Samaria for safety. A few years later the Roman emperor, Augustus, gave Samaria to him. Herod undertook extensive reconstruction of the city that made it the largest and most magnificent to that time. He rebuilt the walls of the city in beautiful fashion, expanding the city to enclose about 160 acres. In honor of Augustus, Herod changed the name of the city to Sebaste (the Greek name of Augustus), although the Jews continued to call it Samaria.

On the highest point of the hill, Herod built a large temple in honor of Augustus. On the terrace north of the temple was a large open court with a broad flight of stairs leading up to the temple. Immediately behind the temple on the south was an apsidal building, with a great hall in the center and a semicircular apse at the south end. West of the temple was a large house with a central court. In the northeast quarter of the city, a large stadium was built in Doric style, measuring about 750 by 200 feet, with rows of columns on three sides.

This magnificent city with its pagan temple stood in contrast to Jerusalem with its beautiful temple to the God of Israel, also remodeled and expanded by Herod. This is the Samaria Jesus visited, the place where Philip the evangelist preached (Acts 8:4-8), the home of Simon Magus (Acts 8:9-25), and the traditional site of John the Baptist's tomb.

When the Jews revolted in AD 66, Sebaste was captured and burned by the rebels. But during the reign of the Roman emperor, Severus (AD 193-211), the city reached its crowning glory. The city was renovated and Severus made the city a *colonia*. The temple to Augustus was rebuilt and expanded, a new portico was added, and the staircase was reconstructed. On the eastern terraces the city forum was built, enclosed with a colonnade and with a basilica at its western end.

When Christianity became the official religion of the Roman empire, the pagan temples of Sebaste fell into disuse, and the forum basilica was converted into a cathedral. In 634, the Arabs conquered the city and it fell into ruins. Eventually the city was covered with soil so that the area could be used for agriculture. This fulfilled the prophecy of Micah:

For further information on Samaria see:

Crowfoot, J. W. and G. M. Crowfoot. *Early Ivories from Samaria* (1938).

Crowfoot, J. W., K. M. Kenyon, and E. L. Sukenik. *The Buildings at Samaria* (1942).

Crowfoot, J. W., G. M. Crowfoot, and K. M. Kenyon. *The Objects from Samaria* (1957).

Jack, J. W. *Samaria in Ahab's Time: Harvard Excavations and Their Results* (1929).

Reisner, G. A., C. S. Fisher, and D. G. Lyon. *Harvard Excavations at Samaria 1908-1910*. 2 Vols. (1924).

Wright, G. E. "Israelite Samaria and Iron Age Chronology." *Bulletin of American Schools of Oriental Research* 15 (1959), 13-29.

J. D. P.

CHAPTER TWENTY-TWO

SEVEN CITIES OF ASIA MINOR

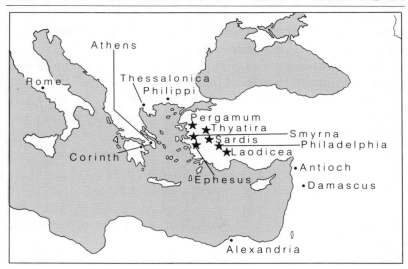

The circumstances of John's exile on Patmos—"for the word of God and the testimony of Jesus"—are not explained in Rev. 1:9. There are good grounds for accepting the traditional view that he was the victim of persecution in the last years of the emperor Domitian (AD 81-96). The term "persecution" may however cover diverse kinds of official or unofficial pressure. It may be that the sufferings of the churches in the cities of Asia were initiated not so much by a formal and deliberate assault upon the faith as by the progressive outworking in the official policy of pressures, the incidence of which can in part be traced in the local and particular situations.

"Asia" here is to be understood of the Roman province of "proconsular Asia" in the west of the land later called Asia Minor. It included some of the Aegean islands and probably Patmos within its bounds. John's exile may then have been the work not of the emperor in person but of the local proconsul, who had wide discretion in the apportionment of penalties and may have used an isolated island within his jursidiction as a place of deportation.

John, whether the apostle or a namesake, clearly had an intimate knowledge of the cities of Asia and their churches. In his exile, perhaps under the traumatic impact of hard labor on an aged body, his vision responded to his urgent meditation and prayer for these churches, and his application to them of Old Testament scriptures that fitted the particularities of their needs. This was the background of ecstatic experience. It means that the local circumstances of the churches are often of great significance for the interpretation of the letters.

Sir William Ramsay first offered the very important observation that the seven cities addressed lie in order on a circular route round the inner, urbanized territories of the province, and that they probably served as postal centers for the churches of the province as a whole. They may even have had this function since the time of Paul. If Ephesians was a circular letter, as often thought, it may have followed a similar path of distribution from its primary destination in Ephesus. So a messenger from Patmos landed at Ephesus, traveled north through Smyrna to Pergamum, and thence southeast through the other four cities, leaving a copy of the book in each for secondary circulation in its district. The number "seven" is of course constantly used in the symbolism of the book of Revelation, but this fact should not be allowed to obscure the circumstance that the book is addressed to seven actual churches in cities ideally placed to serve as the distribution points. The spiritual character of each church reflected its response to its individual environment. Church and city are sometimes closely identified. The vision of Christ in Revelation 1 presents him with the attributes uniquely able to overcome their individual disabilities, and in the end the New

Jerusalem shows that victory complete in the perfect city. Together the seven letters give a penetrating analysis of the various strengths and weaknesses of the churches, a paradigm to apply thoughtfully to modern situations.

Ephesus   Ephesus was a city of great antiquity, traditionally believed to have been founded by Ionian Greeks, but centered upon the shrine of the native goddess identified with the Greek Artemis or Roman Diana; originally here an oriental goddess of fertility, represented by a many-breasted image and symbolized by such emblems of wild nature as the queen bee and the palm tree.

Ephesus suffered many vicissitudes in its early history, and destruction by successive conquerors. It is remarkable that these crises occasioned successive changes of site, often associated with periods of alternating Greek and Anatolian ascendancy. Thus from the time of Croesus of Lydia (560 BC) the city clustered near the great temple of Artemis that he built, but in 287 BC the dynast Lysimachus used the flooding of that low-lying site to impel the population to migrate to his new Ephesus, focusing on the harbor over a mile distant. This latter move laid the foundation for the commercial prosperity of Ephesus in Hellenistic and Roman times, when it became one of the great cities of the world, with a population probably exceeding a quarter of a million. Its fame then rested both on its commerce and on the continuing influence of the cult of its goddess. The Hellenistic Temple of Artemis was one of the seven wonders of the world. As the great cosmopolitan city of Roman Asia, Ephesus was the leading city of the province, though Pergamum was, at least initially, the actual seat of the governor. The one serious problem that afflicted Ephesus was the progressive silting of its harbor by the river Cayster, threatening eventually to block its access to the sea. Today the coastline has retreated six miles, and the ruins of the city are stranded inland.

The remains of Ephesus are now the most impressive in Asia Minor. The city is remarkably well preserved, and one can walk

Theater next to Marble street

Marble street at Ephesus

through streets between the ruins of splendid buildings, often reconstructed by the Austrian excavators. The many stone-cut inscriptions, often surviving *in situ*, give vivid insight into details of the city's life, of industrial disputes, of the proud titles of the city, which indulged in bitter rivalry with Smyrna and Pergamum for precedence, and even the names of people contemporary with the New Testament, among which can be seen those of men named Tyrannus and Trophimus (compare Acts 19:9; 21:29). Many of these inscriptions refer to the *grammateus* (town clerk), the chief, annually-elected executive official of the city, whose title and function Luke renders so accurately in Acts 19:35ff.

The local force of the imagery of Revelation is less striking for this cosmopolitan city than for most of the others. Ephesus was brilliantly successful but threatened ultimately with choking by silt. Its church was orthodox and flourishing, but had lost is "first love." It is called urgently and repeatedly to repentance, on pain of being "moved," perhaps to lose its great opportunities, to fall under the sway of pagan cult in a time of change. The great temple offered asylum for the unrepentant criminal about the sacred tree-shrine of the goddess. The true "tree of life" recalls the cross of Christ as the refuge of the repentant.

Agora at Ephesus

Agora at Smyrna

Ephesus today is deserted, and is represented only by the small Turkish town of Selcuk, next to the hill of Ayasoluk near the temple.

Smyrna Smyrna has now taken over the former role of Ephesus as the great emporium of the west coast. As Turkish Izmir it is the third largest city in Turkey and the largest in Asia Minor until overtaken by the even faster growth of the new capital Ankara. It stretches many miles around the head of a deep gulf, forty miles north of Ephesus.

Smyrna was another early Greek colony, which rose to pride and prosperity before 600 BC. About that time it was overthrown by Alyattes, king of Lydia in the hinterland. The city of that period was situated on a small island or peninsula at the head of the gulf, now a low hill a half mile inland in the modern suburb of Bayrakli. Excavations at this Old Smyrna (Eski Izmir) have revealed the remains of the actual siege-engines that were used in its capture. In his determination to prevent the resurgence of this troublesome city Alyattes, according to the geographer Strabo, destroyed its civic identity by dispersing its

—— 239 ——

surviving inhabitants to live in small villages. Smyrna was then in eclipse for nearly four centuries until the successors of Alexander the Great refounded it on the slopes of the conical hill of Pagus about two miles south of the old site. The new city became famous for its beauty, proud of being the city which had "died and lived again." The symmetrical view of the hill adorned with fine buildings and rising to a crown of battlements above the sea suggested images like that of a garlanded statue. The crown, or wreath, symbolic of victory or festivity, became a constant theme of its coins and monuments.

Christ appeals to the church in Smyrna as the one who suffered, died, and lived again. The very name "Smyrna" is identical with the ordinary Greek word for "myrrh," the word used of the wise men's gift in Matthew 2:11. That is not a true etymology, but it was seen as significant, and the symbolism of myrrh, of suffering, death, burial, and resurrection, seemed especially appropriate to the city. The church too was marked by suffering. It must endure "faithful unto death." Its sufferings are brief when its Lord controls the issues of eternity. He will bestow the victor's "crown" of life.

Turkish Izmir (Smyrna)

The most famous early Christian in Smyrna was Polycarp, who may have been a young man in the community that first received this letter, and his life aptly illustrates it. Many years later as a very old man he was burned for his faith here in Smyrna. In the stadium on Pagus, where athletes were accustomed to compete for a crown of leaves that faded, he won a victory through death into life.

Pergamum   Pergamum is represented today by the relatively small town of Bergama at the foot of the dominating mountain acropolis of the ancient city. Pergamum boasted none of the great antiquity of the two previous cities. It became a stronghold of Lysimachus, until his commander Philetaerus rebelled and placed himself under the protection of the rival Seleucid kingdom. Philetaerus' successors Eumenes I, Attalus I (241-197 BC, who took the titles "king" and *Soter*, "savior," after defeating the Gauls), Eumenes II, and Attalus II extended his principality until it had the appearance of a major power, but on sufferance of the true and rising world-power of Rome. Attalus III, the last of the Attalids, finally bequeathed his kingdom to Rome in 133 BC, and it became the Roman province of Asia.

The kings had developed national cults of the gods Zeus, Athena, Dionysus, and Asclepius, and had themselves accepted divine honors. They built a great sculptured altar of Zeus Soter, but their characteristic god was Asclepius Soter, the god of healing, whose emblem of the serpent has attached itself to later medicine, but which was for the Christians the symbol of Satan. While these cults are vividly illustrative of the religious background of the city, the crucial issue was the primacy of Pergamum in emperor worship. The temple of Rome and Augustus established here in 29 BC was the first such temple officially sanctioned. The Christians in Pergamum faced a stark choice between Christ and Caesar, where Caesar claimed such titles as "Lord" and "Savior." Under Domitian the imperial cult was rigorously enforced except among Jews who paid a tax as the price of exemption. Pergamum was the seat of Roman power in Asia, where the proconsul wielded the "power of the sword."

Altar of Zeus at Pergamum

Pergamum remains a dramatically impressive site: the wind-swept mountain of dark granite, with its rock-cut terraces of magnificent public buildings and honorific inscriptions engraved incongruously on white marble, the serpent motifs of its art, the famous library whose use of sheeps' skins as a writing material gave the city's name to "parchment," and the great Asclepius shrine and amphitheater below the hill.

The letter to Pergamum is a solemn warning against compromise under pressure, such as seems to have been advocated by the Nicolaitans. The final appeal is rich in symbolism. The idea of the inscribed "white stone" (strictly "pebble" or "token") may have evoked various associations. It was the pledge of acquittal and new relationship with Christ, who held the true ultimate authority to judge.

Thyatira Six of the seven cities are in different ways historically or scenically remarkable. Thyatira, now called Akhisar, is an unremarkable industrial town of forty thousand people on a level site in a broad valley. It had had a continuous history of occupation, but there are few visible antiquities, and it has not been excavated, for the modern town covers it. Yet the church here received the longest and most difficult of the seven letters.

In Attalid times Thyatira was a military outpost of the kingdom of Pergamum, though extremely vulnerable. Inscriptions of the Roman period attest the presence of an unusually large number of influential trade-guilds, including notably the dyers (compare Acts 16:14). Some of the same trades are practiced in the modern town, and the use of the vegetable dye "Turkey red" is attested from within the last hundred years.

The problem for the Christian in Thyatira touched his everyday working life. At Pergamum his life was at stake; here his livelihood. The guilds were integrated into the structure of pagan society and involved idolatry and immorality, but it may have seemed impossible to practice a trade without belonging to a guild. "Jezebel" was apparently a symbolic name for a woman in the church who advocated membership in the circumstances, and deployed plausible arguments for bowing to the necessity of compromise. But Christ speaks here as the true patron of the craftsman in his daily work, his feet clad in the finest brass like that made in Thyatira.

Sardis   Thirty miles southeast of Thyatira rise the theatrical mountain pinnacles of Sardis, glowing an unnatural orange in the morning sun. The ancient citadel of Sardis became the capital of the kings of Lydia, and the last of their number, Croesus (560-46 BC), the son of Alyattes, became proverbial for wealth and success. The little river Pactolus was streamed for gold, and the first money was minted here. But Croesus became the classic case of pride before a fall. Herodotus tells the traditional story. Each of his boasted resources in turn failed him in war with Persia, until he found himself blockaded in his acropolis by Cyrus the Persian. But to capture the citadel of Sardis was proverbially impossible. The mountain was composed of a crumbling earthen conglomerate, breaking into precipices and pinnacles that no enemy could climb. Yet Sardis fell, for nobody was on guard when Cyrus came.

The Roman city of Sardis lay below the mountain. It was still prosperous, but its greatness belonged to the distant past. Sardis

—— 243 ——

had been an important center of the Jewish dispersion since early times, and the third-century AD synagogue, now reconstructed, is the most opulent known from the ancient world, and testifies to a considerable integration of the Jewish community into the gentile city.

The church in Sardis had a reputation for being alive but was dead. Its apparent success had been won at the cost of assimilation to its pagan environment, and would be exposed as a sham in time of crisis. Christ calls the negligent to watch for his coming. Then those few in Sardis who had been alert, waiting, and uncorrupted should walk with him in the white robes of purity and victory in his triumphal procession.

Roman gym at Sardis

Temple of Artemis

The goddess Diana (Artemis)

Philadelphia

The city and the church of Sardis seemed strong and was found weak; Philadelphia seemed weak and proved strong in time of testing. Philadelphia was a small town, sloping down from a low, three-peaked hill to the level plain. It was an Attalid foundation, and its name commemorated the "brotherly love" of the brothers Eumenes II and Attalus II. When Eumenes offended the Romans, they transferred their favor to Attalus, and they would have installed him as king in his brother's place if not frustrated by his loyal refusal. Attalus won the title "Philadelphus" (loving his brother), and the city was named after him. He succeeded to the kingship only on his brother's death in 159 BC.

Philadelphia stood on fertile, volcanic soil as an outpost of the later, enlarged Attalid kingdom. Ramsay called it the "missionary city," commanding the routes to the Phrygian hinterland. In AD 17, with other cities of Asia, it was destroyed in a great earthquake. Philadelphia suffered repeated later tremors. Strabo, a contemporary, describes it as a city "full of earthquakes," where people continued living in the fields. He expresses amazement that they persisted there at all.

The church in Philadelphia had "little strength." It struggled to survive in a dangerous and impoverished environment. It faced persecution, here apparently initiated (as at Smyrna) from the Jewish rather than the pagan side, meeting rejection and

—— 245 ——

denunication from those who officially represented the people of God in the eyes of Roman authority. The letter expresses Christ's warmest love for the weak who abide at the post of danger. A great vision is held before them: the heavenly city is for those who dwell in a place of trembling ruins, the assurance of strength and stability for those who then "shall no more go outside."

Philadelphia remained a stronghold of Christianity in Asia Minor even after other greater cities had fallen to the Muslim Turks. The modern town, the Turkish Alasehir, covers the old and has grown beyond the remnants of the square enclosure of its Byzantine walls. It was near the epicenter of an earthquake in 1969.

Laodicea   The valley of the river Lycus, sixty-five miles southeast of Philadelphia, contained three New Testament cities: Laodicea and Hierapolis are mentioned together in Paul's letter to Colossae (Col. 4:13). Laodicea was founded by the Seleucids of Syria in the third century BC, and it grew to affluence as a commercial city at a major crossroads of the country. It had one serious disadvantage; namely the lack of good drinking wa-

City gate at Laodicea

Byzantine church at Laodicea

ter, for nearly all the many streams of the district are from hot springs, clouded with calcareous and other impurities.

The Roman historian Tacitus tells that when Laodicea, too, was destroyed by earthquake in AD 60, the people recovered "by their own resources," without the customary Roman help. Individual citizens donated a stadium and other splendid buildings from their private wealth. It is interesting to trace the sources of their prosperity. Laodicea was a great banking center, but Christ counsels the church to buy "gold" of him; it made woolen garments from a locally developed breed of "black" sheep, but he will provide "white clothing"; it was a medical center specializing in ophthalmology, which evidently made money from the sale of eye ointments, but they need his "eyesalve" to give them spiritual sight.

The most striking image in this letter is that of being "lukewarm." With characteristic enterprise, the Laodiceans had attempted to remedy the badness of their water by bringing a supply through an aqueduct, the stone pipes of which are preserved on the south side of the site. The rings of lime deposit inside the pipes testify plainly after nineteen hundred years to the fact that this water too was warm and so impure that it must have made the traveler vomit. Hierapolis had hot medicinal waters forming the unique petrifying cascades of Pamukkale, one of the natural wonders of the world. Colossae, alone in the valley, had pure, cold, perennial water. The waters of Laodicea were a man-made substitute, inadequate on both counts. The significance of "lukewarm" may be "ineffective" rather than "half-hearted."

Christ turns finally at Laodicea in loving appeal to the individual. Though a rich freedman had donated a three-arched, turreted gate from his own resources and the city could exclude the unwanted stranger, he pleads with the individual who will open the door.

The three cities today are all deserted, replaced by the large town of Denizli, but the scenic splendour of Hierapolis had made its cliffs a famous tourist resort.

For further information on the Seven Cities of Asia see:

Akurgal, E. *Ancient Civilizations and Ruins of Turkey* (1973 ed.).
Cadoux, C. J. *Ancient Smyrna* (1938).
Jones, A. H. M. *Cities of the Eastern Roman Provinces* (1971 ed.).
Magie, S. *Roman Rule in Asia Minor.* 2 vols. (1950).
Ramsey, W. M. *The Letters to the Seven Churches of Asia* (1904).

C. J. H.

THEBES

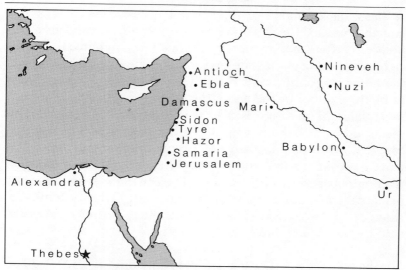

Located on the banks of the Nile River approximately four hundred miles south of Cairo is Luxor, or Thebes as it was known to the Greeks. The name Luxor is derived from the Arabic *El-uqsur*, meaning "the castles" due to the many monuments that have survived from ancient times. There is uncertainty as to exactly why the Greeks referred to this site after the name of the leading city in Boeotia. It has been suggested that the name of Luxor Temple, *t'ipt*, might have sounded close enough to Grecian "Thebes" that a correlation could be made.

Name
The ancient name of Thebes is *w'st*, which applied both to the nome (district) as well as to the city that served as the seat of government. The Theban nome measured approximately twenty miles in length on both banks of the Nile. To this day, reference is made to East Bank and West Bank Thebes. The nome consisted of four major cult centers with surrounding settlements; these include Armant, Tod, Medamud, and Thebes itself. Reckoning from the south, Waset was the fourth Upper Egyptian nome. The first nome began at the First Cataract which is located at the modern city of Aswan, or biblical Syene (Ezek. 29:10, 30:6).

Waset as the name of the nome is attested as early as the Fourth Dynasty (*ca.* 2490-472 BC) on a triad of Menkaure (the builder of the smallest of the famous Giza pyramids). To the right of the king stands the personified figure of the nome with the nome standard on his head. This nome standard continues to be the symbol of the nome throughout its history. The phonetic value of this sign is *w's*, which means "dominion." This seems to be a foreshadowing of the future greatness of this city, for from it was to come some of Egypt's greatest monarchs. It is from the root *w's* that the name *w'st* is derived (the *t* indicates the feminine gender of the word). The earliest record of the city being called Waset dates back to the Sixth Dynasty tombs located on the West Bank. In the mythology however, Waset is said to have come into being at creation.

Tombs and Temples
During the Old Kingdom (*ca.* 2600-2150 BC) Thebes played no significant role in the political or religious picture of Egypt. In fact, Thebes during the Old Kingdom has been described as "an insignificant village." There are Sixth Dynasty tombs of the Theban monarchs located in western Thebes, which served as the necropolis for the provincial capital for most of its history. These tombs were cut into the rock in an area called Khokha in Arabic and is situated less than a mile east of Deir el-Bahri. Although Montu, the Hawk-headed war god,

was the patron deity in the Theban nome, the god Amun is also mentioned in these texts. Virtually nothing can be said about the site of Thebes, probably because much of the ancient town is covered by Luxor. No known temples have survived from the Old Kingdom except that there may have been a brick chapel built by Userkaef (Fifth Dynasty) at Tod. With the demise of the Old Kingdom, the primary capital of which was Memphis at the base of the delta, Egypt fell into its first "dark age" known as the First Intermediate period. According to the Manethonian tradition, the Ninth and Tenth Dynasties' seat of power was located at Heracleopolis, about fifty miles south of Memphis. The rise of the Heracleopolitan kings was followed by the emergence of Thebes, as political rivalry developed, which led to decades of civil war between the two. This general period of turmoil is recalled in some of Egypt's finest literature which came out of this period or just after. Meryibre Khety I, one of the Heracleopolitan kings, confesses to his son in the so called "Wisdom for Merikare" that his troops had attacked the southland and had defiled the sacred area of Alydos in the process.

This incursion of the northern kings took them just seventy-five miles north of the Thebaid. The Theban chieftains, of course, grew concerned with these developments and led a series of campaigns to remove the invaders. Wah-Ankh Intef II (*ca.* 2100-2070 BC) records that he succeeded in gaining control of upper Egypt as far north as the tenth nome, which included the liberation of Abydos.

But it was left to Montuhotep Nebhepetre to complete the task of terminating the Heracleopolitan supremacy. According to the Turin Canon of Egyptian kings, Montuhotep reigned fifty-one years, *ca.* 2060-2010 BC. The process of Egypt's reunification can be traced in the changing Horus names of Montuhotep. Initially his name was "Making the Heart of the Two Lands Live." Some time before his thirty-ninth year he took the name "Lord of the White Crown," which undoubtedly signaled that he had gained control as far north as Memphis (known as the "Balance of the Two Lands") or Upper Egypt. By his thirty-ninth year a third name appears, suggesting that he had succeeded in bringing all

Temple of Queen Hatshepsut

of Egypt under the kingship of Thebes, for he called himelf "Uniter of the Two Lands."

The reunification of Egypt involved military activity as witnessed in some of the fragmentary reliefs of Montuhotep's mortuary temple at Deir el-Bahri, next to the renowned temple of queen Hatshepsut, in western Thebes. Further evidence of military activity during this period was the gruesome discovery of a common tomb containing sixty slain soldiers of Montuhotep. The corpses were riddled with arrows and other signs of wounds that were inflicted by weapons. The cost was dear, but for the first time, Thebes was the capital of Egypt, and Montu, its patron deity was "pacified" (Montuhotep means "Montu is pacified").

The unification of Egypt ushered in the Middle Kingdom. In just a matter of decades Egypt was to be ruled by a new dynasty. The last Montuhotep apparently died without a successor, and his vizier, Amenemhet, acceded to the throne, establishing Egypt's Twelfth Dynasty (1991-1786 BC). Apparently for political reasons, Amenemhet moved the capital to a new site called Itjtawy "Seizer of the Two Lands" or modern Lisht. It might have been thought that Egypt could be better governed from this neutral spot, twenty miles south of Memphis, rather than favoring

Thebes or the old northern capital Memphis. But Thebes was by no means deserted by these kings, for the earliest evidence of building activity at Karnak temple can be traced to the outset of the Twelfth Dynasty.

Karnak temple is so named because of the village that now surrounds the complex. In Egyptian this temple is known as *ipt swt* "most select of places." A stone altar found at Karnak bearing the name of Amenemhet I is the oldest object found to date and may reflect the beginnings of what was to become the largest temple complex in Egypt. The earliest temple to have survived is the so-called "White Chapel" of Senusret I (1961-28 BC), which was actually found in the Third Pylon, built by Amenhotep III (*ca.* 1419-1382).

The reuse of earlier blocks by later kings may reflect the desire to transfer the sacredness of the previous structure to the new one or to establish a continuity in kingship. Apparently the new Dynasty had a special preference for Amun, for Amun is a central figure in the "White Chapel," as is Re the sun-god, and Amun-Re the coalescence of the two. The name Amenemhet means "Amun is foremost." From this point Thebes would be

Temple of Amun at Karnak

known as the cultic center of Amun-Re, which might be considered the imperial god during the Eighteenth and Nineteenth Dynasties (1570-1225 BC) when nearly every king made some sort of contribution to the complex. Thus it became ideologically and economically the most important temple establishment in the whole of Egypt.

Undoubtedly it was the importance of the temple and Amun-Re that led to Thebes being called *niwt imn* "City of Amun" and *iwnw rsy* "Southern Heliopolis," for Heliopolis was perhaps the most important cult center in Egypt.

With the fall of the Twelfth Dynasty Egypt fell into the Second Intermediate Period, characterized by the breakdown of centralized authority, which permitted the so called *Hyksos* ("foreign rulers") kings to gain control of the Delta. From the end of the Hyksos period, King Kamose informs us that Apophis, the Hyksos king, controlled Egypt as far south as Cusae (twenty-five miles north of Assiut).

The Theban kings from the end of the Seventeenth Dynasty began the process of regaining control of middle Egypt. Seqenere Tao's mummy reveals wounds made by an arrow and a battle-axe. This has led to the suggestion that he initiated the liberation of Egypt and lost his life in the process. Kamose, the succeeding king, also launched campaigns which are recorded in his stela that was discovered at the Karnak temple. He claims to have plundered Avaris, the Hyksos capital. His accomplishment seems dubious since the third of these kings, Ahmose, attacked Avaris. Ahmose pursued the Hyksos to Palestine, thus ridding Egypt of these "foreign rulers" and inaugurating the New Kingdom or Empire period, and founding the Eighteenth Dynasty.

The New Kingdom was the period of Thebes' greatest prosperity and growth. Amun-Re, the imperial god of Karnak, is credited with giving victories to the pharaohs who extended Egypt's sphere of influence beyond the Euphrates. The campaigns into Western Asia and Nubia brought great wealth to Egypt, and many a thankful king built temples and erected stelas in commemoration of his accomplishments. The temple of

Amun at Karnak benefited especially. Most of the Eighteenth Dynasty kings left their mark at Karnak in the form of pylons, chapels, massive temples, statues, and even a sacred lake. Karnak is actually divided into four major sections. The largest area, and most central, is the precinct of Amun with its renowned hypostyle hall built by Horemheb, Seti I, and Ramses II. To the north of the temenos wall around the Amun precinct is the temple of Montu, the early Theban god, which was apparently founded by Thutmose I (*ca.* 1508-04 BC). To the south is the Mut complex begun by Hatshepsut (*ca.* 1504-1481 BC). Excavations from 1975 to the present at the east of the Amun complex have revealed the original location of Akhenaton's several temples to Aton. These were violently destroyed and most of the blocks removed by Horemhab at the close of the Amarna age (*ca.* 1350-20 BC).

While Karnak enjoyed its greatest period of wealth and growth during the New Kingdom, it continued to be a place where kings built, made additions, decorated, and left their statues all the way through Ptolemaic times and into the Roman period.

The second major temple complex in eastern Thebes is Luxor temple, just over a mile south of Karnak. Built by Amenhotep III, Tutankhamun, and Ramses II, *ipt rsyt* or "the southern harim," served primarily for the celebration of the Opet festival, when the bark of Amun-Re would fare up stream bringing the cult image of Amun to visit the "southern harim" where his consort resided.

During the New Kingdom, West Bank Thebes took on a new significance. Through most of Egyptian history, the Royal necropoli were located in the vicinity of Memphis. But these Theban kings chose to be buried in their own nome. The Seventeenth Dynasty kings had been buried in the area south of Montuhotep's mortuary complex at Deir el-Bahri. Beginning with Thutmose I, the Valley of the Kings served as the royal necropolis for the remainder of the New Kingdom.

Each king had a mortuary temple built near the desert's edge of Western Thebes. Most of these were destroyed in antiquity and the blocks reused by later kings. Only the temples of Hatshepsut, Ramses II, and Ramses III have survived. The famous "Colossi of Memnon," actually statues of Amenhotep III, stand at what was originally the entrance to his mortuary temple. The blocks of the superstructure were completely removed.

Thebes and the Bible   Despite the importance of Thebes in Egyptian history, it has little prominence in the Old Testament. When the Israelites settled in Egypt (Gen. 47:6, 11), they were located in the Delta. During the reigns of the Israelite kings, Egypt's power base was Memphis, Tanis (biblical Zoan), and Sais. But Thebes remained influential in Egypt, and Amun-Re's significance was not diminished. This is why Thebes is mentioned several times by the prophets Nahum, Jeremiah, and Ezekiel.

In his oracle against Nineveh, Nahum (3:8) asks, "Are you better than Thebes that sat by the Nile with water around her, her rampart a sea, and water her wall?" This statement undoubtedly refers to the sack of Thebes in 663 BC at the hands of the Assyrian king, Ashurbanipal. This represents the first time in its nearly two thousand year history that Thebes had fallen to a foreign foe. If Thebes, which was proud of its legacy and impregnability, could have been destroyed, then surely Nineveh could likewise be despoiled. Thebes, in the Hebrew text, is written as *no' 'amon*, which means "city of Amun." This is probably a shortened form of the expression "Waset City of Amun." But "City of Amun" was a well-known designation for Thebes in the New Kingdom.

Jeremiah 46:25 (LXX 26:25) contains a denunciation of Thebes in which God says, "I am bringing punishment upon Amon in Thebes." The Greek renders this as "I will avenge Ammon her son." Apparently the LXX translators understood the Hebrew *amon bno'* as *'amon bnah*. (The *b* in the Hebrew or *m* for *min* as actually preserved in the manuscripts was undoubtedly in the text used by the LXX translators.) The Greek understanding does not make sense in the context. Clearly Amun of Thebes is in the mind of the writer.

Ezekiel 30:14, 16 refer to Thebes by simply writing *no'*. This usage was known as early as the Eighteenth Dynasty, and was perhaps a more abbreviated form for "Waset City of Amun." In the Assyrian texts of the Seventh century, they refer to Thebes as *Ni-i'*. The Hebrew and Assyrian words are clearly Egyptian *Niw(t)*. The *t* was the feminine element which was not pronounced in Late Egyptian. *Ne* is the survival of this word in Coptic. The LXX translates *no'* as Diospolis, "City of Zeus," for they equate Amun with Zeus their chief god.

Even though Thebes does not directly influence written Old Testament history a great deal, its importance to Egypt was so great that indirectly it played a significant role in the events of the Hebrew peoples, for there was much contact between Egypt and Israel from Genesis onward.

For further information on Thebes see:

Baines, J. and J. Malek. *Atlas of Ancient Egypt* (1980).
Gardiner, A. H. *Egypt of the Pharaohs* (1961).
Nims, C. F. *Thebes of the Pharaohs* (1965).
Steindorff, G. and K. Seele, *When Egypt Ruled the East* (1942).
Winlock, H. E. *The Rise and Fall of the Middle Kingdom in Thebes* (1947).

J. K. H.

THESSALONICA

For the contemporary reader of the Bible, Thessalonica is important because of its connection with the apostle Paul: there he "preached the gospel of God" (1 Thess. 2:9) as part of his so-called second missionary journey, and to the church that resulted from his labors he addressed the two letters now contained in the New Testament canon. But from a first-century Greco-Roman perspective (as in keeping with Paul's apparent strategy of concentrating on significant urban centers), Thessalonica was an important city in its own right.

**Origin and
Location**
According to the geographer Strabo, the city owes its origin to the Macedonian king Cassander, who was one of the successors of Alexander the Great. Probably in the interests of administrative efficiency, he followed a policy of amalgamating clusters of neighboring villages into single cities established on the Greek city-state model. Thessalonica, founded in 316 or 315 BC and named after Cassander's wife (who also happened to be Alexander's half-sister), was the most elaborate of these amalgamations, incorporating as it did the inhabitants of some twenty-six villages.

The geographical setting of the new city ensured a quick rise to prominence. Centrally located at the head of the Thermaic Gulf, on or near the site of the earlier village of Thermē (one of the twenty-six), it was easily accessible from all parts of Macedonia. This, together with its excellent natural harbor, made it ideally suited as a channel for the growing trade and travel between Macedonia and the new world of the Hellenistic east that followed in the wake of Alexander's conquests. By the onset of Roman rule in 168 BC, Thessalonica was a flourishing commercial center, spreading out in the shape of an amphitheater on the slopes surrounding the bay, secure behind sturdy walls and an impregnable acropolis, and boasting all the edifices and institutions (agora, hippodrome, gymnasium, temples) characteristic of a thriving Hellenistic city.

**Socio-economic
Structures**
With the arrival of the Romans, the prominence of the city was enhanced, for in addition to its continuing economic prosperity, it came to possess political and strategic importance as well. After defeating the Macedonian king Perseus in 168 BC, Rome, following a policy of divide-and-rule, organized Macedonia into four self-governing districts, with Thessalonica the capital of the second of these. After quelling a Macedonian uprising in 149 BC, Rome decided that firmer control of the territory was necessary. Macedonia was made a province with Thessalonica as its capital. A military highway, the *Via Egnatia*, was built across the province, from Apollonia and

Dyrrhachium on the Adriatic coast to Thessalonica on the Aegean. This highway not only allowed Rome to consolidate its hold on the new province but also, especially when it was extended to Philippi/Neapolis and later to Byzantium, provided a vital line of communication with the provinces to the east, particularly in the winter when navigation was impossible.

Because of its strategic position on the *Via Egnatia*, Thessalonica could not avoid being affected during periods of conflict. It suffered greatly during the Mithridatic and civil wars, and it would have suffered even more if Brutus had defeated Antony and Octavian. Because of the city's support for the latter, Brutus had promised his troops that they could plunder it if they were victorious in battle. But for the most part, and especially in the era of the empire, Thessalonica flourished under Roman rule. Roman docks were built in the harbor to facilitate the ever-increasing flow of people and goods to and from the Mediterranean east. In addition to the *Via Egnatia*, the city found itself as the terminus for another military and commercial land route, this time to the north, as Roman sovereignty began to expand up to the Danube and beyond. It is not surprising, then, that Strabo could describe Thessalonica at the end of the first century BC as the most populous city in Macedonia.

In this period Thessalonica also enjoyed the status of a "free city," a rare honor shared, according to Pliny, with only a handful of other Macedonian cities. Numismatic evidence suggests that this honor was bestowed by Antony and Octavian in gratitude for the city's support during the civil war that followed Julius Caesar's death. The privileges pertaining to such a status varied somewhat, but generally they included freedom from taxation and the billeting of Roman troops, the right to strike coins and to levy taxes, and the right to self-government according to ancestral customs. With respect to this last item, Thessalonica's status meant that it was free to conduct its internal affairs according to the democratic pattern characteristic of the Greek *polis*: an assembly (*ekklēsia*) of all citizens, in which, at least in principle, ultimate authority was vested; the smaller elected council (*boulē*), where most of the real work of governing was carried on; and the board of magistrates, who were officials responsible for specific aspects of administration. In Acts 17:6-8, Luke refers to the magistrates of Thessalonica as "politarchs." While this term appears nowhere else in Greek literature, Luke's accuracy has been confirmed by inscriptional evidence, which indicates that this was the common title for magistrates not only in Thessalonica but in Macedonia as a whole. In keeping with Thessalonica's free status, it was these politarchs (five or six in number), rather than any Roman official, who heard the case against Paul and his companions (Acts 17:6-9).

Paul and Thessalonian Religions It was to this bustling, prosperous, cosmopolitan city that Paul and his coworkers came with their Christian message in AD 50 or so, having traveled the ninety miles from Philippi along the *Via Egnatia*. To Paul, the message that he came to proclaim was "the gospel" of the one "living and true God" (compare 1 Thess. 1:9, 2:2). But to the casual Thessalonian observer, Paul's "gospel" would have appeared as but one more religious import in an already crowded market. Along with such commodities as wheat and iron, spices and silk, the Mediterranean trade routes served as conduits for less tangible intellectual and religious cargo, borne along not only by itinerant preachers and philosophers engaged in full time propagation but also by merchants, sailors, soldiers, colonists, and others caught up in the everyday life of a mobile society. The result, in a city like Thessalonica, was a profuse and highly variegated religious life, as foreign cults put down roots alongside the more traditional philosophic schools and indigenous forms of worship.

Worship of the Olympian pantheon of gods was part of Thessalonian life from the very beginning. A late fourth century BC inscription speaks of the "Priest of the Gods," who presided over the civic cult, a cult in which Apollo, Athena, and Hercules were especially prominent. Native Greek mystery religions also flourished in Thessalonica. The cult of Dionysus, with its savage and ecstatic rituals, was well established by the second century BC, and that of the Cabiri, originating in Samothrace, was gaining a following among the upper classes a century or so later. The Greek intellectual tradition, quasi-religious in nature, was also well represented. The praise which Lucian of Samosata heaped on the city in the second century AD for its active schools of rhetoric and philosophy would have been just as appropriate a century earlier.

Religions of foreign origin found a home in Thessalonica as well. After the great fire of 1917, workmen engaged in reconstruction discovered a temple for the worship of the Egyptian gods Sarapis and Isis, originally built in the late third century BC. In 1939 a similar temple from the Roman period was found nearby. Thus, no later than a century after Alexander's conquests, Egyptian deities were being worshiped in Thessalonica. A stele found in the Sarapeum, bearing an excerpt from a declaration of Philip V, indicates that at least by 187 BC the cult was well enough established to have engaged the attention of the king. An inscription from a later period gives evidence of a religious society dedicated to the worship of the Egyptian god Anubis.

The God of Israel was worshiped in the city as well. According to Acts 17:1-2, Thessalonica (in contrast to Philippi; Acts 16:13) contained a synagogue to which Paul made his way when he arrived. While archaeological evidence for Jewish presence in the city is scanty, it is quite probable that Jews arrived in the city not long after the Egyptians. A fourth-century AD inscription also suggests the presence of a Samaritan community, but its date of origin cannot be ascertained.

The arrival of the Romans also had religious repercussions. Even before the onset of emperor worship, civic cults, presided over by the "Priest of Zeus Eleutherios and Rome" or the "Priest of Rome and the Benefactor Romans," were instituted in honor of Rome.

Despite the variety of religious options already present in the city, Paul's message was embraced by a surprising number of Thessalonians, of whom the majority were Gentiles (1 Thess.

1:9; compare Acts 17:4). Believers would agree with Paul that such success was due to the Holy Spirit and the power of the gospel itself (compare 1 Thess. 1:5). Nevertheless, in Thessalonica as in other Hellenistic cities, sociological, cultural, and related factors made for especially fertile ground.

The growth and development of Thessalonica during the Hellenistic and Roman periods was just one aspect of a wider process of urbanization. Throughout the Mediterranean world a whole new kind of urban existence was emerging, as Alexander's dream of a unified worldwide society (*oikoumenē*) was realized in a modified way through Augustus' *pax Romana*. This new city-centered social milieu was characterized by a common culture—a cosmopolitan Hellenism in which a combination of Greek ideals and oriental ways was held together within the infrastructure of the Greek *polis*. Several aspects of this "cosmopolitan Hellenism" as it was manifested in Thessalonica have already been observed in passing. With respect to one of the most important elements of the common infrastructure, the Greek language, it might be noted that despite its significance in the Roman scheme of things, Thessalonica remained a decidedly Greek city. Of the more than one thousand extant inscriptions, all but fourteen are in Greek.

Another aspect of this new urban social reality was the emergence of a growing middle class—artisans, merchants, traders, manual workers and others, whose livelihood, unlike the aristocracy who owned the land surrounding the city and the rural slaves who worked it, was made possible by the city itself. Paul's injunctions to the Thessalonian Christians that they follow his example of earning a living with his own hands (1 Thess. 4:10-12; 2 Thess. 3:6-12) suggest that his converts were largely drawn from this group. In addition, the changing social conditions within the city environment provided unprecedented opportunities for women to acquire wealth and influence. This was especially true in Macedonia; in both Philippi (Acts 16:13-18; Phil 4:2f.) and Thessalonica (Acts 17:4) we find such women figuring prominently among Paul's converts.

If the emergence of a common urban milieu and Paul's skills

Galerius Arch

as an artisan made it possible for him to move easily from city to city with his message, several less desirable features of urban life produced the kind of social discontent often conducive to the success of new religious messages. One of these was a sense of alienation and insecurity. Smaller, traditional, ethnically-cohesive societies provided a feeling of stability and identity that was easily lost in the cosmopolitan, mobile, and rapidly changing environment of a city like Thessalonica. To counteract this, city residents sought a sense of belonging within the various religious associations and trade-guilds common in Thessalonica and elsewhere. In fact, the "assembly" (*ekklēsia*; 1 Thess. 1:1; 2 Thess. 1:1) that Paul founded in Thessalonica would have appeared to the casual onlooker as just another of these voluntary associations. Its success was due in part to its ability, rooted in the gospel itself, to provide a sense of security in an uncertain world.

Paul was forced to make a premature and hasty retreat from Thessalonica (Acts 17:10), but the church, like the city itself (known today as Salonika), has survived in unbroken succession to the present day. Because of the continuous occupation of the site since the city's foundation, archaeological discoveries have been the result more of chance than of systematic investigation. Mention has been made of the Sarapeum and related discoveries, and of various numismatic and inscriptional remains. In 1962 archaeologists uncovered the Roman forum or marketplace, whose buildings date from New Testament times or a little later. The original layout of the city is probably preserved, at least in part, in present-day Salonika. Some stretches of the city wall, built in Byzantine times but resting on earlier foundations, still stand. The *Via Egnatia* continues to be one of the city's main streets. Of the two Roman arches that stood at either entrances, one, built to honor Emperor Galerius for a victory in 297 AD, still stands; the other, Vardar Gate, which may have been in existence when Paul made his departure, was demolished in 1876. Perhaps the most important things to survive from ancient Thessalonica—valuable alike for their insight into early Christianity and for their enduring witness to the gospel— are those first-century letters now known as 1 and 2 Thessalonians.

For further information on Thessalonica see:

Burton, E. D. "The Politarchs." *American Journal of Theology* 2 (1898), 598-632.

Edson, C. "Macedonia I: A Dedication of Philip V." *Harvard Studies in Classical Philology* 51 (1940), 125f.

———— . "Macedonia II: State Cults of Thessalonica", *ibid.*, 127-136.

———— . "Macedonia III: Cults of Thessalonica." *Harvard Theological Review* 41 (1948), 153-204.

Meeks, W. A. *The First Urban Christians: The Social World of the Apostle Paul* (1983).

Vacalopoulos, A. E. *A History of Thessaloniki*, trans. T. F. Carney (1972).

Vickers, M. "Hellenistic Thessaloniki." *Journal of Hellenic Studies* 92 (1972), 156-70.

T. L. D.

TYRE AND SIDON

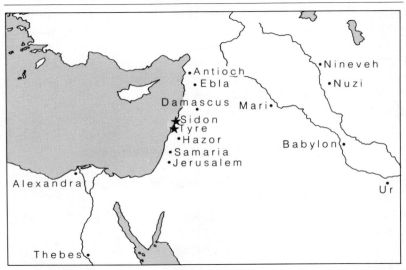

Despite the ravages of modern warfare, southern Lebanon remains as one of the world's finest corners of natural beauty. The region south of Beirut is dominated by a range of mountains extending north-south and parallel to the coast, its western flanks leveling into a narrow plain alongside the Mediterranean Sea. The coast is rocky, broken by occasional beaches and by the mouths of rivers bearing the runoff waters from the mountains. On the coast itself are two towns that have little current importance in the economy of Lebanon. Saida, located on a promontory jutting west into the Mediterranean, is a small city of a little more than fifty thousand persons. Some twenty miles to the south of Saida is Sur, with approximately five thousand inhabitants in the town proper, which stretches westward into the sea on a small peninsula. Today, Sur is essentially a large fishing village.

Occasionally the names of these Lebanese towns catch the attention of the international press. In November, 1983 a pick-up truck loaded with explosives swerved off the highway, kamikaze fashion, into the Israeli military post at Sur and exploded; the young driver of the truck and some sixty other persons died in the explosion. Briefly Sur was in the news, but as quickly it was forgotten. Sur and Saida, nowadays, are not the focal point of world attention. Thus it is not easy to imagine that in biblical times these two places, then named Tyre and Sidon, were for a while among the world's most famous cities.

Location and
Excavation
The southern city, Tyre, was situated on the Lebanese coast just south of the spot where the river Litani flows into the Mediterranean. Its site had been chosen because of a small rocky island, located half a mile out from the shore. Part of the city had been built on the mainland, part on the island, with the double location offering its citizens both military protection and excellent port facilities. Above all, Tyre was a maritime city. Its fame was based on the ocean with its traffic and trade. Tyre's sister city, Sidon, had a similar location further north on the coast. Just south of where the Awali River flows into the sea, a promontory protruded from the coastline; the promontory itself was protected from ocean storms by a rocky reef offshore, so that to the north of the promontory there were port facilities sheltered by the reef, and to its south a natural bay provided safe harbor. East of Sidon, the foothills of the Lebanese mountains enclosed a small plain, famous then as now for its citrus orchards. But Sidon, like Tyre, was essentially a maritime city.

Neither Tyre nor Sidon has been a major focal point of modern archaeological activity, in part no doubt because the two sites continue to be occupied, making extensive excavation difficult. There has been considerable exploration in the general vicinity of Sidon, but the results, though rewarding, have not made the ancient city a center of interest. In 1855, an accidental discovery was made by a French amateur archaeologist, M. Peretié, just south of the city. A large sarcophagus, constructed from black stone and measuring approximately eight feet by four feet, was found in a mound. Its inscription stated that it belonged to Eshmunazar, king of Sidon. This discovery prompted further exploration. Between 1861 and 1863, Napoleon III commissioned Ernest Renan, a distinguished French scholar and man of letters, to direct further explorations in the vicinity of Sidon. The members of his staff found several sarcophagi and the remains of ancient cemeteries, but for the most part the discoveries were not exceptional. Exploration continued in a desultory fashion into the twentieth century, and early in the century a temple once dedicated to the god Eshmun was excavated, as well as various burial chambers in the environs of the city.

Both Tyre and Sidon became the focal point for a while of the newly developed techniques of underwater exploration, their respective harbor facilities offering unusual scope in this respect.

Harbor at Sidon

The waters of the Mediterranean have risen considerably over more than two millennia, and parts of the original harbors of the cities lay at depths more than forty feet below the surface. The port facilities at Sidon were examined both underwater and with the help of aerial photography, between 1946 and 1950; Tyre's harbor was examined at an earlier date (1934-37). Soil excavations at Tyre have uncovered a number of important structures, including an ancient theater, though they are relatively late (Graeco-Roman) and tell little of the city's earliest history. But, compared with other ancient cities such as Ebla and Babylon, Tyre and Sidon have not survived primarily on the basis of modern archaeological discoveries, rather as a consequence of the multitude of references to them in ancient texts.

Socio-economic Structures Although both Tyre and Sidon are known to have flourished in the second millennium BC, being referred to in both the Ugaritic texts and the letters from Amarna in Egypt, they came into prominence in the first millennium BC with the rise of Phoenicia to a central place in world history. Phoenicia, a territory generally similar to modern Lebanon in scope, was not so much a nation as a collection of city-states. Four were of particular importance: Byblos, Arwad, Tyre, and Sidon. In the latter half of the second millennium BC, Byblos held pride of place among these coastal cities, but by the beginning of the first millennium Tyre had assumed pre-eminence, until later, in the Persian period (sixth century BC), Sidon was to become first among the Phoenician cities.

Throughout the biblical period, the two cities lived an existence that was partly colonial and partly independent. They passed successively under the suzerainty or influence of the various superpowers of their time, being for a while under Egyptian control, then Assyrian, Neo-Babylonian, Persian, Greek, and Roman. (And their situation has changed very little during the last two millennia; only the identities of the superpowers have changed.) But throughout these successive periods of foreign influence, sometimes as a colony and sometimes merely as a partner in treaty, Tyre and Sidon retained a large degree of autonomy, principally as a consequence of the wealth and influence they acquired through trade. And Tyre for a while had its own empire of sorts, scattered throughout the Mediterranean world in the form of settlements and trading posts.

A number of factors contributed to the greatness of Tyre and Sidon in past centuries, but it was above all their coastal location and their development of trade that led to greatness. Many a coastal settlement never rises above the status of fishing village (indeed, Julian Huxley was to write in 1954: "Proud Tyre is now a broken-down fishing port." *From an Antique Land*, p. 72), but these two cities in biblical times capitalized on their locations by developing both trade and local industries. They exported timber (cedar and cypress), oil, wine, and dyed materials; they traded in linen, ivory, and precious metals from Egypt, in copper from Cyprus, and in other commodities from the world's remote corners, always profiting from the exchange. But the Phoenicians, and especially the citizens of Tyre, were not content simply to become a part of the mercantile world as it then was; they developed it still further.

As early as the ninth century BC, the Tyrian fleets had opened up sea routes to Spain, exploiting the rich mineral resources of that land (copper, tin, and silver). They established trading colonies in North Africa, one of which, Carthage, was to become a significant state in its own right. About 600 BC, Phoenician sailors under a Tyrian admiral circumnavigated Africa, preceding Vasco da Gama's famous voyage by some two millennia. In the fifth century BC, Tyrian sailors from Carthage sailed to Britain, perhaps searching for a suitable sea route for the transportation of tin from the Cornish mines. During the biblical period, Tyre and the Phoenicians had for a time a maritime empire akin to that of the British in the nineteenth and early twentieth centuries.

The local industries in Tyre and Sidon also contributed to their wealth. Cedar provided not only valuable exports but also the resources for a strong shipbuilding industry. (The cedar, though it remains the national symbol of modern Lebanon, has now virtually been eliminated from that part of the world.) And certain kinds of sea-snails, species of *murex* that flourished in the coastal waters, provided the raw material from which valuable purple and scarlet dyes were manufactured. Today, in Saida (Sidon), a great hill (some 150 feet high) can still be seen in the southern part of the city adjoining the medieval castle which is commonly known as Murex Hill; it is the refuse heap of snail shells from the ancient dye industry. As Julian Huxley remarked, the dye industry in ancient Sidon was the precursor of the great chemical industries of our own time, I.C.I. or I.G. Farben (*From an Antique Land*, pp. 73-75).

Tyre in Biblical Literature   During both the Old and New Testament periods, the histories of Tyre and Sidon intersected frequently with the history of the Hebrews, and later of the early Christians. It was Hiram, king of Tyre, who sent cedar, along with carpenters and masons, to assist David in the construction of his palace in Jerusalem (2 Sam. 5:11). And Solomon sent a messenger to

Tyre Colonnade

the same Hiram when he made preparations for the construction of the temple. "Now therefore command that cedars of Lebanon be cut for me; and my servants will join your servants, and I will pay you for your servants such wages as you set; for you know that there is none among us who knows how to cut timber like the Sidonians" (*RSV*, 1 Kings 5:6). But relations between Tyre, Sidon, and Israel were not always to retain the happy note of the time of the united monarchy; Ahab's marriage to Jezebel, daughter of the ruler of Tyre, introduced into Israel a warning note of the danger of Tyre's pagan faith for the purity of Israel's religion.

By the time of the great prophets, the happy relationships of the time of David and Solomon were long forgotten. Tyre and Sidon were condemned by the prophets for their arrogance. Isaiah, Jeremiah, Ezekiel, and others pointed to the cruelty of the citizens of Tyre and Sidon and their violations of the human rights of others. Ezekiel, for example, in a series of extraordinarily powerful poems (or oracles) addressed to Tyre and Sidon, declared God's condemnation on the two cities for their arrogance and hubris, and he announced their coming judgment and destruction (Ezekiel 26-28). Not long after Ezekiel's preaching, beginning in 586 BC, the Babylonians began a thirteen-year siege of Tyre, destroying its mainland territories. The island sector of the city was destroyed later by Alexander the Great, who built a causeway to the island, breaching its classic defense against land-based attack (332 BC). (The peninsular part of modern Sur was originally an island, but the accumulation of sand around Alexander's causeway converted it to its modern form.) Sidon, too, was conquered by the Babylonian emperor Nebuchadrezzar (*ca.* 587 BC), but both cities recovered from devastation to flourish for further centuries into the New Testament period, when something of their earlier influence over maritime trade was reasserted within the domain of the Roman empire.

Jesus, during the years of his preaching ministry, visited the coastal region of Tyre and Sidon, which was not too far distant from his native Galilee. It was in the vicinity of Tyre and Sidon that he healed the daughter of a Syro-Phoenician woman (Mark

7:24-30). And when he preached and taught, people from the cities of Tyre and Sidon were among those who thronged to hear him (Mark 3:8; Luke 6:17). Paul and Luke, returning from a missionary journey, spent a week in Tyre, where a small Christian community was already established (Acts 21:3-4). And when Paul and his companions finally set sail for Rome, they put in briefly at the port of Sidon and received kind treatment there (Acts 27:3). From David's time to Paul's, Tyre and Sidon are on the map of biblical geography and history, sometimes cast in good light and sometimes more darkly described. But these two remarkable coastal cities had a central role to play in the drama of the biblical narrative.

Having left their mark in the Bible, Tyre and Sidon have also continued to hold a place in Western literature and imagination. Robert Browning, the English poet, composed a poem entitled "Popularity" (1855), at a time when, in early middle-age, he had not yet achieved recognition. Tyre and its dye constitute one of the poem's central themes:

> Who has not heard how Tyrian shells
> > Enclosed the blue, that dye of dyes
> Whereof one drop worked miracles,
> > And coloured like Astarte's eyes
> Raw silk the merchant sells?

But it was Rudyard Kipling, himself a citizen of an empire not unlike that of Tyre, who captured best the spirit of the message of the Hebrew prophets. In his famous poem "Recessional," written in 1897, he penned some words which still convey something of what we can learn from the fate of two remarkable cities in the ancient world.

> Far-called, our navies melt away—
> > On dune and headland sinks the fire—
> Lo, all our pomp of yesterday
> > is one with Nineveh and Tyre!

Judge of the Nations, spare us yet,
Lest we forget—lest we forget!

For further information on Tyre and Sidon see:

Elayi, J. "The Relations between Tyre and Carthage during the Persian Period." *Journal of the Ancient Near Eastern Society* 13 (9181), 15-29.
Harden, D. *The Phoenicians* (1962).
Jidejian, N. *Tyre through the Ages* (1969).
_____ . *Sidon through the Ages* (1971).
Katzenstein, H. J. *The History of Tyre* (1973).
_____ . "Tyre in the Early Persian Period." *Biblical Archaeologist* 42 (1979), 23-34.
For the poems quoted: Loucks, J. F. ed. *Robert Browning's Poetry* (1979), p. 216; and Rudyard Kipling, *The Recessional, Departmental Ditties and the Vampire* (1909).

P. C. C.

UR

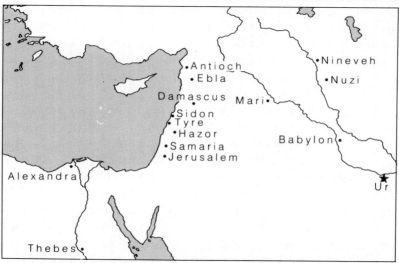

"Ur of the Chaldees" (or "Chaldeans") is the Bible's term for the place where Abraham was born (Gen. 11:28, 31; 15:7; Neh. 9:7; compare Acts 7:4, "land of the Chaldeans"). Apart from occasional references to it being "beyond the river" (the Euphrates; for example, Josh. 24:2-3), it is not located more precisely, and two main traditions have developed over the centuries. One places it somewhere in northern Mesopotamia, most often at Urfa in southern Turkey, the important early Christian center of Edessa, or possibly at one of several towns named Ura in Asia Minor. An even older tradition, going back to Berossus in the third century BC, placed Ur in southern Mesopotamia. The northern tradition predominated for many years, but two factors have swung informed opinion very much in favor of the southern location. Firstly in the 1850s, the distinguished pioneer cuneiformist, Henry C. Rawlinson, was able to identify the impressive remains called Tell el-Muqayyar ("Mound of Pitch," so called because the bricks were bonded by bitumen rather than mortar) as the ancient city of Ur. Secondly excavations in the mid-nineteenth and early twentieth centuries at the site, culminating in the Joint Expedition of the British Museum and the Museum of the University of Pennsylvania from 1922-34, under the direction of Sir Leonard Woolley, showed conclusively that this Ur was one of the major cities of the ancient world. The designation "of the Chaldees" refers to the Kaldu tribe who lived in Babylonia from at least the end of the second millennium and gave their name to the Babylonian dynasty of the late seventh and sixth centuries.

The modern visitor to Ur cannot fail to be impressed by the dominating remains of the great ziggurat, a vast towering temple on whose summit once stood a shrine to the moon god. Standing on top of the ruins, one can see for many miles in every direction over the unending flatness of the land, and so gain some impression of the awe which the ziggurat must have inspired in the population. Ur is now a completely deserted site, about ten miles southwest of the town of Nasiriya on the modern course of the Euphrates, but in ancient times the river flowed through Ur itself. It was a thriving city with dependent towns and villages, linked by land and sea, not only with the great cities of the north such as Ashur and Mari but through its trading contacts with part of northern Africa, Asia Minor, and Afghanistan.

The Sumerian Period Ur's earliest known inhabitants lived in the Ubaid period, one of the earliest phases of prehistoric civilization in southern Iraq dating to before 4000 BC. Already there was a village-based peasant economy in the area, and the settlements at Ur itself and at Ubaid, about four miles to the northwest; also

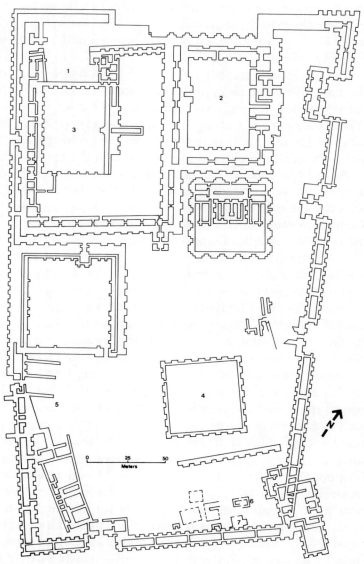

CITY PLAN OF UR

1: Shrine of Nannar
2: Court of Nannar
3: Ziggurat

4: Palace of Ur-Nammu and Shulgi
5: Dungi temple of Nimin-Tabba
6: Tomb of Queen Pu-abi
7: Great Death Pit

show marked signs of continuity with the flowering of Sumerian culture in the third millennium. Ur's own apogee also belonged to the third millennium, in two stages under the First and Third Dynasties of Ur.

The wealth and tragedy of the First Dynasty, to be placed in the Early Dynastic III period and dated *ca.* 2700-2500 BC, have been revealed through the extraordinary discoveries in the "Royal Cemetery." Contemporary documentary evidence for the kings of Ur also appears for the first time in this period, when writing was still in comparative infancy. In the reign of Sargon of Akkad (*ca.* 2300 BC), a custom is attested, which still continued nearly two thousand years later in the reign of Nabonidus, whereby the ruler of all Sumer held the right of appointment of the high-priestess of Ur's chief deity, the moon god. Sargon, like many of his successors, appointed his daughter to the position. Since the temple was at the center of economic and administrative life, especially in the third millennium, a prominent role for the city was ensured, even when politically it was less powerful.

Under the Third Dynasty (*ca.* 2112-2004 BC), Ur's control extended to much of Mesopotamia as well as the cities of Sumer. Its two most notable rulers were the dynasty's founder Ur-Nammu and his son Shulgi. Apart from founding an empire Ur-Nammu's main achievement was his building work in Ur. The mighty ziggurat is the most obvious sign of this, but he also renewed the associated temple complex and constructed the city wall twenty-six feet in height, so solidly that the rampart which acted as a retaining wall was discovered to be seventy-seven feet thick at its base. The fragments preserved of the Laws of Ur-Nammu also proclaim him as the earliest lawgiver and law collector known to us. Shulgi's comparatively peaceful reign of nearly half a century deserves comment for the king's patronage of culture, particularly as a lover of music and an inspirer of royal hymns, and for the large number of bureaucratic texts (usually known as "business documents") which have been preserved.

The sack of Ur and subsequent fall of the Third Dynasty in the reign of Ibbi-Sin was an event greatly lamented, whose memory reverberated throughout Mesopotamia for many centuries. Even the identity of those responsible for the devastation still remains uncertain, though the Elamites, Subarians, and Gutians from the north and east were certainly involved. So were the Amorites from the west, against whom Ibbi-Sin's father Shu-Sin had constructed a defensive wall some 170 miles long, but some responsibility must rest with one of Ibbi-Sin's own governors, Ishbi-Erra. By treachery and diplomacy, he contributed to Ur's downfall from within and succeeded in founding a new dynasty based at the city of Isin. Although Ur continued to flourish under external rulers of the Old Babylonian era, its chief glory had already departed. *Circa* 1740 BC the citizens of Ur joined a rebellion of various southern cities against their Babylonian overlords, but Ur was quickly recaptured by Samsuiluna, the king of Babylon, who dismantled the walls and burnt the city.

Thereafter, Ur was rebuilt periodically, sometimes even on a grand scale, but it never again attained the heights of the Sumerian period. Three restorations are worthy of note. Firstly *ca.* 1400 BC, the Kassite monarch Kurigalzu I rebuilt many of the old public buildings, including the major temples, and then in the first half of the seventh century, for a short while it became an important financial and religious center under its Neo-Assyrian governor Sin-balassu-iqbi. Finally, the Neo-Babylonian kings, Nebuchadnezzar and Nabonidus were assiduous builders, particularly on the *temenos*, the sacred area. Nabonidus' extensive repair of the ziggurat was an especially notable achievement. Ur's final decline took place under Persian rule, though the last dated inscription extends to the twelfth year of Alexander the Great.

Monuments The most striking discoveries at Ur were uncovered in the "Royal Cemetery," though very little is now preserved at the site, since excavation is often necessarily a work of destruction. Out of a total of 1,850 graves, sixteen stood out by their wealth and their distinctive structure. These special graves

were found to contain a "death pit," where the remains of between sixty and seventy-four people were uncovered, as well as
a stone or brick vaulted tomb, where the principal body lay.
With the bodies lay many objects of extraordinary beauty and
value, including decorated ox-carts with the oxen still in har-
ness. Among the treasures were a golden-winged helmet, exqui-
site animal-headed harps and lyres with mosaic borders and
gold-headed nails, and many ordinary objects wrought in gold
and silver such as beads, hair-ribbons, combs, and ear-rings. A
magnificent headdress was recovered from a queen's grave,
comprising three overlapping wreaths of gold pendants in the
shape of beech-leaves with ornaments of lapis lazuli and carnelian, a gold "comb" topped with gold rosettes in place on the
back of the head, and enormous gold lunate ear-rings. Also recovered from the cemetery was one of the most elaborate works
of art from this early period, the so-called "Standard of Ur." It
has four mosaic panels, with the two main faces divided into
three registers portraying "War" and "Peace." The evidence
clearly suggests a short-lived practice of human sacrifice on a
lavish scale, where a monarch was accompanied on the journey
to the underworld by a group of retainers. The fine dress and
peaceful order of the servants show that they went quietly to
their deaths. One lady, for instance, was poignantly found with
her fingers still on the strings of her harp, apparently playing
solemn music until the very moment of her dying breath. The
means of death was apparently poison, as may be deduced from
small cups found near many of the bodies, taken as they stood
in position in the pit once the king or queen had been laid to
rest. The burials are quite unique in Mesopotamian archaeology, and detailed explanation is not possible. Similar practices
are alluded to only briefly in one Sumerian text, and in scattered
indications from First Dynasty Egypt, the Scythian kings, and
among the Lucians. Some of the occupants of these tombs can,
however, be identified. One group comprises king A-kalam-
dug, a certain Mes-kalam-dug, and queen Pu-abi or Shub-ad.
These three are probably earlier than a second group comprising kings Mes-ane-pada and his son A-ane-pad, whose names

U R

Lyre from Ur

Ruins at Ur

were already known from the Sumerian King List as the first two kings of the First Dynasty of Ur. The latter also provide a synchronism with the famous Gilgamesh of Erech, while A-ane-pada was the builder of the early dynastic temple at Ubaid.

Another outstanding feature of Ur is of course the ziggurat. The present building is primarily the work of Ur-Nammu, though he certainly enlarged an earlier version that may well go back to the time of the First Dynasty. The base of Ur-Nammu's ziggurat, which measures about 200 by 170 feet, is still very well preserved after four thousand years, being constructed of a solid core of unbaked brick surrounded by an eight–foot skin of baked brick set in bitumen. It was built with a deliberate slight curve so that one can see along the walls only to the center, which along with the pronounced batter gives an even greater impression of solidity and strength. Three staircases of one hundred steps lead up to a great gate-tower giving access to the two upper stories and the shrine at the summit. The brickwork was painted black on the lower stages and red on the upper stages, while the shrine was covered in blue glazed tiles. The terraces were also apparently lined with trees and shrubs as a kind of hanging gardens, and the colors and vegetation must have added considerably to the image of the ziggurat as a "mountain of god."

The best examples of private houses date from the Old Baby-lonian period, and in the words of the excavator, "many of them were so well preserved that it was easy to picture them as having been deserted but yesterday." They were constructed of good burnt brickwork in the lower courses with mudbrick above. Some of the houses were surprisingly large, with rooms round a paved courtyard and two stories. Sometimes there were small private chapels in the houses themselves, whereas others must have frequented the wayside shrines in the narrow, winding streets. Whether or not this was the period in which Abraham actually lived, as is often claimed, the homeliness and quaint-ness of the housing quarter provides a fascinating foil to the grandeur of other parts of Ur.

The region of Ur is not rich in natural resources. Prosperity

Ziggurat

had of necessity to be derived from the Euphrates, and so Ur-Nammu designed a system of canals branching out from an irrigation dam to the north of the city. This extensive irrigation system supported huge flocks and herds and extensive crops of grain and dates. The major industry was textiles, especially wool. Ur's wealth, however, was really derived from her trading activities. It is not impossible that in ancient times, an arm of the Persian Gulf extended to Ur and its two harbors on the north and west, where import taxes were collected at the registry. The large number of business documents of the Third Dynasty demonstrates how meticulous was the administration of Ur-Nammu and his successors. Many of the imported raw materials were turned into manufactured goods by craftsmen of all kinds, who were employed mainly in the temples. One tablet lists eight different tradesmen with their own workshops, including a chisel-worker, jeweller, mason, carpenter, smith, leatherworker, fuller, and basketmaker. To what extent Terah and his three sons were involved in these industries will almost certainly never be

—— 283 ——

known. Abraham's possessions of flocks and herds, however, allow us to imagine their owning possibly quite large flocks that were sold in the markets of Ur, and from which were made some of the woolen clothing so familiar in Sumerian art.

The case of Abraham shows that the value of Ur for biblical interpretation is indirect. An even more tenuous link occurs with the Flood. Woolley initially claimed that an eight-foot layer of clay discovered above the Ubaid strata at Ur was the actual evidence on which the flood stories of Mesopotamia and Israel were based. Excavation has also uncovered evidence of serious floods at three other sites in Mesopotamia (including Farah/Shuruppak, the city mentioned in Sumerian and Akkadian flood stories), but they belong to different eras and therefore presumably derive only from major, localized inundations.

Of more direct interest is the boast, discovered at Ur, by Cyrus king of Persia, that "Sin-Nanna [the Semitic and Sumerian names of Ur's chief deity, the moon god] of heaven and earth delivered the four quarters of the world into my hands with his favourable omen, and I returned the gods to their shrines" (UET, 1, 307). It is a remarkable echo of Cyrus' edict proclaimed to the Jewish exiles: "The Lord, God of the heavens, has delivered to me all the kingdoms of the world, and has appointed me to rebuild his temple in Jerusalem" (Ezra 1:2). The response of many of those exiles, some perhaps even living in Ur and its environs, in retracing Abraham's steps of faith and returning to Palestine, shows that despite Ur's glories, it was for the Israelites a city to be left behind for the sake of God's even better promises.

For further information on Ur see:

Woolley, C. L. *Excavations at Ur* (1954).
_____ . *et. al., Ur Excavations*. Vols. 1-10 (1927-51).
Gadd, C. J., *et. al. Ur Excavations Texts*. Vols. 1-9 (1928-76).
Mallowan, M. E. L. and D. J. Wiseman, ed. *Ur in Restrospect* (1960).

M. J. S.

A-ane-pad, 280, 282
Adijah, 53
Abraham, 55, 56, 194, 197, 275, 284
Abu-Kemal, 158
Accad, 33
Achaea, 218
Achaia, 85
Ada, 114
Adad-Nimri III, 228
Ada-Nirari, 35
Adad, nirari III, 185
Adamma, 115
Adonis, 60
Aegean, islands of, 235
Aegean Sea, 22
Aelia Capitolina, 152
Aetolia, 199
Africa, 218
Agabus, 68
Agade, 33
Agrippa I, 13, 69
Agum II, 34
Ahab, 53, 101, 102, 124, 126, 127,
   191, 225, 226, 272
Ahaz, 230
Ahaziah, 227
Ai, 51, 52, 54, 56
Akhisar, 242
A-Kalmdug, 280
Akkad, 110 - 111, 159, 194, 278
Alalakh, 195
Alasehir, 246
Albright, W. F., 55, 192, 196
Alciphron, 94
Aleppo, 111, 190
Alexander Jannaeus, 64
Alexander River, 67
Alexander the Great, 1, 4, 9, 40, 46
   105, 144, 198, 203, 231, 240, 259,
   272
Alexandria, 1 - 7, 9, 15, 71, 77
Alps (Roman province), 218
Alyattes, 239, 243
Amarna, 269
Amaziah, 53, 228
Amenemhet I, 252, 253
Amenhotep II, 99
Amenhotep III, 253, 255, 256

Amenophis IV, 97
Amos, 53, 191
Amosis, 135
Amran-Jumjuma, 42
Amun, 251, 253, 255
Amunhotep II, 120, 127
Amun-Re, 253, 254
Anaitis. See Artemis
Ananias, 106
Anatolia, 110
Andrae, W., 43
Antakiya, 9
Anthony, Mark, 105, 200, 260
Antioch of Syria, 8 - 11, 65, 87, 105
Antiochus (a Jew), 15
Antiochus I, 12, 104
Antiochus I Soter, 10
Antiochus III, 12
Antiochus IV Epiphanes, 12, 14, 144,
   145
Antiochus XII, 105
Antonia, 203
Antonius Felix, 69
Ansud, 159
Apamea, 10, 15
Aphrodite, 64, 91, 92, 93
Apollo, 23, 26, 90, 91, 212, 261
Apollos, 6
Apollos Patroon, 25
Apuleius, 85
Aquila, 219
Aramea, 99-100
Aratus of Cilicia, 30
Archelaus, 67
Ar-Ennum, 110
Ares, 23, 25
Aretas III, 105
Aristarchus, 3, 68, 69
Aristobulus, 219
Arius, 7
Arkha, 39
Arraphe, 190 - 197
Artaxerxes Longimanus, 231
Artemidorus, 64
Artemis, 9, 200, 203, 204, 236
Arwad, 269
Asa, 100
Asclepius, 93, 241

Cybele, 203
Cyrenaica, 218
Cyrenius, 218
Cyrus, 38, 39, 60, 143, 243, 284
Cyrus Cylinder, 38
Cythera, island of, 83

Dadusha, 165
Dagan, 113, 114, 115
Damascus, 76, 96 - 106, 121, 123, 228, 230
Damu, 116
Dan, 53
Daniel, 36
Daphne, 10, 15, 18
Darius, 39
David, 52, 58, 59, 64, 100, 130, 140, 141, 142, 271
Dead Sea, 49, 133
Deborah, 52, 121
Deinocrates, 2
Deir el-Bahri, 252, 255
Demeter, 91
Demetrius, 199
Demetrius I, 105
Demetrius II, 105
Denizli, 248
de Vaux, R., 196
Diana, 203, 236
Dio Cassius, 84
Dio Chrysostom, 87
Diogenes, 40
Dionysius, 23, 26, 144, 241, 261
Domitian, 16, 234, 241
Drusilla, 68, 69
Dussand, René, 157

Ebla, 96, 98, 107 - 118, 159, 191, 194, 269
Ebrium, 110, 113
Edessa, 275
Egypt, 1 - 7, 67, 99, 104, 120, 187, 218, 249 - 257
Elagabalus, 18
Elam, 187
Eliezer, 99, 194
Eligah, 53, 137
Emar, 109, 110
En-Nasira, 172
Enlil, 157
Enna-Daga, 159
Ephesus, 235, 236 - 239

Ephraim, 195
Epimenides, 30
Eratosthanes, 3
Erech, 33
Esarhaddon, 36, 187
Esau, 195
Esdraelon, plain of, 170, 171
Eshmunazar, 268
Eshtar, 109, 114
Eski Izmir, 239
Euclid, 3
Eumenes I, 241
Eumenes II, 241, 245
Euphanor, 24, 25
Euphrates River, 38, 44, 270, 275
Euripides, 30
Eusebius, 6, 54, 56, 71, 220, 222
Evil-merodach, 37
Ezekiel, 256, 272
Ezra, 54, 60
Farah, 284
Faustia, 203
Felix, 69

Gabrinius, 232
Gaius, 68, 222
Galatia, 218
Galerius, 206, 207, 265
Galilee, 72 - 82, 170 - 179
Galilee, Sea of, 119, 171
Gangites River, 199
Garstang, John, 122, 131
Gasur, 194
Gaul, 218
Gaumata (pseudo-Smerdis), 39
Gedaliah, 59
Gennesaret, plain of, 73
Gessius Florus, 70
Gethsemane, garden of, 151
Gibeah, 50
Gihon, spring of, 139, 140, 143
Gilgamesh, 282
Gneaus Babius Phillinus, 91
Golgotha, 153, 154
Great Rift Valley, 133
Greece, 22 - 31, 83 - 95, 198
Gubarus, 38
Gulf of Corinth, 83, 93
Hadadezer, 100
Hadrian, 15, 18
Hagar, 196
Hamazi, 110

Mount Symbolon, 199
Mukin-zeri, 35
Mursilis I, 112

Nabonidus, 37, 38, 39, 278, 279
Nabopolassar, 36, 42, 45, 46, 47, 188
Nahal Hadera, 67
Nahal Tanninim, 67
Nahum, 189, 256
Nahum (unknown Galilean), 72
Napoleon III, 268
Naram-Sin, 111
Narcissus, 219
Nasiriya, 270
Nathan, 141
Nazareth, 170 - 179
Neopolis, 56
Nebi-Yunus, 181, 184
Nebo, 186
Nebuchadnezzar, 10, 34, 36, 37, 44,
    45, 47, 143, 189, 279
Nebuchadnezzar III, 39
Nebuchadnezzar IV, 39
Negeb, the, 58
Nehemiah, 56, 60, 143, 231
Nemean River, 86
Neptune, 91
Nergal-Sharezer, 37
Neriglissar, 37
Nero, 65, 110, 209
Nicolaus of Antioch, 18
Nidintu-Bel, 39
Nile River, 249
Nimrod, 33, 184
Nimrud, 186
Nineveh, 180 - 189, 191
Ninmah, 43, 47
Ninurta, 47
Nippur, 191
Nisroch, 187
Nuzi, 190 - 197

Octavian. *See* Augustus
Omri, 101, 223, 224, 227
Oppert, Jules, 42
Origen, 7, 19, 71, 150
Orontes River, 8, 9, 10, 11, 12
Osnapper, 187
Osorkon II, 226

Pactolus River, 243
Pamphilius, 71

Parmenio, 104
Parrot, André, 157, 161, 184
Parthia, 40
Patmos, 234, 235
Paul, 6, 16, 17, 22, 24, 25, 27, 29, 30,
    65, 68, 69, 86 - 94, 106, 146, 202 -
    207, 219, 220, 221, 246, 258, 260,
    262, 264, 273
Paul of Samosata, 19
Pausanias, 24, 25, 84, 86, 89, 92, 93
Pergamum, 235, 236, 238, 241 - 242,
    243
Pekah, 230
Pekahiah, 230
Peloponnesus, 83, 84
Penuel, 223
Pericles, 23, 26, 27, 29
Perseus, 199, 259
Persia, 38 - 40, 104, 243, 284
Peter, 41, 68, 79, 80, 219, 221
Pettinato Giovanni, 108, 109
Pharos, island of, 1, 2
Phidias, 23, 26, 27
Philadelphia, 245 - 246
Philetaerus, 241
Philip, 68, 198
Philip V, 199, 262
Philip the evangelist, 233
Philippi, 193 - 207
Philistia, 50
Philo, 6, 64, 90
Phoenicia, 266 - 274
Piraeus, 24
Pliny, 64, 260
Plutarch, 93
Polycarp, 241
Pompey, 13, 105, 146, 200, 212, 232
Pontius Pilate, 66, 67, 152, 153, 218
Pontus, 218
Porcius Festus, 69
Poseidon, 29, 91
Ptolemy II Philadelphus, 4, 5, 64
Pu-abi, 281

Qarqar, 227

Rachel, 59, 196
Rahab, 130
Ramaliah, 230
Ramoth Gilead, 227
Ramsey, William, 235
Ramses II, 255, 256